WORDSWORTH CLASSICS
OF WORLD LITERATURE

General Editor: Tom Griffith MA, MPhil

THE NICOMACHEAN ETHICS

Aristotle

The Nicomachean Ethics

Translated with Notes by Harris Rackham

With an Introduction by Stephen Watt

WORDSWORTH CLASSICS
OF WORLD LITERATURE

This edition published 1996 by Wordsworth Editions Limited
Cumberland House, Crib Street, Ware, Hertfordshire SG12 9ET

ISBN I 85326 461 X

Typeset in Great Britain by Antony Gray
Printed and bound in Denmark by Nørhaven

The paper in this book is produced from pure wood
pulp, without the use of chlorine or any other substance
harmful to the environment. The energy used in its
production consists almost entirely of hydroelectricity
and heat generated from waste material, thereby
conserving fossil fuels and contributing little
to the greenhouse effect.

CONTENTS

INTRODUCTION

1. Why read the Ethics?

Aristotle's own answer to this question is clear: studying the Ethics will help us to live better. But why should we believe him? It was written over two thousand years ago in a society which relied on slavery for its existence, regarded women as inferior to men and valued military prowess far more than we would today think wise or necessary. Aristotle lived in a very different world from ours, and his work is shot through with the values and concerns of that world. Why bother to read him?

One answer is that Aristotle's writings, including the Ethics, have been extremely influential historically. During the mediaeval period in particular, Islamic, Jewish and Christian philosophers adopted his views in their own works: such was Aristotle's importance that he became known simply as 'the Philosopher'. In the Christian West, the most important figure in this movement was Thomas Aquinas (1224–74), who used Aristotle to provide a rational underpinning of Christian teaching. The philosophy which resulted, known as Thomism, remains a living tradition, particularly within the Roman Catholic Church, and has exercised a profound influence on Western thought.

Another, better answer is that Aristotle's ideas might help us solve some of the questions and problems which trouble us today. However, before turning to consider some of the philosophical issues in detail, we need to consider the historical background to Aristotle's work in general and to the Ethics in particular. In what follows, the reader should note that, as is customary, references to the Ethics are given according to the page and line numbers of Bekker's edition of the complete works. (In the translation, the line numbers of the corresponding text are shown at the top of each page.)

2. Historical background

Aristotle was born in 384 BC in the Macedonian town of Stagira. His father, Nicomachus, was a physician at the court of Philip of Macedon. Between 367 and 347 he studied and later taught at Plato's Academy in Athens, only leaving when Plato died, perhaps driven out by anti-Macedonian feeling or by pique at his failure to assume leadership of the Academy. Between 347 and 334 he remained outside Athens teaching and pursuing his researches in various parts of the Greek world. For about two years from 343, he is supposed to have acted as tutor to Philip of Macedon's son, Alexander the Great. In 334 he returned to Athens to set up his own school at the Lyceum, leaving in 323 possibly again as a result of anti-Macedonian feeling. He died shortly after in 322.

Most of Aristotle's works which we now possess, including the Ethics, were probably composed in the period when he was teaching in the Lyceum. They cover non-philosophical areas – for example, zoology, history, aesthetics, physics and astronomy – as well as the strictly philosophical topics of logic, metaphysics and ethics. The work contained in this volume – the Nicomachean Ethics – is one of several works which have been attributed to Aristotle in the field of ethics and politics. Of the others, the most important are the Eudemian Ethics, a work which covers similar ground to the Nicomachean Ethics, and whose precise relationship to the present volume is a matter of dispute; and the Politics, which forms, with the Ethics, a complete course in political science (see 1181b12–23). The reason for the full title, the Nicomachean Ethics, is uncertain, a plausible explanation being that Aristotle's son, Nicomachus, edited the book from Aristotle's lecture notes.

3. The Ethics

The Ethics contains ten books which are further subdivided into chapters. Whatever the truth about the composition of the Ethics, it is certain that the structure of books and chapters has been imposed on the material by later editors. The reader should accordingly not allow herself to be misled into regarding in particular the division into chapters as necessarily reflecting the true shape of the argument.

A very rough sketch of the content of the books is as follows:

Book I	Everyone aims at what he thinks is happiness. Understanding the virtues will help us understand happiness.
Book II	What in general is a virtue?
Books III–V	The particular virtues are examined.
Book VI	The intellect, practical and theoretical.
Book VII	Weakness of will and pleasure.
Books VIII–XI	Human relationships.
Book X	After a further discussion of pleasure, happiness is defined as the exercise of theoretical reason. To attain happiness, people have to be brought up in a good society, so we need to study good societies – the content of the succeeding volume called the Politics.

Although this gives some idea of the shape of the work, the reader should note that various treatments of the same topic are scattered throughout the books. Thus Book III, as well as containing an examination of particular virtues, also has much to say on the practical intellect.

My aim in what follows is to give the reader an idea of some of the areas of interest in the Ethics. As mentioned above, one theory about the work is that it was assembled from Aristotle's lecture notes by his son: it is in any case certainly true that the Ethics resembles a patchwork of incomplete essays with no clear connection between them. It has even been compared to the contents of an academic's wastepaper basket. The typical approach of philosophers this century in the Anglo-American tradition has been to treat the Ethics as a quarry from which discrete arguments can be hewn and examined rather than to make an attempt to descry an overall theme, an approach which fits in well with the understanding of the Ethics as a patchwork. This strategy is in complete opposition to that of, say, Thomas Aquinas, who treated the Ethics as having a rigorous and logical overall structure. My own view is that there is a coherent structure behind the apparent disorder, but that much of the interest of the Ethics lies in the detail underpinned by that structure rather than the structure itself. Accordingly, the reader should be aware that in what follows many topics of interest contained in its pages will have to be overlooked and many of the debates surrounding the areas

I do address will have been simplified or ignored. One reason why the Ethics is such a wonderful book is that, despite often having the appearance of great simplicity, the interpretation of its argument is invariably contentious and difficult. The following explanations should, therefore, be treated as a stimulus to further inquiry rather than the final word on any particular matter.

4.   The philosophy of the Ethics

i   *The practical purpose of the Ethics*

Two very good questions to ask of the Ethics are: 'What is Aristotle setting out to do?' and 'How does he set out to do this?' For most philosophical works, the answer to the first question will be something along the lines of trying to provide a true account, or improve our understanding, of some pàrticular field of knowledge. In the case of the Ethics, however, this sort of answer won't do: as we have already noted, Aristotle makes it very clear that ethics is a practical study intended to make its students good rather than just knowledgeable (e.g. 1095a5–6). So let us move on to the second question: how does Aristotle intend to make the students of ethics good? The obvious answer to this would be that he intends to make them more knowledgeable and thus better at being good in the same way that a more knowledgeable lawyer is going to be better at being a lawyer. The problem with this answer is that it seems to be contradicted by the argument of Book X chapter ix, where the attainment of goodness is held to be almost entirely a matter of being brought up correctly: if the intended audience of the Ethics are adults – which according to 1095a3–11 must be the case – the likely effect of an academic work such as the Ethics on their behaviour would seem to be negligible.

So we have a problem. The Ethics aims to make you good, but it is hard to see how, in Aristotle's eyes, it could do this. This confronts us with the first of many preconceptions we shall have to abandon in reading the Ethics: that of moral goodness as a distinct class of goodness. Consider Machiavelli's book *The Prince*. This is a book which argues, broadly, that if you want to be a good prince, you can't act morally: you have to bump off your opponents, terrorise civilians and so on. For Aristotle, being good is being good at the things human beings need to do or are benefited by doing. If Machiavelli were right in arguing that rulers need, say, to assassinate their opponents, then given that human beings need rulers, it would be good that a ruler practises assassination. In Aristotelian terms, the further question as to whether actions which are good for human beings are also moral simply doesn't exist.

Aristotle is thus out to make his audience good at doing what human beings do, but not necessarily good at everything that human beings do. Aristotle isn't interested in making his audience good at specialised crafts or sciences, however necessary they are to human life (1907a15–b 21). Nor is he trying to produce someone who is good at finding the means to bring about any end, in the way a good government official will be able to put into effect the commands of her political masters, whatever her own political views (1144a23–36). What is left is that Aristotle is concerned with making his audience good at pursuing not just any old end, but the supreme end of human beings.

The key to understanding much of the Ethics is, I suggest, that Aristotle is concerned to produce good statesmen, that is, people who are good at making other people good by running good societies. Given this assumption, the Ethics is concerned with analysing the purpose or end of a good society – the good life – and its companion volume, the Politics, is concerned with the means to achieve that purpose, a well-organised society. This understanding of the purpose of the Ethics is important because what may be a satisfactory answer to the question 'What should a statesman try to produce?' won't necessarily be a satisfactory answer to the question 'How should I lead my life?' It is a failure to be clear about the differences between the two questions which has led, I believe, to some of the difficulties in interpreting Aristotle. I return to this point below in section v.

ii The good character

Given then that the Ethics is concerned with examining the good life, how does it go about this? Most of the Ethics can be described as being broadly concerned with character, indeed 'ethics' in Greek just means 'matters concerned with character'. Some modern philosophers have been attracted to Aristotle's concern with character – broadly, what good people are like – rather than the typical interest of Anglo-American moral philosophy, which has been to provide answers to questions about what agents should do in particular circumstances. I think this difference of emphasis in Aristotle is due rather to his addressing a different sort of question about action – i.e. what should the statesman do? – than to any principled objection to questions about action being dealt with philosophically. But putting that aside, it is worth considering in what ways Aristotle's treatment of character diverges from the interests of modern philosophers interested in what is often known as 'virtue ethics'.

Virtue ethics tries to analyse those qualities which a person needs in order to lead any sort of recognisably human life. For example, she needs to be able to live and work with others; she needs to be able to confront difficulties and threats; she needs to be able to control her desires; and so on. These qualities are called virtues and Aristotle is often set up as the father of this way of doing ethics. Now Aristotle certainly does deal with virtues in Books II–VI and at least some of these virtues bear a superficial resemblance to the virtues which would appear in any modern philospher's list: thus Aristotle talks about courage (1115a6–1117b22) and temperance (1117b23–1119b18), and it is highly plausible that any human being would need to be courageous in confronting dangers and temperate in pursuing pleasures in order to live well. But this apparent congruity between modern ethicists and Aristotle soon disappears upon examination of what qualities he thinks are virtues. Although courage is mentioned, Aristotle defines it not as the characteristic of being able to confront all dangers but narrowly as the virtue displayed by those who face death in battle (1115b32–35). And virtues unknown to the modern list are also found: greatness of soul, for example (1123a24–1125a35), which leads its possessor to be haughty and to have a deep voice (1125a12–16).

To understand how Aristotle arrives at his understanding of the virtues, we need to examine how he goes about doing ethics in more detail.

iii   Aristotle's ethical method

Aristotle's philosophical method in fact explains the content of his virtues. It is evident to even a casual reader that Aristotle's detailed discussion of the individual virtues in Books III–V is an idealised description of the character of a fourth-century-BC Athenian male and not of the qualities required to live any sort of human life. But how could this be otherwise, given that his method is to take as his starting point the common opinions of male Athenians regarding what makes an admirable character? (See, for example, 1105b28–1106a2; 1140a24–25).

This brings us up against a second preconception that needs to be ditched in reading Aristotle. The tendency of western philosophy since Descartes (1596–1650) has been sceptical, that is, it has taken seriously the possibility that all our commonsense everyday knowledge of the world may be wrong: thus Descartes suggested the possibility that what we take to be external reality could be fantasies induced by a malevolent demon; and modern philosophers of a similar temper have advanced the possibility of our being disembodied brains given the illusion of an external world by scientists. Whatever the advantages or disadvantages in such a sceptical approach, it is not Aristotle's. In ethics, this difference in methodology leads Aristotle to accept that what all think to be good is actually good (1172b35–1173a2), where thinking includes not just what people say about what is good, but what they reveal about their understanding of good and bad in their actions. It is this divergence from Descartes' scepticism that is, in part, responsible for the revival of interest in Aristotle among Anglo-American philosophers, particularly in the second half of this century; for it fits in well with the general reaction against such scepticism, a reaction in particular exemplified in the later work of the philosopher Wittgenstein (1889–1951).

That Aristotle is not a sceptical philosopher doesn't mean that he can't distinguish between what seems to be good to any particular person at a particular time and what is actually good, any more than it would lead him to say that there is never a possibility that someone who thinks he is seeing a table is in fact hallucinating. Moreover, it allows the possibility that some agents will be invariably wrong in their judgments, being unable to see the good in a way analogous to the blind being unable to see physical objects (1173b20–25). What it does mean, however, is that people will normally get it right: that what they think, feel and pursue as good will normally actually be good. So there is every reason for him to begin with the common-or-garden views of good character held by his contemporaries and to think that an examination of these views will establish something about what is actually good for human beings.

iv · *Prudence and choice (Books III and VI)*

The word translated in this edition of the Ethics by 'prudence' is used by Aristotle to mean that virtue by which we reason about our actions (1140b4–6). It is therefore sometimes also translated as practical reason and is to be contrasted with wisdom or theoretical reason (1141a9–b 14).

A central term in Aristotle's discussion of prudence is that of what is called in this translation 'choice'. Choice is discussed both in Book VI (1139a21–b 13) and Book III (1111b4–1113a14) and is one of the most important technical terms used in the Ethics. Choice, like prudence itself, is concerned with means not ends (1111b26–27; 1144a7–9), is caused by reasoning and is itself the cause of action (1139a31–33). This suggests the following picture. A desire irrationally pops into my head for an ice-cream. I deliberate for a few moments, wondering whether to steal or buy it, then I choose to buy it and this, rather like throwing a switch, sets my body in motion. Is this Aristotle's picture of action? Well, he doesn't think everything we would call action is like this because animals, children and adults who lack self-restraint don't act on choice (1111b6–10). So let's concentrate on good people and their actions.

There are two major elements in the above account of action. Firstly, reason is held to have no effect on ends: that I desire the end of eating an ice-cream is not a result of my reasoning, even though reasoning is involved in working out the means to get the ice-cream once the desire for one has struck me. Whether Aristotle thought that prudence is involved in the assessment of which ends an agent should pursue has always been debated by scholars. My own view, and this is probably the predominant view at present, is that Aristotle did believe that prudence was involved in assessing ends. Perhaps the best evidence for this is the Ethics itself, which is a work of reason dedicated to arriving at the supreme end for mankind. So whatever Aristotle does mean by saying that prudence and choice are concerned with means and not ends, it should not be assumed that this excludes reason from an assessment of ends.

Secondly, the account assumes that there is always a history to an action: when a person acts, she has always first deliberated, then chosen, and only then finally does she act. But is this always true? Unless you have already been got at by some philosophical theory before reading this, you should be inclined to answer no. Sometimes we just act. After acting, we can explain our actions and provide reasons for what we did, but this doesn't mean that for every action, we first go through a time of deliberation, then there is a mental event which is the choice and then we act: sometimes this is what happens if there is a particularly important and unfamiliar dilemma and we have sufficient time, but not normally in the case of day-to-day actions.

So if this is Aristotle's picture, it looks as if he's got it wrong. Several possibilities exist to save him from this embarrassment. Firstly, Aristotle may only be suggesting that there is choice in the case of those actions where we do have to sit down and think and come to a conscious decision; but that this subset of actions, in some way, typifies all our action. I would reject this explanation on two grounds: firstly, I think it is reasonably clear from the discussions in Books III and VI that Aristotle is talking about a type of action which is our normal way of acting as good adults, and this would rule out his intending solely those actions preceded by the agent's conscious deliberation and decision; secondly, it is hard to understand how a type of action so different from our normal actions could in any sense typify all our actions.

Another possibility is to claim that there is in fact always an event, which we can call a choice, which precedes our action but of which we are normally unaware, perhaps because it occurs so quickly. This, of course, wouldn't explain the deliberation which is supposed to precede the action·unless we also claim that there is an unconscious process of deliberation as well, but put that aside. Whether you are inclined to accept such an explanation will depend on whether you think it is philosophically true. Many modern philosophers do think that a theory along these lines is a contribution to our understanding of human agency. Since I don't believe that it is, I would only be inclined to attribute it to Aristotle if I thought that the text demanded it, and I don't think it does. Within the Ethics, the main reason for assuming that choice is an event which precedes the action is the comment at 1139a31–32, that choice is the efficient cause of action. Talk of efficient causality tends, to the modern mind, to suggest the picture of billiards: the white ball moves towards the red ball, then hits it, and then the red ball moves off. If Aristotle talks of efficient causality, it is argued, then it is this picture he must have in mind, with the choice preceding the movement of the body in the same way that the movement of the white ball precedes the movement of the red. It is, however, quite clear from Aristotle's discussions outside the Ethics that his concept of efficient causality is substantially different from the modern one and, in particular, that he does not assume that the efficient cause always precedes the movement for which it is responsible but that it sometimes coincides with that movement.

A final possibility, and the one which I favour, is to regard Aristotle's concept of choice as seeking to explain actions by giving the reasons for which they were done rather than their causal history. The success of such a strategy depends on being able to distinguish Aristotle's understanding of efficient causality from the billiard ball model mentioned above and also requires an account of how reasons explain actions without providing their causal history. On the assumption that such an account of choice is possible, Aristotle's further claim that deliberation causes choice could then be understood as highlighting the role of intellect in learning, as we grow into adults, to understand our actions as done for reasons.

It must be admitted that these are difficult areas, perhaps the most difficult in the Ethics. For a reader new to Aristotle, the most important point to be grasped is the negative one: that whatever Aristotle does mean, it isn't necessarily the simple 'ice-cream' model sketched above.

v   *The argument from human nature (Books I and X)*

If you threw away Books II to IX of the Ethics, it might be rather easier to suppose that you understood the work. After an introduction (chapters i–iii), Book I states that the common opinion of mankind is that everyone tries in their lives and actions to achieve 'happiness'. Unfortunately, although everyone agrees on what to call it, no one agrees on what it actually is (chapters iii–v). After some digression (vi to vii 1097b21), Aristotle suggests that we might get a grasp on what happiness actually is by considering what the function of man is. He concludes (1098a16–18) that it is an activity in accordance with the best human virtue. We then jump to Book X chapter vii, where, remembering from Book VI the existence of the virtue of wisdom or theoretical reason, we learn that happiness is the exercise of that virtue in contemplation.

The conclusion of this argument has been stigmatised as just what one would expect from a man who had spent all his adult life in an ivory tower. Although its oddness is reduced by Aristotle's further remark that the life of active participation in city life also constitutes happiness, albeit of a secondary, inferior variety (1178a9–10), it has seemed to many philosophers a self-evidently foolish conclusion. What precisely Aristotle thinks is involved in contemplation can be argued over: whatever the details, it clearly involves prizing some sort of academic activity over other goods. Before considering the conclusion in a bit more detail, however, let's consider the argument leading up to it; for if the conclusion is wrong, then the argument must be flawed in some way.

The argument begins by Aristotle making a relatively uncontroversial point. Once we know that the job of a sculptor is to sculpt, we can say that someone who sculpts badly is a bad sculptor; or once we know that the job of an eye is to see, we can say that an eye that sees badly is a bad eye (1097b24–33). So if we could say that human beings, just by virtue of being human beings rather than by being sculptors or carpenters or shoemakers, had a job or, as in this translation, a function, we could conclude that someone who performed that function badly was a bad human being.

So why would we think it appropriate to say that human beings have a function? Well, if human beings were made to do something, in the same way as, say, corkscrews were made to open bottles, it would obviously be appropriate to ascribe them a function. In essence, this is the interpretation of Thomas Aquinas: God made us for a purpose and thereby gave us a function. Despite some metaphorical talk about nature (eg 1097b30), this isn't Aristotle's answer.

At this point, most commentators suggest that Aristotle's ascription of a function to human beings is simply the result of his general metaphysical and scientific system which ascribes functions or purposes to all substances: since we no longer accept his metaphysics and science, we should not be surprised that we are no longer able to accept his ethics. Perhaps. But a number of points need to be made before his argument is so easily dismissed. Firstly, even dropping the part of his argument which relies explicitly on function (1097b22–1098a20), Aristotle might still claim to have proved that the exercise of theoretical reason is the supreme good. Having resumed the function argument from 1098a20 at 1177a12–18, he goes on to say that the results already achieved, presumably via the function argument, must now be compared with the truth; and then goes on to try to show that people, albeit perhaps not explicitly, already regard the exercise of theoretical reason as the highest occupation of humanity. Aristotle here is remaining true to his anti-sceptical assumptions: if he could show that everyone already thought theoretical reason was best or else acted in such a way that they revealed this as an unarticulated assumption, he would have proved that it indeed was best. Nor should we scoff at this. If we think of the vast amount of time and energy spent on academic studies in the world, on the arts, on those aspects of culture which have no practical use but to which the most highly educated tend to attach enormous importance, are we so very far away from Aristotle's conclusion? Don't human beings, as he puts in another work, have a natural desire to know?

Secondly, as noted by modern virtue ethicists (see section ii above), there is a fairly straightforward sense in which human beings, just like all living creatures, have certain needs. Plants, for instance, in order to survive, need water. Analogously, human beings might need to reason. Now, it can't be as straightforward a matter to decide that human beings need to reason as it is to decide that plants need water: waterless plants wilt, but what happens to human beings who don't reason? On the other hand, it still seems quite reasonable to assert that human beings need, say, love, even though unloved human beings don't wilt in precisely the same way as unwatered plants. So if the function argument could be understood as saying that human beings need to reason in order to be happy, Aristotle's claim would seem to be perfectly coherent: whether or not it was in fact true would be, of course, a completely different matter.

Parenthetically, this confronts us with the question of whether 'happiness' is a good translation of the Greek word 'eudaimonia'. Although 'happiness' is the traditional translation – and is the one used in the present version of the Ethics – many philosophers prefer to substitute 'flourishing'. The grounds for this preference can now be seen. Plants need water in order to flourish; human beings, arguably, need to exercise theoretical reason in order to achieve 'eudaimonia'. Neither translation is perfect: 'happiness' can mislead the reader into thinking that Aristotle just means a purely subjective state such as pleasure; 'flourishing' smacks of technicality and obscures the differences between the ways things are good for plants and the ways things are good for human beings.

I hope that the above remarks will have suggested, not that the function argument is certainly valid, but only that it is wrong to dismiss it out of hand as resting on an esoteric metaphysics. But even if the argument is valid, this still leaves the conclusion obscure. Should we pursue academic truth at the expense of all other values? Or should we merely give it pride of place in a balanced life?

Scholars argue over this question, fruitlessly, I believe. In general, Aristotle is not concerned with the predominant interest of modern moral philosophers, namely, the moral dilemma. As he puts it, in a dilemma one should do whatever the good man would do (1106b36–1107a2). Now this lack of interest might be for two reasons. Firstly he might think that, in principle, that is all that can be said: that how the good man comes to a decision as to what he should do cannot be further articulated, at least before the decision is made. Secondly, he might be more interested in how to make good men rather than in what they do once made.

Aristotle certainly does seem to believe that less can be said in advance about how good people should act in difficult circumstances than is nowadays generally assumed: for him, good people simply solve a dilemma correctly, just as people simply identify tables correctly without usually needing to follow a set of explicit rules. Aristotle regards both cases as being examples of 'aisthesis' or perception (1143 b 5). But the primary reason for turning his attention elsewhere is that he is interested not in specifying what a good person does, but rather what the product of a good society should be. For this purpose, to know that a society should regard the exercise of theoretical reason as the supreme good, rather than, say, the expansion of its territory, is to learn something new and of importance. But to expect an answer in the abstract about precisely how a society should realise this supreme good is foolish: it will all depend on the circumstances. Aristotle does, however, suggest a way in which an answer can be approached, namely, by studying how various different societies have arranged their affairs in the past, a study which is begun in the Politics. This answer in respect of a society can be compared with the perfectly sensible advice that might be given to an individual that she might get a better idea how to live her own life by becoming familiar with how other people have lived theirs.

5. Conclusion

I began this introduction by asking why we should read Aristotle. There are, I suggest, three main reasons. Firstly, Aristotle is interested not in 'morality' but in what is good for human beings. This is important because, while we have a grasp of the latter notion, it is hard to understand what a morally good action as opposed to a good action *simpliciter* might be, a difficulty which some philosophers have explained by arguing that in the absence of belief in a God who issues commandments to humanity moral goodness makes no sense as a separate category from goodness.

Secondly, there is his method of doing philosophy. Instead of inventing some theory – such as that we should maximise pleasure or that we should always do our duty – he takes as his starting point what people actually say and do. He then sifts and articulates these views and tries to build them into a coherent whole, a process called by him 'dialectic', a word which in Greek means both argument and conversation. Philosophy accordingly remains engaged with how people actually live and talk about their lives; and its arguments thus retain the possibility of convincing non-philosophers and thereby changing their lives and their actions. In the modern world, philosophy is predominantly an academic discipline with only limited opportunities of and interest in affecting public opinion. Since Aristotle believes that ethics only has importance as a practical and not as a theoretical discipline, he challenges us to consider whether the subject remains important if it has become non-practical, say by becoming too technical to be understood by a layman.

The final reason is the content of Aristotle's ethical philosophy. It rests upon views of people who lived in a world very different from our own and whose outlook is accordingly very different from our own. By taking those views seriously, we are forced to articulate and reconsider the assumptions on which our own views rest. But there is more than this. Just as Greek drama reminds us how some human concerns have remained unchanged over two thousand years, so Aristotle's philosophy should cause us to reflect on what this enduring core of humanity is. Aristotle tells us that human beings need to live in communities and need to exercise reason both in organising these communities and in the study of theoretical truth. He also tells us about some of the qualities required to live in fourth-century Greek society, many of which will be required in any form of society. He says something about what it is to be a mature human being and how we learn to become one. Aristotle says things about human beings that are not found in other writers, and in listening to and arguing with those views is to be discovered both intellectual pleasure and ethical advancement.

STEPHEN WATT
The Open University

SUGGESTIONS FOR FURTHER READING

Introductory
J. L. Ackrill, *Aristotle the Philosopher*, Oxford 1981
J. Barnes, *Aristotle*, Oxford 1982
W. F. R. Hardie, *Aristotle's Ethical Theory*, Oxford 1968

For the more advanced reader
J. Barnes, M. Schofield, R. Sorabji (eds), *Articles on Aristotle,* vol. 2,
    London 1977
S. Broadie, *Ethics with Aristotle*, Oxford 1991
A. O. Rorty, *Essays on Aristotle's Ethics*, Berkeley 1980

Works developing Aristotelian themes
W. Charlton, *Weakness of Will*, Oxford 1988
S. L. Hurley, *Natural Reasons*, Oxford 1989
R. Hursthouse, *Beginning Lives,* Oxford 1987
A. MacIntyre, *Three Rival Versions of Moral Enquiry*, London 1990

Particularly full bibliographies of Aristotelian literature are to be
found in Barnes *et al.* and Broadie above.

NOTE ON THE TRANSLATION

The translation and accompanying notes are by Harris Rackham
(1868–1944), and are based on his revision of the Greek text
published by Immanuel Bekker in 1831.

THE NICOMACHEAN ETHICS

BOOK ONE

Introduction: the nature of the subject

i   Every practical science has an end.

ii   The ultimate end, which is the supreme good, is the end of political science.

iii   Political science not an exact science. Its study is both impossible and useless for the young and immature.

The nature of happiness

iv   Current views stated. Inductive method justified.

v   Current views of the good inferred from typical lives. The life of enjoyment. The life of action. The life of contemplation (X, vii). The life of money-making.

vi   Plato's idea of good refuted as basis for ethics

     (i)   Idea of good disproved by doctrine of categories:

         (a)   'Good' denotes thing, or a quality of a thing, or its relation to another thing; but the last notion is secondary, and cannot be classed with the first under one idea.

         (b)   'Good' may mean 'a good thing', 'excellent', 'enough', 'useful', 'opportune', 'healthy', etc.: but these are not a single notion.

         (c)   Good even in one category is the object of several sciences.

     (ii)   The idea of good superfluous, being the same in essence as the concept 'good'. Its eternity does not affect its essence. (The Pythagorean view.)

     (iii) (supplementing (i) (a))   The idea of good does not even apply to things good in themselves (if any), since even they are good in different ways; though 'good' must denote something – perhaps a certain relation.

     (iv)   The idea of good not relevant to ethics, since a transcendent good is unattainable, and useless even as a guide to the attainment of practicable goods.

vii   Happiness the supreme practical good because

         (a)   perfect or final, and

         (b)   self-sufficient or complete in itself.

Nature of happiness deduced from the function of man. Definition of happiness. Ethics a practical and therefore not an exact science.

Definition of happiness tested

Analysis of definition of happiness
(continues through to Book VI)

i Every art and every investigation, and likewise every practical pursuit or undertaking, seems to aim at some good: hence it has
2 been well said that the good is that at which all things aim. (It is true that a certain variety is to be observed among the ends at which the arts and sciences aim: in some cases the activity of practising the art is itself the end,[1] whereas in others the end is some product over and above the mere exercise of the art; and in the arts whose ends are certain things beside the practice of the arts themselves, these products are essentially superior in value to
3 the activities.) But as there are numerous pursuits and arts and sciences, it follows that their ends are correspondingly numerous: for instance, the end of the science of medicine is health, that of the art of shipbuilding a vessel, that of strategy victory, that of
4 domestic economy wealth. Now in cases where several such pursuits are subordinate to some single faculty – as bridle-making and the other trades concerned with horses' harness are subordinate to horsemanship, and this and every other military pursuit to the science of strategy, and similarly other arts to different arts again – in all these cases, I say, the ends of the master arts are things more to be desired than all those of the arts subordinate to them; since the latter ends are only pursued for the sake of the
5 former. (And it makes no difference whether the ends of the pursuits are the activities themselves or some other thing beside these, as in the case of the sciences mentioned.)

ii   If therefore among the ends at which our actions aim there be one which we wish for its own sake, while we wish the others only for the sake of this, and if we do not choose everything for the sake of something else (which would obviously result in a process *ad infinitum*, so that all desire would be futile and vain), it is clear that this one ultimate end must be the good, and indeed
2 the supreme good. Will not then a knowledge of this supreme good be also of great practical importance for the conduct of life? Will it not better enable us to attain what is fitting, like archers
3 having a target to aim at? If this be so, we ought to make an

attempt to determine at all events in outline what exactly this supreme good is, and of which of the theoretical or practical sciences it is the object.

4 Now it would be agreed that it must be the object of the most authoritative of the sciences – some science which is pre-
5 eminently a master-craft. But such is manifestly the science of
6 politics; for it is this that ordains which of the sciences are to exist in states, and what branches of knowledge the different classes of the citizens are to learn, and up to what point; and we observe that even the most highly esteemed of the faculties, such as strategy, domestic economy, oratory, are subordinate to the
7 political science. Inasmuch then as the rest of the sciences are employed by this one, and as it moreover lays down laws as to what people shall do and what things they shall refrain from doing, the end of this science must include the ends of all the
8 others. Therefore, the good of man must be the end of the science of politics. For even though it be the case that the good is the same for the individual and for the state, nevertheless, the good of the state is manifestly a greater and more perfect good, both to attain and to preserve.[2] To secure the good of one person only is better than nothing; but to secure the good of a nation or a state is a nobler and more divine achievement.

This then being its aim, our investigation is in a sense the study of politics.

iii Now our treatment of this science will be adequate, if it achieves that amount of precision which belongs to its subject matter. The same exactness must not be expected in all departments of philosophy alike, any more than in all the
2 products of the arts and crafts. The subjects studied by political science are moral nobility[3] and justice; but these conceptions involve much difference of opinion and uncertainty, so that they are sometimes believed to be mere conventions and to have no
3 real existence in the nature of things. And a similar uncertainty surrounds the conception of the good, because it frequently occurs that good things have harmful consequences: people have before now been ruined by wealth, and in other cases courage
4 has cost men their lives. We must therefore be content if, in dealing with subjects and starting from premises thus uncertain, we succeed in presenting a broad outline of the truth: when our

subjects and our premises are merely generalities, it is enough if we arrive at generally valid conclusions. Accordingly we may ask the student also to accept the various views we put forward in the same spirit; for it is the mark of an educated mind to expect that amount of exactness in each kind which the nature of the particular subject admits. It is equally unreasonable to accept merely probable conclusions from a mathematician and to demand strict demonstration from an orator.

5　Again, each man judges correctly those matters with which he is acquainted; it is of these that he is a competent critic. To criticise a particular subject, therefore, a man must have been trained in that subject: to be a good critic generally, he must have had an all-round education. Hence the young are not fit to be students of political science.[4] For they have no experience of life and conduct, and it is these that supply the premises and subject

6　matter of this branch of philosophy. And moreover they are led by their feelings; so that they will study the subject to no purpose or advantage, since the end of this science is not knowledge but

7　action. And it makes no difference whether they are young in years or immature in character: the defect is not a question of time, it is because their life and its various aims are guided by feeling; for to such persons their knowledge is of no use, any more than it is to persons of defective self-restraint.[5] But moral science may be of great value to those who guide their desires and actions by principle.

8　Let so much suffice by way of introduction as to the student of the subject, the spirit in which our conclusions are to be received, and the object that we set before us.

iv　To resume, inasmuch as all studies and undertakings are directed to the attainment of some good, let us discuss what it is that we pronounce to be the aim of politics, that is, what is the

2　highest of all the goods that action can achieve. As far as the name goes, we may almost say that the great majority of mankind are agreed about this; for both the multitude and persons of refinement speak of it as happiness,[6] and conceive 'the good life' or 'doing well'[7] to be the same thing as 'being happy'. But what constitutes happiness is a matter of dispute; and the popular account of it is not the same as that given by the philosophers.

3　Ordinary people identify it with some obvious and visible good, such as pleasure or wealth or honour – some say one thing and some another, indeed very often the same man says different things at different times: when he falls sick he thinks health is happiness, when he is poor, wealth. At other times, feeling conscious of their own ignorance, men admire those who propound something grand and above their heads; and it has been held by some thinkers[8] that beside the many good things we have mentioned, there exists another good, that is good in itself, and stands to all those goods as the cause of their being good.

4   Now perhaps it would be a somewhat fruitless task to review all the different opinions that are held. It will suffice to examine those that are most widely prevalent, or that seem to have some argument in their favour.

5   And we must not overlook the distinction between arguments that start from first principles and those that lead to first principles. It was a good practice of Plato to raise this question, and to enquire whether the right procedure was to start from or to lead up to the first principles, as in a race-course one may run from the judges to the far end of the track or reversely. Now no doubt it is proper to start from the known. But 'the known' has two meanings – 'what is known to us', which is one thing, and 'what is knowable in itself', which is another. Perhaps then for us[9] at all

6 events it is proper to start from what is known to us. This is why in order to be a competent student of the right and just, and in short of the topics of politics in general, the pupil is bound to have

7 been well trained in his habits. For the starting-point or first principle is the fact that a thing is so; if this be satisfactorily ascertained, there will be no need also to know the reason why it is so. And the man of good moral training knows first principles already, or can easily acquire them. As for the person who neither knows nor can learn, let him hear the words of Hesiod:[10]

> Best is the man who can himself advise;
> He too is good who hearkens to the wise;
> But who, himself being witless, will not heed
> Another's wisdom, is worthless indeed.

V   But let us continue from the point[11] where we digressed. To judge from men's lives, the more or less reasoned conceptions of the good or happiness that seem to prevail among them are the following. On the one hand the generality of men and the most vulgar identify the good with pleasure, and accordingly are

2 content with the life of enjoyment – for there are three specially prominent lives,[12] the one just mentioned, the Life of politics,

3 and thirdly, the life of contemplation. The generality of mankind then show themselves to be utterly slavish, by preferring what is only a life for cattle; but they get a hearing for their view as reasonable because many persons of high position share the feelings of Sardanapallus.[13]

4   Men of refinement, on the other hand, and men of action think that the good is honour – for this may be said to be the end of the life of politics. But honour after all seems too superficial to be the good for which we are seeking; since it appears to depend on those who confer it more than on him upon whom it is conferred, whereas we instinctively feel that the good must be something proper to its possessor and not easy to be taken away

5 from him. Moreover men's motive in pursuing honour seems to be to assure themselves of their own merit; at least they seek to be honoured by men of judgement and by people who know them, that is, they desire to be honoured on the ground of virtue. It is clear therefore that in the opinion at all events of men of

6 action, virtue is a greater good than honour; and one might perhaps accordingly suppose that virtue rather than honour is the end of the political life. But even virtue proves on examination to be too incomplete to be the end; since it appears possible to possess it while you are asleep, or without putting it into practice throughout the whole of your life; and also for the virtuous man to suffer the greatest misery and misfortune – though no one would pronounce a man living a life of misery to be happy, unless for the sake of maintaining a paradox. But we need not pursue this subject, since it has been sufficiently treated in the ordinary discussions.[14]

7   The third type of life is the life of contemplation, which we shall consider in the sequel.

8   The life of money-making is a constrained[15] kind of life, and clearly wealth is not the good we are in search of, for it is only good as being useful, a means to something else. On this score indeed one might conceive the ends before mentioned to have a better claim, for they are approved for their own sakes. But even

they do not really seem to be the supreme good; however, many arguments have been laid down in regard to them, so we may dismiss them.

vi   But perhaps it is desirable that we should examine the notion of a universal good, and review the difficulties that it involves, although such an enquiry goes against the grain because of our friendship for the authors of the theory of ideas.[16] Still perhaps it would appear desirable, and indeed it would seem to be obligatory, especially for a philosopher, to sacrifice even one's closest personal ties in defence of the truth. Both are dear to us, yet 'tis our duty to prefer the truth.[17]

2   The originators[18] of this theory, then, used not to postulate ideas of groups of things in which they posited[19] an order of priority and posteriority[20] (for which reason they did not construct an idea of numbers in general). But good is predicated alike in the categories of substance, of quality, and of relation; yet the absolute,[21] or substance, is prior in nature to the relative, which seems to be a sort of offshoot or 'accident' of substance; so that there cannot be a common idea corresponding to the absolutely good and the relatively good.

3   Again, the word 'good' is used in as many senses as the word 'is'; for we may predicate good in the category of substance, for instance of god or intelligence; in that of quality – the excellences; in that of quantity – moderate in amount; in that of relation – useful; in that of time – a favourable opportunity; in that of place – a suitable 'habitat';[22] and so on. So clearly good cannot be a single and universal general notion; if it were, it would not be predicable in all the categories, but only in one.

4   Again, things that come under a single idea must be objects of a single science; hence there ought to be a single science dealing with all good things. But as a matter of fact there are a number of sciences even for the goods in one category: for example, opportunity, for opportunity in war comes under the science of strategy, in disease under that of medicine; and the due amount in diet comes under medicine, in bodily exercise under gymnastics.

5   One might also raise the question what precisely they mean by their expression 'the ideal so-and-so',[23] seeing that one and the same definition of man applies both to 'the ideal man' and to 'man',[24] for in so far as both are man, there will be no difference

between them; and if so, no more will there be any difference between 'the ideal good' and 'good' in so far as both are good.

6 Nor yet will the ideal good be any more good because it is eternal, seeing that a white thing that lasts a long time is no whiter than one that lasts only a day.

7 The Pythagoreans[25] seem to give a more probable doctrine on the subject of the good when they place unity in their column of goods; and indeed Speusippus[26] appears to have followed them. But this subject must be left for another discussion.

8 We can descry an objection that may be raised against our arguments on the ground that the theory in question was not intended to apply to every sort of good, and that only things pursued and accepted for their own sake are pronounced good as belonging to a single species, while things productive or preservative of these in any way, or preventive of their opposites, are said to be good as a means to these, and in a different sense.

9 Clearly then the term 'goods' would have two meanings, (1) things good in themselves and (2) things good as a means to these; let us then separate things good in themselves from things useful as means, and consider whether the former are called good

10 because they fall under a single idea. But what sort of things is one to class as good in themselves? Are they not those things which are sought after even without any accessory advantage, such as wisdom, sight, and certain pleasures and honours? for even if we also pursue these things as means to something else, still one would class them among things good in themselves. Or is there nothing else good in itself except the idea? If so, the

11 species will be of no use.[27] If on the contrary the class of things good in themselves includes these objects, the same notion of good ought to be manifested in all of them, just as the same notion of white is manifested in snow and in white paint. But as a matter of fact the notions of honour and wisdom and pleasure, as being good, are different and distinct. Therefore, good is not a general term corresponding to a single idea.

12 But in what sense then are different things called good? For they do not seem to be a case of things that bear the same name merely by chance. Possibly things are called good in virtue of being derived from one good; or because they all contribute to one good. Or perhaps it is rather by way of a proportion:[28] that

is, as sight is good in the body, so intelligence is good in the soul, and similarly another thing in something else.

13   Perhaps however this question must be dismissed for the present, since a detailed investigation of it belongs more properly to another branch of philosophy.[29] And likewise with the idea of the good; for even if the goodness predicated of various things in common really is a unity or something existing separately and absolute, it clearly will not be practicable or attainable by man; but the good which we are now seeking is a good within human reach.

14   But possibly someone may think that to know the ideal good may be desirable as an aid to achieving those goods which are practicable and attainable: having the ideal good as a pattern we shall more easily know what things are good for us, and knowing
15   them, obtain them. Now it is true that this argument has a certain plausibility; but it does not seem to square with the actual procedure of the sciences. For these all aim at some good, and seek to make up their deficiencies,[30] but they do not trouble about a knowledge of the ideal good. Yet if it were so potent an aid, it is improbable that all the professors of the arts and sciences
16   should not know it, nor even seek to discover it. Moreover, it is not easy to see *how* knowing that same ideal good will help a weaver or carpenter in the practice of his own craft, or how anybody will be a better physician or general for having contemplated the absolute idea. In fact it does not appear that the physician studies even health[31] in the abstract; he studies the health of the human being – or rather of some particular human being, for it is individuals that he has to cure.

Let us here conclude our discussion of this subject.

vii   We may now return to the good which is the object of our search, and try to find out what exactly it can be. For good appears to be one thing in one pursuit or art and another in another: it is different in medicine from what it is in strategy, and so on with the rest of the arts. What definition of the good then will hold true in all the arts? Perhaps we may define it as that for the sake of which everything else is done. This applies to something different in each different art – to health in the case of medicine, to victory in that of strategy, to a house in architecture, and to something else in each of the other arts; but in every pursuit or undertaking it describes the end of that pursuit or undertaking, since in all of them it is for the sake of the end that everything else is done. Hence if there be something which is the end of all the things done by human action, this will be the practicable good – or if there be several such ends, the sum of

2 these will be the good. Thus by changing its ground the argument has reached the same result as before.[32] We must attempt however to render this still more precise.

3   Now there do appear to be several ends at which our actions aim; but as we choose some of them – for instance wealth, or flutes,[33] and instruments generally – as a means to something else, it is clear that not all of them are final ends; whereas the supreme good seems to be something final. Consequently if there be some one thing which alone is a final end, this thing – or if there be several final ends, the one among them which is

4 the most final – will be the good which we are seeking. In speaking of degrees of finality, we mean that a thing pursued as an end in itself is more final than one pursued as a means to something else, and that a thing never chosen as a means to anything else is more final than things chosen both as ends in themselves and as means to that thing; and accordingly a thing chosen always as an end and never as a means we call absolutely

5 final. Now happiness above all else appears to be absolutely final in this sense, since we always choose it for its own sake and never as a means to something else; whereas honour, pleasure, intelligence, and excellence in its various forms, we choose indeed for their own sakes (since we should be glad to have each of them although no extraneous advantage resulted from it), but we also choose them for the sake of happiness, in the belief that they will be a means to our securing it. But no one chooses happiness for the sake of honour, pleasure, etc., nor as a means to anything whatever other than itself.

6   The same conclusion also appears to follow from a consideration of the self-sufficiency of happiness – for it is felt that the final good must be a thing sufficient in itself. The term self-sufficient, however, we employ with reference not to oneself alone, living a life of isolation, but also to one's parents and children and wife, and one's friends and fellow citizens in

7 general, since man is by nature a social being.[34] On the other

hand a limit has to be assumed in these relationships; for if the list be extended to one's ancestors and descendants and to the friends of one's friends, it will go on *ad infinitum*. But this is a point that must be considered later on; we take a self-sufficient thing to mean a thing which merely standing by itself alone renders life desirable and lacking in nothing,[35] and such a thing we deem

8 happiness to be. Moreover, we think happiness the most desirable of all good things without being itself reckoned as one among the rest;[36] for if it were so reckoned, it is clear that we should consider it more desirable when even the smallest of other good things were combined with it, since this addition would result in a larger total of good, and of two goods the greater is always the more desirable.

Happiness, therefore, being found to be something final and self-sufficient, is the end at which all actions aim.

9 To say however that the supreme good is happiness will probably appear a truism; we still require a more explicit account

10 of what constitutes happiness. Perhaps then we may arrive at this by ascertaining what is man's function. For the goodness or efficiency of a flute-player or sculptor or craftsman of any sort, and in general of anybody who has some function or business to perform, is thought to reside in that function; and similarly it may be held that the good of man resides in the function of man, if he has a function.

11 Are we then to suppose that, while the carpenter and the shoemaker have definite functions or businesses belonging to them, man as such has none, and is not designed by nature to fulfil any function? Must we not rather assume that, just as the eye, the hand, the foot and each of the various members of the body manifestly has a certain function of its own, so a human being also has a certain function over and above all the functions

12 of his particular members? What then precisely can this function be? The mere act of living appears to be shared even by plants, whereas we are looking for the function peculiar to man; we must therefore set aside the vital activity of nutrition and growth. Next in the scale will come some form of sentient life; but this too appears to be shared by horses, oxen, and animals generally.

13 There remains therefore what may be called the practical[37] life of the rational part of man. (This part has two divisions,[38] one

rational as obedient to principle, the other as possessing principle and exercising intelligence.) Rational life again has two meanings; let us assume that we are here concerned with the active exercise[39] of the rational faculty, since this seems to be the more

14 proper sense of the term. If then the function of man is the active exercise of the soul's faculties[40] in conformity with rational principle, or at all events not in dissociation from rational principle, and if we acknowledge the function of an individual and of a good individual of the same class (for instance, a harper and a good harper, and so generally with all classes) to be generically the same, the qualification of the latter's superiority in excellence being added to the function in his case (I mean that if the function of a harper is to play the harp, that of a good harper is to play the harp well): if this is so, and if we declare that the function of man is a certain form of life, and define that form of life as the exercise of the soul's faculties and activities in association with rational principle, and say that the function of a

15 good man is to perform these activities well and rightly, and if a function is well performed when it is performed in accordance with its own proper excellence – from these premises it follows that the good of man is the active exercise of his soul's faculties in conformity with excellence or virtue, or if there be several human excellences or virtues, in conformity with the best and

16 most perfect among them. Moreover this activity must occupy a complete lifetime; for one swallow does not make spring, nor does one fine day; and similarly one day or a brief period of happiness does not make a man supremely blessed[41] and happy.

17 Let this account then serve to describe the good in outline – for no doubt the proper procedure is to begin by making a rough sketch, and to fill it in afterwards. If a work has been well laid down in outline, to carry it on and complete it in detail may be supposed to be within the capacity of anybody; and in this working out of details time seems to be a good inventor or at all events co-adjutor. This indeed is how advances in the arts have

18 actually come about, since anyone can fill in the gaps. Also the warning given above [42] must not be forgotten; we must not look for equal exactness in all departments of study, but only such as belongs to the subject matter of each, and in such a degree as is

19 appropriate to the particular line of enquiry. A carpenter and a

geometrician both seek after a right angle,[43] but in different ways; the former is content with that approximation to it which satisfies the purpose of his work; the latter, being a student of truth, looks for its essence or essential attributes. We should therefore proceed in the same manner in other subjects also, and not allow side issues to outweigh the main task in hand.

20 Nor again must we in all matters alike demand an explanation of the reason why things are what they are; in some cases it is enough if the fact that they are so is satisfactorily established.[44] This is the case with first principles; and the fact is the primary

21 thing – it *is* a first principle. And principles are studied – some by induction, others by perception, others by some form of

22 habituation, and also others otherwise;[45] so we must endeavour to arrive at the principles of each kind in their natural manner, and must also be careful to define them correctly, since they are

23 of great importance for the subsequent course of the enquiry. The beginning is admittedly more than half of the whole,[46] and throws light at once on many of the questions under investigation.

viii Accordingly we must examine our first principle[47] not only as a logical conclusion deduced from certain premises but also in the light of the current opinions on the subject. For if a proposition be true, all the facts harmonise with it, but if it is false, it is soon found to be discordant with them.

2 Now things good have been divided into three classes, external goods on the one hand, and goods of the soul and of the body on the other;[48] and of these three kinds of goods, those of the soul we commonly pronounce good in the fullest sense and the highest degree. But it is our actions and the soul's active exercise of its functions[49] that we posit (as being happiness); hence so far as this opinion goes – and it is of long standing, and generally accepted by students of philosophy – it supports the correctness of our definition of happiness.

3 It also shows it to be right merely in declaring the end to consist in actions or activities of some sort, for thus the end is included among goods of the soul, and not among external goods.[50]

4 Again, our definition accords with the description of the happy man as one who 'lives well' or 'does well'; for it has virtually identified happiness with a form of good life or doing well.[51]

5   And moreover all the various characteristics that are looked for in happiness are found to belong to the good as we define it. Some people think happiness is goodness or virtue, others 6 prudence, others a form of wisdom; others again say it is all of these things, or one of them, in combination with pleasure, or accompanied by pleasure as an indispensable adjunct; another school include external prosperity as a concomitant factor. Some 7 of these views have been held by many people and from ancient times, others by a few distinguished men, and neither class is likely to be altogether mistaken; the probability is that their beliefs are at least partly, or indeed mainly, correct.

8   Now with those who pronounce happiness to be virtue, or some particular virtue, our definition is in agreement; for 'activity 9 in conformity with virtue' involves virtue. But no doubt it makes a great difference whether we conceive the supreme good to depend on possessing virtue or on displaying it – on disposition, or on the manifestation of a disposition in action. For a man may possess the disposition without its producing any good result, as for instance when he is asleep, or has ceased to function from some other cause; but virtue in active exercise cannot be inoperative – it will of necessity act, and act well. And just as at the Olympic games the wreaths of victory are not bestowed upon the handsomest and strongest persons present, but on men who enter for the competitions – since it is among these that the winners are found – so it is those who *act* rightly who carry off the prizes and good things of life.

10   And further, the life of active virtue is essentially pleasant. For the feeling of pleasure is an experience of the soul,[52] and a thing gives a man pleasure in regard to which he is described as 'fond of' so-and-so: for instance a horse gives pleasure to one fond of horses, a play to one fond of the theatre, and similarly just actions are pleasant to the lover of justice, and acts conforming with 11 virtue generally to the lover of virtue. But whereas the mass of mankind take pleasure in things that conflict with one another,[53] because they are not pleasant of their own nature, things pleasant by nature are pleasant to lovers of what is noble, and so always are actions in conformity with virtue, so that they are pleasant 12 essentially as well as pleasant to lovers of the noble. Therefore their life has no need of pleasure as a sort of ornamental

appendage,[54] but contains its pleasure in itself. For there is the further consideration that the man who does not enjoy doing noble actions is not a good man at all: no one would call a man just if he did not like acting justly, nor liberal if he did not like

13 doing liberal things, and similarly with the other virtues. But if so, actions in conformity with virtue must be essentially pleasant.

But they are also of course both good and noble, and each in the highest degree, if the good man judges them rightly; and his

14 judgement is as we have said. It follows therefore that happiness is at once the best, the noblest, and the pleasantest of things: these qualities are not separated as the inscription at Delos makes out –

> Justice is noblest, and health is best,
> But the heart's desire is the pleasantest –

for the best activities possess them all; and it is the best activities, or one activity which is the best of all, in which according to our definition happiness consists.

15 Nevertheless it is manifest that happiness also requires external goods in addition, as we said; for it is impossible, or at least not easy, to play a noble part unless furnished with the necessary equipment.[55] For many noble actions require instruments for their performance, in the shape of friends or wealth or political

16 power; also there are certain external advantages, the lack of which sullies supreme felicity, such as good birth, satisfactory children, and personal beauty: a man of very ugly appearance or low birth, or childless and alone in the world, is not our idea of a happy man, and still less so perhaps is one who has children or friends[56] that are worthless, or who has had good ones but lost

17 them by death. As we said therefore, happiness does seem to require the addition of external prosperity, and this is why some people identify it with good fortune (though some identify it with virtue).[57]

ix It is this that gives rise to the question whether happiness is a thing that can be learnt, or acquired by training, or cultivated in some other manner, or whether it is bestowed by some divine

2 dispensation or even by fortune. (1) Now if anything that men have is a gift of the gods, it is reasonable to suppose that happiness is divinely given – indeed of all man's possessions it is most likely

3 to be so, inasmuch as it is the best of them all. This subject

however may perhaps more properly belong to another branch of study.[58] Still, even if happiness is not sent us from heaven, but is won by virtue and by some kind of study or practice, it seems to be one of the most divine things that exist. For the prize and end of goodness must clearly be supremely good – it must be
4 something divine and blissful. (2) And also on our view it will admit of being widely diffused, since it can be attained through some process of study or effort by all persons whose capacity for
5 virtue has not been stunted or maimed. (3) Again, if it is better to be happy as a result of one's own exertions than by the gift of fortune, it is reasonable to suppose that this is how happiness is won; inasmuch as in the world of nature things have a natural tendency to be ordered in the best possible way, and the same is
6 true of the products of art, and of causation of any kind, and especially the highest.[59] Whereas that the greatest and noblest of all things should be left to fortune would be too contrary to the fitness of things.

7 Light is also thrown on the question by our definition of happiness, which said that it is a certain kind of activity of the soul; whereas the remaining good things[60] are either merely indispensable conditions of happiness, or are of the nature of
8 auxiliary means, and useful instrumentally. This conclusion[61] moreover agrees with what we laid down at the outset; for we stated that the supreme good was the end of political science, but the principal care of this science is to produce a certain character in the citizens, namely to make them virtuous, and capable of performing noble actions.

9 We have good reasons therefore for not speaking of an ox or horse or any other animal as being happy, because none of these is
10 able to participate in noble activities. For this cause also children cannot be happy, for they are not old enough to be capable of noble acts; when children are spoken of as happy, it is in compliment to their promise for the future. Happiness, as we said,
11 requires both complete goodness and a complete lifetime. For many reverses and vicissitudes of all sorts occur in the course of life, and it is possible that the most prosperous man may encounter great disasters in his declining years, as the story is told of Priam in the epics; but no one calls a man happy who meets with misfortunes like Priam's, and comes to a miserable end.

x   Are we then to count no other human being happy either, as long as he is alive? Must we obey Solon's warning,[62] and 'look to
2   the end'? And if we are indeed to lay down this rule, can a man really be happy after he is dead? Surely that is an extremely strange notion, especially for us who define happiness as a form of activity!
3   While if on the other hand we refuse to speak of a dead man as happy, and Solon's words do not mean this, but that only when a man is dead can one safely call him blessed as being now beyond the reach of evil and misfortune, this also admits of some dispute; for it is believed that some evil and also some good can befall the dead, just as much as they can happen to the living without their being aware of it – for instance honours, and disgraces, and the prosperity and misfortunes of their children and their descendants
4   in general. But here too there is a difficulty. For suppose a man to have lived in perfect happiness until old age, and to have come to a correspondingly happy end: he may still have many vicissitudes befall his descendants, some of whom may be good and meet with the fortune they deserve, and others the opposite; and moreover these descendants may clearly stand in every possible degree of remoteness from the ancestors in question. Now it would be a strange thing if the dead man also were to change[63] with the fortunes of his family, and were to become a happy man at one
5   time and then miserable at another; yet on the other hand it would also be strange if ancestors were not affected at all, even over a limited period, by the fortunes of their descendants .
6   But let us go back to our former difficulty,[64] for perhaps it will
7   throw light on the question[65] we are now examining. If we are to look to the end, and congratulate a man when dead not as actually being blessed, but because he has been blessed in the past, surely it is strange if at the actual time when a man is happy that fact cannot be truly predicated of him, because we are unwilling to call the living happy owing to the vicissitudes of fortune, and owing to our conception of happiness as something permanent and not readily subject to change, whereas the wheel of fortune often turns full circle in the same person's experience. For it is
8   clear that if we are to be guided by fortune, we shall often have to call the same man first happy and then miserable; we shall make out the happy man to be a sort of 'chameleon, or a house built on the sand'.[66]

9 But perhaps it is quite wrong to be guided in our judgement by the changes of fortune, since true prosperity and adversity do not depend on fortune's favours, although, as we said, our life does require these in addition; but it is the active exercise of our faculties in conformity with virtue that causes happiness, and the opposite activities its opposite.

10 And the difficulty just discussed is a further confirmation of our definition; since none of man's functions possess the quality of permanence so fully as the activities in conformity with virtue: they appear to be more lasting even than our knowledge of particular sciences. And among these activities themselves those which are highest in the scale of values are the more lasting, because they most fully and continuously occupy the lives of the supremely happy: for this appears to be the reason why we do not forget them.

11 The happy man therefore will possess the element of stability in question, and will remain happy all his life; since he will be always or at least most often employed in doing and contemplating the things that are in conformity with virtue. And he will bear changes of fortunes most nobly, and with perfect propriety in every way, being as he is 'good in very truth' and 'four-square without reproach'.[67]

12 But the accidents of fortune are many and vary in degree of magnitude; and although small pieces of good luck, as also of misfortune, clearly do not change the whole course of life, yet great and repeated successes will render life more blissful, since both of their own nature they help to embellish it, and also they can be nobly and virtuously utilised;[68] while great and frequent reverses can crush and mar our bliss both by the pain they cause and by the hindrance they offer to many activities. Yet neverthe-less even in adversity nobility shines through, when a man endures repeated and severe misfortune with patience, not owing

13 to insensibility but from generosity and greatness of soul. And if, as we said, a man's life is determined by his activities, no supremely happy man can ever become miserable. For he will never do hateful or base actions, since we hold that the truly good and wise man will bear all kinds of fortune in a seemly way, and will always act in the noblest manner that the circumstances allow; even as a good general makes the most effective use of the

forces at his disposal, and a good shoemaker makes the finest shoe possible out of the leather supplied him, and so on with all the
14 other crafts and professions. And this being so, the happy man can never become miserable; though it is true he will not be supremely blessed if he encounters the misfortunes of a Priam. Nor yet assuredly will he be variable and liable to change; for he will not be dislodged from his happiness easily, nor by ordinary misfortunes, but only by severe and frequent disasters, nor will he recover from such disasters and become happy again quickly, but only, if at all, after a long term of years, in which he has had time to compass high distinctions and achievements.

15 May not we then confidently pronounce that man happy who realises compete goodness in action, and is adequately furnished with external goods? Or should we add, that he must also be destined to go on living not[69] for any casual period but throughout a complete lifetime in the same manner, and to die accordingly, because the future is hidden from us, and we conceive happiness as an end, something utterly and absolutely
16 final and complete? If this is so, we shall pronounce those of the living who possess and are destined to go on possessing the good things we have specified to be supremely blessed, though on the human scale of bliss.

So much for a discussion of this question.

xi That the happiness of the dead is not influenced at all by the fortunes of their descendants and their friends in general seems
2 too heartless a doctrine, and contrary to accepted beliefs. But the accidents of life are many and diverse, and vary in the degree in which they affect us. To distinguish between them in detail would clearly be a long and indeed endless undertaking, and a
3 general treatment in outline may perhaps be enough. Even our own misfortunes, then, though in some cases they exercise considerable weight and influence upon the course of our lives, in other cases seem comparatively unimportant; and the same is true
4 of the misfortunes of our friends of all degrees. Also it makes a great difference whether those who are connected with any occurrence are alive or dead, much more so than it does in a tragedy whether the crimes and horrors are supposed to have
5 taken place beforehand or are enacted on the stage. We ought therefore to take this difference also into account, and still more

perhaps the doubt that exists whether the dead really participate in good or evil at all. For the above considerations seem to show that even if any good or evil does penetrate to them, the effect is only small and trifling, either intrinsically or in relation to them, or if not trifling, at all events not of such magnitude and kind as to make the unhappy happy or to rob the happy of their blessedness.

6   It does then appear that the dead are influenced in some measure by the good fortune of their friends, and likewise by their misfortunes, but that the effect is not of such a kind or degree as to render the happy unhappy or *vice versa*.

xii   These questions being settled, let us consider whether happiness is one of the things we praise or rather one of those that we honour';[70] for it is at all events clear that it is not a mere potentiality.[71]

2   Now it appears that a thing which we praise is always praised because it has a certain quality and stands in a certain relation to something. For we praise just men and brave men, in fact good men and virtue generally, because of their actions and the results they produce; and we praise the men who are strong of body, swift of foot and the like on account of their possessing certain natural qualities, and standing in a certain relation to something 3 good and excellent. The point is also illustrated by our feeling about praises addressed to the gods: it strikes us as absurd that the gods should be referred to our standards, and this is what praising them amounts to, since praise, as we said, involves a reference of 4 its object to something else. But if praise belongs to what is relative, it is clear that the best things merit not praise but something greater and better: as indeed is generally recognised, since we speak of the gods as blessed and happy,[72] and also 'blessed' is the term that we apply to the most godlike men; and similarly with good things – no one praises happiness as one praises justice, but we call it 'a blessing', deeming it something higher and more divine than things we praise.

5   Indeed it seems that Eudoxus[73] took a good line in advocating the claims of pleasure to the prize of highest excellence, when he held that the fact that pleasure, though a good, is not praised, is an indication that it is superior to the things we praise, as god and the good are, because they are the standards to which everything else is referred.

6   For praise belongs to goodness, since it is this that makes men capable of accomplishing noble deeds, while encomia[74] are for deeds accomplished, whether bodily feats or achievements of the
7   mind. However, to develop this subject is perhaps rather the business of those who have made a study of encomia. For our purpose we may draw the conclusion from the foregoing
8   remarks, that happiness is a thing honoured and perfect. This seems to be borne out by the fact that it is a first principle or starting-point, since all other things that all men do are done for its sake; and that which is the first principle and cause of things good we agree to be something honourable and divine.

xiii   But inasmuch as happiness is a certain activity of soul in conformity with perfect goodness, it is necessary to examine the nature of goodness. For this will probably assist us in our
2   investigation of the nature of happiness. Also, the true statesman seems to be one who has made a special study of goodness, since
3   his aim is to make the citizens good and law-abiding men – witness the lawgivers of Crete and Sparta, and the other great legislators of history; but if the study of goodness falls within the
4   province of political science, it is clear that in investigating goodness we shall be keeping to the plan which we adopted at the outset.

5   Now the goodness that we have to consider is clearly human goodness, since the good or happiness which we set out to seek
6   was human good and human happiness. But human goodness means in our view excellence of soul, not excellence of body;
7   also our definition of happiness is an activity of the soul. Now if this is so, clearly it behoves the statesman to have some acquaintance with psychology, just as the physician who is to heal the eye or the other parts of the body[75] must know their anatomy. Indeed a foundation of science is even more requisite for the statesman, inasmuch as politics is a higher and more honourable art than medicine; but physicians of the better class devote much attention to the study of the human body. The
8   student of politics[76] therefore as well as the psychologist must study the nature of the soul, though he will do so as an aid to politics, and only so far as is requisite for the objects of enquiry that he has in view: to pursue the subject in further detail would doubtless be more laborious than is necessary for his purpose.

9   Now on the subject of psychology some of the teaching current in extraneous discourses[77] is satisfactory, and may be adopted here: namely that the soul consists of two parts, one
10   irrational and the other capable of reason.[78] (Whether these two parts are really distinct in the sense that the parts of the body or of any other divisible whole are distinct, or whether though distinguishable in thought as two they are inseparable in reality, like the convex and concave sides of a curve, is a question of no
11   importance for the matter in hand.) Of the irrational part of the soul again one division appears to be common to all living things, and of a vegetative nature: I refer to the part that causes nutrition and growth; for we must assume that a vital faculty of this nature exists in all things that assimilate nourishment, including embryos – the same faculty being present also in the fully-developed organism (this is more reasonable than to assume a different
12   nutritive faculty in the latter). The excellence of this faculty therefore appears to be common to all animate things and not peculiar to man; for it is believed that this faculty or part of the soul is most active during sleep, but when they are asleep you cannot tell a good man from a bad one (whence the saying that for half their lives there is no difference between the happy and
13   the miserable). This is a natural result of the fact that sleep is a cessation of the soul from the activities on which its goodness or badness depends – except that in some small degree certain of the sense-impressions may reach the soul during sleep, and consequently the dreams of the good are better than those of
14   ordinary men. We need not however pursue this subject further, but may omit from consideration the nutritive part of the soul, since it exhibits no specifically human excellence .

15   But there also appears to be another element in the soul, which, though irrational, yet in a manner participates in rational principle. In self-restrained and unrestrained[79] people we approve their principle, or the rational part of their souls, because it urges them in the right way and exhorts them to the best course; but their nature seems also to contain another element beside that of rational principle, which combats and resists that principle.
16   Exactly the same thing may take place in the soul as occurs with the body in a case of paralysis: when the patient wills to move his limbs to the right they swerve to the left; and similarly in

unrestrained persons their impulses run counter to their principle. But whereas in the body we see the erratic member, in the case of the soul we do not see it; nevertheless it cannot be doubted that in the soul also there is an element beside that of principle, which opposes and runs counter to principle (though in what

17 sense the two are distinct does not concern us here). But this second element also seems, as we said, to participate in rational principle; at least in the self-restrained man it obeys the behest of principle – and no doubt in the temperate and brave man it is still more amenable, for all parts of his nature are in harmony with principle.

18 Thus we see that the irrational part, as well as the soul as a whole, is double. One division of it, the vegetative, does not share in rational principle at all; the other, the seat of the appetites and of desire in general, does in a sense participate in principle, as being amenable and obedient to it (in the sense in fact in which we speak of 'paying heed' to one's father and friends, not in the sense of the term 'rational' in mathematics).[80] And that principle can in a manner appeal to the irrational part is indicated by our practice of admonishing delinquents, and by our employment of rebuke and exhortation generally.

19 If on the other hand it be more correct to speak of the appetitive part of the soul also as rational, in that case it is the rational part which, as well as the whole soul, is divided into two, the one division having rational principle in the proper sense and in itself, the other obedient to it as a child to its father.

20 Now virtue also is differentiated in correspondence with this division of the soul. Some forms of virtue are called intellectual virtues, others moral virtues: wisdom or intelligence and prudence[81] are intellectual, liberality and temperance are moral virtues. When describing a man's moral character we do not say that he is wise or intelligent, but gentle or temperate; but a wise man also is praised for his disposition, and praiseworthy dispositions we term virtues.

1 Aristotle gives flute-playing as an instance of an art the practice of which is an end in itself, in contrast with the art of building, the end of which is the house built (*Magna Moralia*, 1211 b 27 ff.).

2 or perhaps 'both to ascertain and to secure'.

3 καλόν is a term of admiration applied to what is correct, especially (1) bodies well shaped and works of art or handicraft well made, and (2) actions well done (see III, vii, 6); it thus means (1) beautiful, (2) morally right. For the analogy between material and moral correctness see II, vi, 9.

4 Quoted in *Troilus and Cressida*, II, ii, 165:
> young men, whom Aristotle thought
> Unfit to hear moral philosophy.

5 The argument is, that even if the young could gain a knowledge of ethics (which they cannot, because it requires experience of life), they would not use it as a guide to conduct, because they are led by their passions and appetites; and therefore the study is of no value for them, since ethics, being a practical science, is only pursued for the sake of its practical application.

6 This translation of εὐδαιμονία can hardly be avoided, but it would perhaps be more accurately rendered by 'well being' or 'prosperity'; and it will be found that the writer does not interpret it as a state of feeling but as a kind of activity.

7 The English phrase preserves the ambiguity of the Greek, which in its ordinary acceptation rather means 'faring well' than 'acting well', though in the sequel Aristotle diverts it to the active sense.

8 Plato and the Academy; see chapter vi.

9 in contrast apparently with the school of Plato.

10 *Works and Days*, 293 ff.

11 iv, 4.

12 The doctrine of the three lives goes back to Pythagoras, who compared the three kinds of men to the three classes of strangers who went to the games: traders, competitors and spectators (Iamblichus, *Vit. Pythagoras*, 58). This apologue brings out the metaphor underlying the phrase θεωρητικὸς βίος, lit. 'the life of the spectator' (Burnet).

13 The last two words of the Greek look like a verse passage loosely

quoted. Sardanapallus was a mythical Assyrian king; two versions of his epitaph are recorded by Athenaeus (336, 530), one containing the words 'Eat, drink, play, since all else is not worth that snap of the fingers'; the other ends 'I have what I ate; and the delightful deeds of wantonness and love which I did and suffered; whereas all my wealth is vanished.'

14 It is not certain whether this phrase refers to written treatises (whether Aristotle's own dialogues and other popular works, now lost, or those of other philosophers), or to philosophical debates like those which Plato's dialogues purport to report (as did doubtless those of Aristotle). Cf. De caelo 279 a 30 ἐν τοῖς ἐγκυκλίοις φιλοσοφήμασι, 'in the ordinary philosophical discussions', and De anima 407 b 29 τοῖς ἐν κοινῷ γινομένοις λόγοις, 'the discussions that go on in public'; and see note 77 for similar references to 'extraneous discussions'.

15 Literally 'violent': the adjective is applied to the strict diet and laborious exercises of athletes, and to physical phenomena such as motion, in the sense of 'constrained', 'not natural'. The text here has been suspected.

16 The translation 'forms' is perhaps less misleading: εἶδος is not a psychological term.

17 probably a verse quotation.

18 or perhaps 'importers' from the Pythagoreans of southern Italy.

19 Perhaps 'we posit', if a variant reading of the text is adopted.

20 A is 'prior in nature' (though not necessarily in time) to B, when A can exist without B but not B without A; and they cannot then be on a par as members of one class.

21 literally 'that which is by itself'.

22 δίαιτα is used of the habitat of a species of animals, De mundo 398b 32; though it has been taken here to mean 'a favourable climate' for human beings.

23 literally 'so-and-so itself'.

24 i.e. 'the ordinary notion of man' – the concept of man in general which we form from our experience of particular men, but do not regard as a thing existing independently of them – or perhaps 'a particular man'.

25 This parenthetical note might come better after § 4. The Pythagoreans, instead of (like Plato) saying the good was one, more wisely said the one was good (or akin to the good). Some of them (Metaphysics A, 986 a 22) taught that there were ten pairs of opposing principles, which they ranged in two columns – limit and the unlimited, odd and even, unity and plurality, right and left, male and female, resting and moving, straight and crooked, light

and darkness, good and bad, square and oblong. They also held (*ibid.* A, 1072 b 32) that good and beauty were not original, but appeared in the collapse of the evolution of the world; hence perhaps the late position of good in the list of opposites. The phrase 'column of goods' is inexact, as good was only one of the things in the column – unless it means the column to which good things among others belong; but doubtless all the positive principles were regarded as akin.

26 Speusippus was Plato's nephew, and succeeded him as head of the Academy.

27 *i.e.*, the species or class of things good in themselves will be a class to which nothing belongs (for the idea is not *in* the class).

28 Aristotle's own solution: when different things are called good, it means they each bear the same relation to (contribute to the welfare of) certain other things, not all to the same thing.

29 *i.e.*, first philosophy or metaphysics.

30 Or perhaps 'to supply what is lacking of it' (the good at which they aim); *cf.* vii, 17.

31 *i.e.*, the particular good which is the end of his own science.

32 *cf.* ii, 1.

33 Perhaps a note on 'instruments', interpolated.

34 literally 'a political thing'. *Politics*, 1253 a 2 adds ζῷον, 'a political animal'.

35 A probable emendation gives 'renders life sufficient, that is, lacking in nothing'.

36 *sc.* but as including all other good things as the end includes the means.

37 'Practice' for Aristotle denotes purposeful conduct, of which only rational beings are capable; *cf.* VI, note 6.

38 This anticipation of xiii, 19 is irrelevant, and states decisively a point there left doubtful. Also on grounds of Greek this parenthesis has been suspected as an interpolation and perhaps we should leave it out and render the preceding words 'the practical life of a rational being'.

39 in contrast with the mere state of possessing the faculty.

40 Literally 'activity of soul'; ψυχή however has a wider connotation than either 'soul' or 'mind', and includes the whole of the vitality of any living creature.

41 The word μακάριος, rendered 'blessed' or 'supremely happy', is a derivative of μάκαρ, the adjective applied in Homer and Hesiod to the gods and to those of mankind who have been admitted after death to the Islands of the Blest. See x, 16 and xii, 4.

42 iii, 1–4.

43 or 'straight line'.

44 *cf.* iv, 7.

45 This is usually taken 'that is, different ones in different ways', but καὶ . . . δέ seems to refer to other classes as well.

46 The usual form of the proverb is 'The beginning is half of the whole'. Aristotle applies it by a sort of play on words to ἀρχή in its technical sense of a general principle of science, which is a 'beginning' in the sense that it is the starting point of deductive reasoning. There is a reminiscence of Hesiod, *Works and Days* 30, πλέον ἥμισυ παντός, 'The half is more than the whole', though the meaning of that is entirely different.

47 *i.e.* our definition of the good for man, or happiness.

48 The turn of phrase associates 'bodily goods' with 'goods of the soul', both being personal, in contrast with the third class, 'external goods'. But it at once appears that the important distinction is between 'goods of the soul' on the one hand and all the rest ('the goods in the body and those outside and of fortune', VII, xiii, 2) on the other. Hence in §3 'external goods' must include 'bodily goods', as also §§15 f., where 'external goods' are subdivided into the instruments and the indispensable conditions of well-being (and so in more scientific language, ix, 7), the latter subdivision including beauty, the only bodily good there specified.

49 See the definition, vii, 15.

50 See note 48.

51 See note 7.

52 Not an experience of the body (*cf.* x, iii, 6), even in the case of 'bodily pleasures'. This brings pleasure within the definition of happiness as 'an activity of the soul'.

53 Morally inferior people like things that are only pleasant 'accidentally', *i.e.* owing not to some quality inherent in the thing but to something extraneous to it: some depravity of taste or temporary affection in the person. Hence not only do different people think different things pleasant but the same person thinks the same thing pleasant at one time and unpleasant at another – and so repents to-day of his indulgence yesterday; or he desires two incompatible things at once, or desires a thing with one part of his nature that he dislikes with another, so that there is a conflict between his desires, or between his desire for pleasure and his wish for what he thinks good (see IX, iv, especially §§ 8–10, and contrast § 5).

54 The word is especially used of an amulet hung round the neck or fastened round a limb.

55 It was one of the public duties of rich citizens at Athens to equip the chorus and actors of a drama at their own expense. One so doing was called χορηγός (chorus-leader, as no doubt originally he was), and the dresses, etc., he supplied, χορηγία. The latter term is frequently used by Aristotle to denote the material equipment of life, and has almost or quite ceased to be felt as a metaphor.

56 Perhaps 'or friends' is slipped in because of 'alone in the world' just above, but friends should not be mentioned here among the indispensable conditions of happiness, as they were included just above among its instruments (see note 48).

57 This irrelevant addition looks like an interpolation.

58 *i.e.*, theology, but Aristotle does not reopen the question in the *Metaphysics* or elsewhere.

59 *i.e.*, the intelligence of man.

60 *cf.* viii, 15–16 and note 48.

61 namely, that happiness depends on us and not on fortune, the answer implied by the foregoing arguments to the question raised in § 1.

62 See Herodotus, i, 30–33. Solon visited Croesus, king of Lydia, and was shown all his treasures, but refused to call him the happiest of mankind until he should have heard that he had ended his life without misfortune; he bade him 'mark the end of every matter, how it should turn out'.

63 *i.e.*, if our estimate of his life as happy or the reverse had to change. There is no idea of the dead being conscious of what happens to their descendants (*cf.* § 3 fin.), though this is inconsistently suggested by the wording of § 5.

64 that raised in § 1.

65 that raised in § 4.

66 perhaps a verse from an unknown play.

67 From the poem of Simonides quoted and discussed in Plato, *Protagoras*, 339.

68 This distinction of the two values of good fortune recalls the two classes of external goods defined in viii, 15 and 16; and ix, 7.

69 The clause 'not . . . lifetime' stands above after 'external goods' in the manuscripts: editors have transposed it for reasons of sense.

70 The definition of happiness is now shown to be supported by the current terms of moral approbation; apparently ἐπαινετόν, 'praise-worthy' or 'commendable', was appropriate to means, or things having relative value, and τίμιον, 'valued' or 'revered', to ends, or things of absolute value.

71 *i.e.*, not merely a potentiality of good but an actual good, whether as means or end.

72 but we do not praise them.

73 For a criticism of the hedonism of this unorthodox pupil of Plato see X, ii, iii.

74 Encomia or laudatory orations are the chief constituent of epideictic or declamatory oratory, one of the three branches (the others being deliberative and forensic) into which rhetoric is divided by Aristotle (*Rhetoric*, i, iii).

75 The context seems to disprove the alternative rendering 'just as to cure eyes the oculist must have a general knowledge of the structure of the whole of the body as well'. The illustration is a reminiscence of Plato, *Charmides*, 156 b–e, but does not follow that passage exactly.

76 πολιτικός means for Aristotle both 'political scientist' and 'statesman'; for him they are the same thing, since πολιτική is a practical science.

77 These ἐξωτερικοὶ λόγοι are also mentioned in VI, iv, 2 and six other places in Aristotle (see Ross on *Met.* 1076 a 28). In *Politics*, 1323 a 22 they are appealed to for the tripartite classification of goods which in viii, 2 above is ascribed to current opinion 'of long standing and generally accepted by students of philosophy'. The phrase therefore seems to denote arguments or doctrines (whether familiar in philosophic debates, for which see note 14, or actually recorded in books) that were not peculiar to the peripatetic school; in some cases, as here, it may refer specially to the tenets of the Academy.

78 literally 'having a plan or principle'.

79 For these terms see the beginning of Book VII.

80 This parenthetical note on the phrase 'to have *logos*' is untranslatable, and confusing even in the Greek. According to the psychology here expounded, the intellect 'has a plan or principle', in the sense of understanding principle, and being able to reason and make a plan: in other words, it is fully rational. The appetitive part of man's nature 'has a plan or principle' in so far as it is capable of following or obeying a principle. It happens that this relationship of following or obeying can itself be expressed by the words 'to have *logos*' in another sense of that phrase, 'to take account of, pay heed to'. To be precise the writer should say that the appetitive part λόγον ἔχει τοῦ λόγου, 'has *logos,* (takes account) of the *logos*'. The phrase has yet a third sense in mathematics, where 'to have *logos*' (*ratio*) means 'to be rational' in the sense of commensurable.

81 *i.e.*, practical, as distinguished from speculative, wisdom.

BOOK TWO

Nature of moral virtue

Table of Virtues and Vices (1107a32–1108b10)

Class of action or feeling	Excess	Mean	Deficiency
fear and confidence	rashness	courage	cowardice
pleasure and pain	profligacy	temperance	insensitivity
giving and getting small amounts of money	prodigality	liberality	meanness
giving and getting large amounts of money	vulgarity	magnificence	paltriness
major honour and dishonour	vanity	greatness of soul	smallness of soul
minor honour and dishonour	ambitiousness	[proper ambition]	unambitiousness
anger	irascibility	gentleness	spiritlessness
truthfulness about one's own merits	boastfulness	truthfulness	self-depreciation
pleasantness in social amusement	buffoonery	wittiness	boorishness
pleasantness in social conduct	obsequiousness	friendliness	surliness
shame	bashfulness	modesty	shamelessness
pleasure in others' misfortunes	envy	righteous indignation	malice

i Virtue being, as we have seen, of two kinds, intellectual and moral, intellectual virtue is for the most part both produced and increased by instruction, and therefore requires experience and time; whereas moral or ethical virtue is the product of habit (*ethos*), and has indeed derived its name, with a slight variation of

2 form, from that word.[1] And therefore it is clear that none of the moral virtues is engendered in us by nature, for no natural property can be altered by habit. For instance, it is the nature of a stone to move downwards, and it cannot be trained to move upwards, even though you should try to train it to do so by throwing it up into the air ten thousand times; nor can fire be trained to move downwards, nor can anything else that naturally behaves in one way be trained into a habit of behaving in another

3 way. The virtues[2] therefore are engendered in us neither by nature nor yet in violation of nature; nature gives us the capacity to receive them, and this capacity is brought to maturity by habit.

4 Moreover, the faculties given us by nature are bestowed on us first in a potential form; we exhibit their actual exercise afterwards. This is clearly so with our senses: we did not acquire the faculty of sight or hearing by repeatedly seeing or repeatedly listening, but the other way about – because we had the senses we began to use them, we did not get them by using them. The virtues on the other hand we acquire by first having actually practised them, just as we do the arts. We learn an art or craft by doing the things that we shall have to do when we have learnt it:[3] for instance, men become builders by building houses, harpers by playing on the harp. Similarly we become just by doing just acts, temperate by doing temperate acts, brave by doing brave acts.

5 This truth is attested by the experience of states: lawgivers make the citizens good by training them in habits of right action – this is the aim of all legislation, and if it fails to do this it is a failure; this is what distinguishes a good form of constitution from a bad

6 one. Again, the actions from or through which any virtue is produced are the same as those through which it also is

destroyed – just as is the case with skill in the arts, for both the good harpers and the bad ones are produced by harping, and similarly with builders and all the other craftsmen: as you will become a good builder from building well, so you will become a
7 bad one from building badly. Were this not so, there would be no need for teachers of the arts, but everybody would be born a good or bad craftsman as the case might be. The same then is true of the virtues. It is by taking part in transactions with our fellow-men that some of us become just and others unjust; by acting in dangerous situations and forming a habit of fear or of confidence we become courageous or cowardly. And the same holds good of our dispositions with regard to the appetites, and anger; some men become temperate and gentle, other profligate and irascible, by actually comporting themselves in one way or the other in relation to those passions. In a word, our moral dispositions are
8 formed as a result of the corresponding activities. Hence it is incumbent on us to control the character of our activities, since on the quality of these depends the quality of our dispositions. It is therefore not of small moment whether we are trained from childhood in one set of habits or another; on the contrary it is of very great, or rather of supreme, importance.

ii   As then our present study, unlike the other branches of philosophy, has a practical aim (for we are not investigating the nature of virtue for the sake of knowing what it is, but in order that we may become good, without which result our investigation would be of no use), we have consequently to carry our enquiry into the region of conduct, and to ask how we are to act rightly; since our actions, as we have said, determine the quality of our dispositions.

2   Now the formula 'to act in conformity with right principle' is common ground, and may be assumed as the basis of our discussion. (We shall speak about this formula later,[4] and consider both the definition of right principle and its relation to the other virtues.)

3   But let it be granted to begin with that the whole theory of conduct is bound to be an outline only and not an exact system, in accordance with the rule we laid down at the beginning,[5] that philosophical theories must only be required to correspond to their subject matter; and matters of conduct and expediency have

nothing fixed or invariable about them, any more than have
4 matters of health. And if this is true of the general theory of
ethics, still less is exact precision possible in dealing with
particular cases of conduct; for these come under no science or
professional tradition, but the agents themselves have to consider
what is suited to the circumstances on each occasion, just as is the
5 case with the art of medicine or of navigation. But although the
discussion now proceeding is thus necessarily inexact, we must
do our best to help it out.

6 First of all then we have to observe, that moral qualities are so
constituted as to be destroyed by excess and by deficiency – as we
see is the case with bodily strength and health (for one is forced
to explain what is invisible by means of visible illustrations).
Strength is destroyed both by excessive and by deficient exercises, and similarly health is destroyed both by too much and by
too little food and drink; while they are produced, increased and
7 preserved by suitable quantities. The same therefore is true of
temperance, courage, and the other virtues. The man who runs
away from everything in fear and never endures anything
becomes a coward; the man who fears nothing whatsoever but
encounters everything becomes rash. Similarly he that indulges in
every pleasure and refrains from none turns out a profligate, and
he that shuns all pleasure, as boorish persons do, becomes what
may be called insensitive. Thus temperance and courage are
destroyed by excess and deficiency, and preserved by the
observance of the mean.

8 But[6] not only are the virtues both generated and fostered on
the one hand, and destroyed on the other, from and by the same
actions, but they will also find their full exercise in the same
actions. This is clearly the case with the other more visible
qualities, such as bodily strength: for strength is produced by
taking much food and undergoing much exertion, while also it is
the strong man who will be able to eat most food and endure
9 most exertion. The same holds good with the virtues. We
become temperate by abstaining from pleasures, and at the same
time we are best able to abstain from pleasures when we have
become temperate. And so with courage: we become brave by
training ourselves to despise and endure terrors, and we shall be
best able to endure terrors when we have become brave.

iii   An index of our dispositions is afforded by the pleasure or pain that accompanies our actions. A man is temperate if he abstains from bodily pleasures and finds this abstinence itself enjoyable, profligate if he feels it irksome; he is brave if he faces danger with pleasure or at all events without pain, cowardly if he does so with pain.

In fact pleasures and pains are the things with which moral virtue is concerned.

2   For (1) pleasure causes us to do base actions and pain causes us to abstain from doing noble actions. Hence the importance, as Plato points out, of having been definitely trained from childhood to like and dislike the proper things; this is what good education means.

3   (2) Again, if the virtues have to do with actions and feelings, and every feeling and every action is attended with pleasure or pain, this too shows that virtue has to do with pleasure and pain.

4   (3) Another indication is the fact that pain is the medium of punishment; for punishment is a sort of medicine, and it is the nature of medicine to work by means of opposites.[7]

5   (4) Again, as we said before, every formed disposition of the soul realises its full nature[8] in relation to and in dealing with that class of objects by which it is its nature to be corrupted or improved. But men are corrupted through pleasures and pains, that is, either by pursuing and avoiding the wrong pleasures and pains, or by pursuing and avoiding them at the wrong time, or in the wrong manner, or in one of the other wrong ways under which errors of conduct can be logically classified. This is why some thinkers[9] define the virtues as states of impassivity or tranquillity, though they make a mistake in using these terms absolutely, without adding 'in the right (or wrong) manner' and 'at the right (or wrong) time' and the other qualifications.

6   We assume therefore that moral virtue is the quality of acting in the best way in relation to pleasures and pains, and that vice is the opposite.

7   But the following considerations also will give us further light on the same point.

(5) There are three things that are the motives of choice and three that are the motives of avoidance; namely, the noble, the expedient, and the pleasant, and their opposites, the base, the

harmful, and the painful. Now in respect of all these the good man is likely to go right and the bad to go wrong, but especially in respect of pleasure; for pleasure is common to man with the lower animals, and also it is a concomitant of all the objects of choice, since both the noble and the expedient appear to us pleasant.

8   (6) Again, the susceptibility to pleasure has grown up with all of us from the cradle. Hence this feeling is hard to eradicate, being engrained in the fabric of our lives.

9   (7) Again, pleasure and pain are also[10] the standards by which we all, in a greater or less degree, regulate our actions. On this account therefore pleasure and pain are necessarily our main concern, since to feel pleasure and pain rightly or wrongly has a great effect on conduct.

10   (8) And again, it is harder to fight against pleasure than against anger (hard as that is, as Heraclitus[11] says); but virtue, like art, is constantly dealing with what is harder, since the harder the task the better is success. For this reason also therefore pleasure and pain are necessarily the main concern both of virtue and of political science, since he who comports himself towards them rightly will be good, and he who does so wrongly, bad.

11   We may then take it as established that virtue has to do with pleasures and pains, that the actions which produce it are those which increase it, and also, if differently performed, destroy it, and that the actions from which it was produced are also those in which it is exercised.

iv   A difficulty may however be raised as to what we mean by saying that in order to become just men must do just actions, and in order to become temperate they must do temperate actions. For if they do just and temperate actions, they are just and temperate already, just as, if they write correctly or play in tune, they are scholars or musicians.

2   But perhaps this is not the case even with the arts. It is possible to write something correctly by chance, or because someone else prompts you; hence you will be a scholar only if you write correctly in the scholar's way, that is, in virtue of the scholarly knowledge which you yourself possess.

3   Moreover the case of the arts is not really analogous to that of the virtues. Works of art have their merit in themselves, so that it

is enough if they are produced having a certain quality of their own; but acts done in conformity with the virtues are not done justly or temperately if they themselves are of a certain sort, but only if the agent also is in a certain state of mind when he does them: first he must act with knowledge;[12] secondly he must deliberately choose the act, and choose it for its own sake; and thirdly the act must spring from a fixed and permanent disposition of character. For the possession of an art, none of these conditions is included, except the mere qualification of knowledge; but for the possession of the virtues, knowledge is of little or no avail, whereas the other conditions, so far from being of little moment, are all-important, inasmuch as virtue results from

4 the repeated performance of just and temperate actions. Thus although actions are entitled just and temperate when they are such acts as just and temperate men would do, the agent is just and temperate not when he does these acts merely, but when he does them in the way in which just and temperate men do them.

5 It is correct therefore to say that a man becomes just by doing just actions and temperate by doing temperate actions; and no one can have the remotest chance of becoming good without doing

6 them. But the mass of mankind, instead of doing virtuous acts, have recourse to discussing virtue, and fancy that they are pursuing philosophy and that this will make them good men. In so doing they act like invalids who listen carefully to what the doctor says, but entirely neglect to carry out his prescriptions. That sort of philosophy will no more lead to a healthy state of soul than will the mode of treatment produce health of body.

V   We have next to consider the formal definition of virtue.

A state of the soul is either (1) an emotion, (2) a capacity, or (3) a disposition; virtue therefore must be one of these three

2 things. By the emotions, I mean desire, anger, fear, confidence, envy, joy, friendship, hatred, longing, jealousy, pity; and generally those states of consciousness which are accompanied by pleasure or pain. The capacities are the faculties in virtue of which we can be said to be liable to the emotions, for example, capable of feeling anger or pain[13] or pity. The dispositions are the formed states of character in virtue of which we are well or ill disposed in respect of the emotions; for instance, we have a bad disposition in regard to anger if we are disposed to get angry

too violently or not violently enough, a good disposition if we habitually feel a moderate amount of anger; and similarly in respect of the other emotions.

3   Now the virtues and vices are not emotions because we are not pronounced good or bad according to our emotions, but we are according to our virtues and vices; nor are we either praised or blamed for our emotions – a man is not praised for being frightened or angry, nor is he blamed for being angry merely, but for being angry in a certain way – but we are praised or blamed

4 for our virtues and vices. Again, we are not angry or afraid from choice, but the virtues are certain modes of choice, or at all events involve choice. Moreover, we are said to be 'moved' by the emotions, whereas in respect of the virtues and vices we are not said to be 'moved' but to be 'disposed' in a certain way.

5   And the same considerations also prove that the virtues and vices are not capacities; since we are not pronounced good or bad, praised or blamed, merely by reason of our capacity for emotion. Again, we possess certain capacities by nature, but we are not born good or bad by nature: of this however we spoke before.

6   If then the virtues are neither emotions nor capacities, it remains that they are dispositions.

Thus we have stated what virtue is generically.

vi   But it is not enough merely to define virtue generically as a disposition; we must also say what species of disposition it is. It

2 must then be premised that all excellence has a twofold effect on the thing to which it belongs: it not only renders the thing itself good, but it also causes it to perform its function well. For example, the effect of excellence in the eye is that the eye is good *and* functions well; since having good eyes means having good sight. Similarly excellence in a horse makes it a good horse, and also good at galloping, at carrying its rider, and at facing the

3 enemy. If therefore this is true of all things, excellence or virtue in a man will be the disposition which renders him a good man

4 and also which will cause him to perform his function well. We have already indicated[14] what this means; but it will throw more light on the subject if we consider what constitutes the specific nature of virtue.

Now of everything that is continuous[15] and divisible, it is possible to take the larger part, or the smaller part, or an equal part, and these parts may be larger, smaller, and equal either with respect to the thing itself or relatively to us; the equal part being a

5 mean between excess and deficiency.[16] By the mean of the thing I denote a point equally distant from either extreme, which is one and the same for everybody; by the mean relative to us, that amount which is neither too much nor too little, and this is not

6 one and the same for everybody. For example, let 10 be many and 2 few; then one takes the mean with respect to the thing if one takes 6; since 6 - 2 = 10 - 6, and this is the mean according

7 to arithmetical proportion.[17] But we cannot arrive by this method at the mean relative to us. Suppose that 10 pounds of food is a large ration for anybody and 2 pounds a small one: it does not follow that a trainer will prescribe 6 pounds, for perhaps even this will be a large ration, or a small one, for the particular athlete who is to receive it; it is a small ration for a Milo,[18] but a

8 large one for a man just beginning to go in for athletics. And similarly with the amount of running or wrestling exercise to be taken. In the same way then an expert in any art avoids excess and deficiency, and seeks and adopts the mean – the mean, that

9 is, not of the thing but relative to us. If therefore the way in which every art or science performs its work well is by looking to the mean and applying that as a standard to its productions (hence the common remark about a perfect work of art, that you could not take from it nor add to it – meaning that excess and deficiency destroy perfection, while adherence to the mean preserves it) – if then, as we say, good craftsmen look to the mean as they work, and if virtue, like nature, is more accurate and better than any form of art, it will follow that virtue has the

10 quality of hitting the mean. I refer to moral virtue,[19] for this is concerned with emotions and actions, in which one can have excess or deficiency or a due mean. For example, one can be frightened or bold, feel desire or anger or pity, and experience

11 pleasure and pain in general, either too much or too little, and in both cases wrongly; whereas to feel these feelings at the right time, on the right occasion, towards the right people, for the right purpose and in the right manner, is to feel the best amount of them, which is the mean amount – and the best amount is of

12 course the mark of virtue. And similarly there can be excess,

deficiency, and the due mean in actions. Now feelings and actions are the objects with which virtue is concerned; and in feelings and actions excess and deficiency are errors, while the mean amount is praised, and constitutes success; and to be praised

13 and to be successful are both marks of virtue. Virtue, therefore, is

14 a mean state in the sense that it is able to hit the mean. Again, error is multiform (for evil is a form of the unlimited, as in the old Pythagorean imagery,[20] and good of the limited), whereas success is possible in one way only (which is why it is easy to fail and difficult to succeed – easy to miss the target and difficult to hit it); so this is another reason why excess and deficiency are a mark of vice, and observance of the mean a mark of virtue:

Goodness is simple, badness manifold.[21]

15 Virtue then is a settled disposition of the mind determining the choice[22] of actions and emotions, consisting essentially in the observance of the mean relative to us, this being determined by principle, that is,[23] as the prudent man would determine it.

16 And it is a mean state between two vices, one of excess and one of defect. Furthermore, it is a mean state in that whereas the vices either fall short of or exceed what is right in feelings and in

17 actions, virtue ascertains and adopts the mean. Hence while in respect of its substance and the definition that states what it really is in essence virtue is the observance of the mean, in point of excellence and rightness it is an extreme.[24]

18 Not every action or emotion however admits of the observance of a due mean. Indeed the very names of some directly imply evil, for instance malice,[25] shamelessness, envy, and, of actions, adultery, theft, murder. All these and similar actions and feelings are blamed as being bad in themselves; it is not the excess or deficiency of them that we blame. It is impossible therefore ever to go right in regard to them – one must always be wrong; nor does right or wrong in their case depend on the circumstances, for instance, whether one commits adultery with the right woman, at the right time, and in the right manner; the

19 mere commission of any of them is wrong. One might as well suppose there could be a due mean and excess and deficiency in acts of injustice or cowardice or profligacy, which would imply that one could have a medium amount of excess and of

deficiency, an excessive amount of excess and a deficient amount
20 of deficiency. But just as there can be no excess or deficiency in
temperance and justice, because the mean is in a sense an
extreme,[26] so there can be no observance of the mean nor excess
nor deficiency in the corresponding vicious acts mentioned
above, but however they are committed, they are wrong; since,
to put it in general terms, there is no such thing as observing a
mean in excess or deficiency, nor as exceeding or falling short in
the observance of a mean.

vii We must not however rest content with stating this general
definition, but must show that it applies to the particular virtues.
In practical philosophy, although universal principles have a
wider application,[27] those covering a particular part of the field
possess a higher degree of truth; because conduct deals with
particular facts, and our theories are bound to accord with these.
    Let us then take the particular virtues from the diagram.[28]

2   The observance of the mean in fear and confidence is courage.
The man that exceeds in fearlessness is not designated by any
special name (and this is the case with many of the virtues and
vices); he that exceeds in confidence is rash; he that exceeds in
3 fear and is deficient in confidence is cowardly. In respect of
pleasures and pains – not all of them, and to a less degree in
respect of pains[29] – the observance of the mean is temperance, the
excess profligacy. Men deficient in the enjoyment of pleasures
scarcely occur, and hence this character also has not been assigned
4 a name, but we may call it insensitive. In regard to giving and
getting money, the observance of the mean is liberality; the excess
and deficiency are prodigality and meanness,[30] but the prodigal
man and the mean man exceed and fall short in opposite ways to
one another: the prodigal exceeds in giving and is deficient in
getting, whereas the mean man exceeds in getting and is deficient
5 in giving. For the present then we describe these qualities in
outline and summarily, which is enough for the purpose in hand;
but they will be more accurately defined later.

6   There are also other dispositions in relation to money, namely,
the mode of observing the mean called magnificence (the
magnificent man being different from the liberal, as the former
deals with large amounts and the latter with small ones), the excess
called tastelessness or vulgarity, and the defect called paltriness.

These are not the same as liberality and the vices corresponding to it; but the way in which they differ will be discussed later.

7   In respect of honour and dishonour, the observance of the mean is greatness of soul, the excess a sort of vanity, as it may be
8 called, and the deficiency, smallness of soul. And just as we said that liberality is related to magnificence, differing from it in being concerned with small amounts of money, so there is a certain quality related to greatness of soul, which is concerned with great honours, while this quality itself is concerned with small honours; for it is possible to aspire to minor honours in the right way, or more than is right, or less. He who exceeds in these aspirations is called ambitious, he who is deficient, unambitious; but the middle character has no name, and the dispositions of these persons are also unnamed, except that that of the ambitious man is called ambitiousness. Consequently the extreme characters put in a claim to the middle position, and in fact we ourselves sometimes call the middle person ambitious and sometimes unambitious: we sometimes praise a man for being ambitious,
9 sometimes for being unambitious. Why we do so shall be discussed later; for the present let us classify the remaining virtues and vices on the lines which we have laid down.

10   In respect of anger also we have excess, deficiency, and the observance of the mean. These states are virtually without names, but as we call a person of the middle character gentle, let us name the observance of the mean gentleness, while of the extremes, he that exceeds may be styled irascible and his vice irascibility, and he that is deficient, spiritless, and the deficiency spiritlessness.

11   There are also three other modes of observing a mean which bear some resemblance to each other, and yet are different; all have to do with intercourse in conversation and action, but they differ in that one is concerned with truthfulness of speech and behaviour, and the other with pleasantness, in its two divisions of pleasantness in social amusement and pleasantness in the general affairs of life. We must then discuss these qualities also, in order the better to discern that in all things the observance of the mean is to be praised, while the extremes are neither right nor praiseworthy, but reprehensible. Most of these qualities also are unnamed, but in these as in the other cases we must attempt to coin names for them ourselves, for the sake of clearness and so

that our meaning may be easily followed.

12   In respect of truth then, the middle character may be called truthful, and the observance of the mean truthfulness;[31] pretence in the form of exaggeration is boastfulness, and its possessor a boaster; in the form of understatement, self-depreciation, and its possessor the self-depreciator.

13   In respect of pleasantness in social amusement, the middle character is witty and the middle disposition wittiness; the excess is buffoonery and its possessor a buffoon; the deficient man may be called boorish, and his disposition boorishness. In respect of general pleasantness in life, the man who is pleasant in the proper manner is friendly, and the observance of the mean is friendliness; he that exceeds, if from no interested motive, is obsequious, if for his own advantage, a flatterer; he that is deficient, and unpleasant in all the affairs of life, may be called quarrelsome and surly.

14   There are also modes of observing a mean in the sphere of and in relation to the emotions. For[32] in these also one man is spoken of as moderate and another as excessive – for example the bashful man whose modesty takes alarm at everything; while he that is deficient in shame, or abashed at nothing whatsoever, is shame-less, and the man of middle character modest. For though modesty is not a virtue, it is praised, and so is the modest man.

15   Again, righteous indignation is the observance of a mean between envy and malice,[33] and these qualities are concerned with pain and pleasure felt at the fortunes of one's neighbours. The righteously indignant man is pained by undeserved good fortune; the jealous man exceeds him and is pained by all the good fortune of others;[34] while the malicious man so far falls short of being pained that he actually feels pleasure.

16   These qualities however it will be time to discuss in another place. After them we will treat justice,[35] distinguishing its two kinds – for it has more than one sense – and showing in what way each is a mode of observing the mean. [And we will deal similarly with the logical virtues.][36]

viii   There are then three dispositions – two vices, one of excess and one of defect, and one virtue which is the observance of the mean; and each of them is in a certain way opposed to both the others. For the extreme states are the opposite both of the middle state and of each other, and the middle state is the opposite of

2 both extremes; since just as the equal is greater in comparison with the less and less in comparison with the greater, so the middle states of character are in excess as compared with the defective states and defective as compared with the excessive states, whether in the case of feelings or of actions. For instance, a brave man appears rash in contrast with a coward and cowardly in contrast with a rash man; similarly a temperate man appears profligate in contrast with a man insensitive to pleasure and pain, but insensitive in contrast with a profligate; and a liberal man seems prodigal in contrast with a mean man, mean in contrast
3 with one who is prodigal. Hence either extreme character tries to push the middle character towards the other extreme; a coward calls a brave man rash and a rash man calls him a coward, and correspondingly in other cases.

4   But while all three dispositions are thus opposed to one another, the greatest degree of contrariety exists between the two extremes. For the extremes are farther apart from each other than from the mean, just as great is farther from small and small from
5 great than either from equal. Again[37] some extremes show a certain likeness to the mean – for instance, rashness resembles courage, prodigality liberality, whereas the extremes display the greatest unlikeness to one another. But it is things farthest apart from each other that logicians define as contraries, so that the farther apart things are the more contrary they are.

6   And in some cases the defect, in others the excess, is more opposed to the mean; for example cowardice, which is a vice of deficiency, is more opposed to courage than is rashness, which is a vice of excess; but profligacy, or excess of feeling, is more opposed to temperance than is insensitivity, or lack of feeling.
7 This results from either of two causes. One of these arises from the thing itself; owing to one extreme being nearer to the mean and resembling it more, we count not this but rather the contrary extreme as the opposite of the mean; for example, because rashness seems to resemble courage more than cowardice does, and to be nearer to it, we reckon cowardice rather than rashness as the contrary of courage; for those extremes which are more remote from the mean are thought to be more contrary to it.
8 This then is one cause, arising out of the thing itself. The other cause has its origin in us: those things appear more contrary to the

mean to which we are ourselves more inclined by our nature. For example, we are of ourselves more inclined to pleasure, which is why we are prone to profligacy [more than to propriety].[38] We therefore rather call those things the contrary of the mean, into which we are more inclined to lapse; and hence profligacy, the excess, is more particularly the contrary of temperance.

ix   Enough has now been said to show that moral virtue is a mean, and in what sense this is so, namely that it is a mean between two vices, one of excess and the other of defect; and that it is such a mean because it aims at hitting the middle point in feelings and in

2   actions. This is why it is a hard task to be good, for it is hard to find the middle point in anything: for instance, not everybody can find the centre of a circle, but only someone who knows geometry. So also anybody can become angry – that is easy, and so it is to give and spend money; but to be angry with or give money to the right person, and to the right amount, and at the right time, and for the right purpose, and in the right way – this is not within everybody's power and is not easy; so that to do these things properly is rare, praiseworthy, and noble.

3   Hence the first rule in aiming at the mean is to avoid that extreme which is the more opposed to the mean, as Calypso advises – [39]

> Steer the ship clear of yonder spray and surge.

4   For of the two extremes one is a more serious error than the other. Hence, inasmuch as to hit the mean extremely well is difficult,[40] the second best way to sail,[41] as the saying goes, is to take the least of the evils; and the best way to do this will be the way we enjoin.

The second rule is to notice what are the errors to which we are ourselves most prone (as different men are inclined by nature

5   to different faults) – and we shall discover what these are by observing the pleasure or pain that we experience; then we must drag ourselves away in the opposite direction, for by steering wide of our besetting error we shall make a middle course. This is the method adopted by carpenters to straighten warped timber.

6   Thirdly, we must in everything be most of all on our guard against what is pleasant and against pleasure; for when pleasure is

on her trial we are not impartial judges. The right course is therefore to feel towards pleasure as the elders of the people felt towards Helen,[42] and to apply[43] their words to her on every occasion; for if we roundly bid her be gone, we shall be less likely to err.

7   These then, to sum up the matter, are the precautions that will best enable us to hit the mean. But no doubt it is a difficult thing to do, and especially in particular cases: for instance, it is not easy to define in what manner and with what people and on what sort of grounds and how long one ought to be angry; and in fact we sometimes praise men who err on the side of defect in this matter and call them gentle, sometimes those who are quick to anger
8   and style them manly. However, we do not blame one who diverges a little from the right course, whether on the side of the too much or of the too little, but one who diverges more widely, for his error is noticed. Yet to what degree and how seriously a man must err to be blamed is not easy to define on principle. For in fact no object of perception is easy to define; and such questions of degree depend on particular circumstances, and the decision lies with perception.

9   Thus much then is clear, that it is the middle disposition in each department of conduct that is to be praised, but that one should lean sometimes to the side of excess and sometimes to that of deficiency, since this is the easiest way of hitting the mean and the right course.

1   It is probable that ἔθος, 'habit' and ἦθος, 'character' (whence 'ethical', moral) are kindred words.

2   ἀρετή is here as often in this and the following Books employed in the limited sense of 'moral excellence' or 'goodness of character', *i.e.*, virtue in the ordinary sense of the term.

3   Or possibly 'For things that we have to learn to do [in contrast with things that we do by nature], we learn by doing them.'

4   *i.e.*, in Book VI; for the sense in which 'the right principle' can be said to *be* the virtue of prudence see VI, note 87 on p. 167.

5   See I, iii, 1.

6   We here resume from the end of i. The preceding paragraphs, repeating from Book I the caution as to method, and introducing the doctrine of the mean, which is to be developed below, are parenthetical.

7   The contrary maxim to *similia similibus curantur* or homoeopathy. Fever, caused by heat, is cured by cold. Hence if the remedy for wickedness is pain, it must have been caused by pleasure.

8   *i.e.*, is actively exercised when fully developed, *cf.* ii, 8.

9   The reference is probably to Speusippus, although in the extant remains of Greek philosophy *apathy*, or freedom from passions or emotions, first appears as an ethical ideal of the Stoics.

10 *sc.*, as well as being the sources of our feelings.

11 Heraclitus, Fr. cv (Bywater) 'it is hard to fight with anger. Whatever it wishes to get, it purchases at the cost of life.'

12 See III, i, where this is interpreted as meaning both knowledge of what he is doing (the act must not be unconscious or accidental), and knowledge of moral principle (he must know that the act is a right one).

13 Probably for 'pain' we should emend the Greek text to read 'fear'.

14 ii, 8 f.

15 *i.e.*, without distinct parts, and so (if divisible at all) divisible at any point, as opposed to what is διῃρημένον, 'discrete', or made up of distinct parts and only divisible between them.

16 Greek comparatives, 'larger', 'smaller', etc., may also mean 'too large', 'too small', etc.; and there is the same ambiguity in the

words translated 'excess' and 'deficiency'. Again μέσον, 'middle' or 'mean', is used as a synonym for μέτριον, 'moderate' or of the right amount, and ἴσον 'equal' can mean 'equitable'. Hence 'to take an equal part with respect to the thing itself' means to take a part equal to the part left, *viz.* a half; 'to take an equal part relatively to us', means to take what is a fair or suitable amount. The former is a mean as being exactly in the middle between all and none – if the thing in question is represented by a line, this is bisected at a point equidistant from its two ends; the latter is a mean in the sense of being the right amount for the recipient, and also of lying somewhere between any two other amounts that happen to be too much and too little for him.

17 We should rather call this an arithmetical progression.

18 a famous wrestler.

19 The formula of the mean does not apply to the intellectual virtues.

20 *cf.* I, vi, 7.

21 This verse from an unknown source would come in better just before or just after the last parenthesis.

22 προαίρεσις, 'choice' or 'purpose', is discussed in III, ii, where see note 15 on p. 78.

23 A variant reading gives 'determined by principle, or whatever we like to call that by which the prudent man would determine it'.

24 *cf.* III, iv, 8.

25 See vii, 15. The word means 'delight at another's misfortune', *Schadenfreude*.

26 See § 17.

27 or 'have a wider acceptance'.

28 See p. 32. Apparently the lecturer displayed a table of virtues (like the one in *Eudemian Ethics* II, 122 b 37), exhibiting each as a mean between two vices of excess and defect in respect of a certain class of action or feeling. This is developed in detail in III, vi to end and IV.

29 This parenthesis looks like an interpolation from III, x, 1.

30 The Greek word is the negative of that translated liberality, but 'illiberality' and 'illiberal' we do not usually employ with reference to money.

31 From IV, vii it appears that the quality intended is sincerity of speech and conduct in the matter of asserting one's own merits. The observance of the mean in this respect is there said to have no name; and here the form of expression apologises for using 'truthfulness' in so limited a sense. The defect in this respect Aristotle expresses by εἰρωνεία, a word specially associated with the

affectation of ignorance practised by Socrates. Neither this nor its other shades of meaning correspond very closely to that of its English derivative *irony*.

32 This sentence in the manuscript follows the next one.

33 See vi, 18 (and note 25): there envy and 'rejoicing-in-evil' come in a list of emotions in which a due mean is impossible; and in *Rhetoric*, II, ix, 1386 b 34 they are said to be two sides of the same character. The present attempt to force them into the scheme as opposite extremes is not very successful, and it is noteworthy that this group of qualities is omitted in Book IV.

34 It is difficult not to think that some words have been lost here, such as 'and the righteously indignant man is pained by the undeserved misfortune of others'.

35 in Book VI.

36 Grant rightly rejects this sentence, since the intellectual virtues are nowhere else thus designated by Aristotle, nor does he regard them as modes of observing a mean.

37 This sentence should perhaps follow the next one, as it gives a second test of opposition, *viz.* unlikeness. However, unlikeness and remoteness are blended together in § 7.

38 These words are probably an interpolation, since the sense requires 'more than to insensitivity'.

39 *Odyssey*, xii, 219: really the words are said by Odysseus conveying to his steersman Circe's advice, to avoid the whirlpool of Charybdis which will engulf them all, and steer nearer to the monster Scylla who will devour only some of them.

40 or 'to hit the mean is extremely difficult'.

41 A proverb, meaning to take to the oars when the wind fails.

42 *Iliad*, iii, 156–160.

43 or 'repeat'.

i Virtue however is concerned with emotions and actions, and it is only voluntary actions for which praise and blame are given; those that are involuntary are condoned, and sometimes even pitied. Hence it seems to be necessary for the student of ethics to define the difference between the voluntary and the involuntary[1]; and this will also be of service to the legislator in assigning rewards and punishments.

2 It is then generally held that actions are involuntary when done (a) under compulsion or (b) through ignorance; and that (a) an act is compulsory when its origin is from without, being of such a 3 nature that the agent, who is really passive, contributes nothing to it: for example, when he is carried somewhere by stress of 4 weather, or by people who have him in their power. But there is some doubt about actions done through fear of a worse alternative, or for some noble object – as for instance if a tyrant having a man's parents and children in his power commands him to do something base, when if he complies their lives will be spared but if he refuses they will be put to death. It is open to 5 question whether such actions are voluntary or involuntary. A somewhat similar case is when cargo is jettisoned in a storm; apart from circumstances, no one voluntarily throws away his property, but to save his own life and that of his shipmates any sane man 6 would do so. Acts of this kind, then, are 'mixed' or composite;[2] but they approximate rather to the voluntary class. For at the actual time when they are done they are chosen or willed; and the end or motive of an act varies with the occasion, so that the terms 'voluntary' and 'involuntary' should be used with reference to the time of action; now the actual deed in the cases in question is done voluntarily, for the origin of the movement of the parts of the body instrumental to the act lies in the agent; and when the origin of an action is in oneself, it is in one's own power to do it or not. Such acts therefore are voluntary, though perhaps involuntary apart from circumstances – for no one would choose to do any such action in and for itself.

7 Sometimes indeed men are actually praised[3] for deeds of this 'mixed' class, namely when they submit to some disgrace or pain as the price of some great and noble object; though if they do so without any such motive they are blamed, since it is contemptible to submit to a great disgrace with no advantage or only a trifling one in view. In some cases again, such submission though not praised is condoned, when a man does something wrong through fear of penalties that impose too great a strain on human

8 nature, and that no one could endure. Yet there seem to be some acts which a man cannot be compelled to do,[4] and rather than do them he ought to submit to the most terrible death: for instance, we think it ridiculous that Alcmaeon in Euripides' play[5] is

9 compelled by certain threats to murder his mother. But it is sometimes difficult to decide how far we ought to go in choosing to do a given act rather than suffer a given penalty, or in enduring a given penalty rather than commit a given action; and it is still more difficult to abide by our decision when made, since in most of such dilemmas the penalty threatened is painful and the deed forced upon us dishonourable, which is why praise and blame are bestowed according as we do or do not yield to such compulsion.

10 What kind of actions then are to be called 'compulsory'? Used without qualification, perhaps this term applies to any case where the cause of the action lies in things outside the agent, and when the agent contributes nothing. But when actions intrinsically involuntary are yet in given circumstances deliberately chosen in preference to a given alternative, and when their origin lies in the agent, these actions are to be pronounced intrinsically involuntary but voluntary in the circumstances, and in preference to the alternative. They approximate however rather to the voluntary class, since conduct consists of particular things done,[6] and the particular things done in the cases in question are voluntary. But it is not easy to lay down rules for deciding which of two alternatives is to be chosen, for particular cases differ widely.

11 To apply the term 'compulsory' to acts done for the sake of pleasure or for noble objects, on the plea that these exercise constraint on us from without, is to make every action compulsory. For (1) pleasure and nobility between them supply the motives of all actions whatsoever. Also (2) to act under compulsion and unwillingly is painful, but actions done for their pleasantness or

nobility are done with pleasure. And (3) it is absurd to blame
external things, instead of blaming ourselves for falling an easy
prey to their attractions; or to take the credit of our noble deeds
to ourselves, while putting the blame for our disgraceful ones
12 upon the temptations of pleasure. It appears therefore that an act
is compulsory when its origin is from outside, the person
compelled contributing nothing to it.

13   (b) An act done through ignorance is in every case not
voluntary,[7] but it is involuntary only when it causes the agent
pain and regret: since a man who has acted through ignorance
and feels no compunction at all for what he has done, cannot
indeed be said to have acted voluntarily, as he was not aware of
his action, yet cannot be said to have acted involuntarily, as he is
14 not sorry for it. Acts done through ignorance therefore fall into
two classes: if the agent regrets the act, we think that he has acted
involuntarily; if he does not regret it, to mark the distinction we
may call him a 'non-voluntary' agent – for as the case is different
it is better to give it a special name. Acting *through* ignorance
however seems to be different from acting *in* ignorance; for
when a man is drunk or in a rage, his actions are not thought to
be done through ignorance but owing to one or other of the
conditions mentioned, though he does act without knowing,
and *in* ignorance. Now it is true that all wicked men are ignorant
of what they ought to do and refrain from doing, and that this
15 error is the cause of injustice and of vice in general. But the term
'involuntary' does not really apply to an action when the agent is
ignorant of his true interests. The ignorance that makes an act
blameworthy is not ignorance displayed in moral choice[8] (that
sort of ignorance constitutes vice) – that is to say, it is not general
ignorance (because that is held to be blameworthy), but particular
ignorance, ignorance of the circumstances of the act and of the
things[9] affected by it; for in this case the act is pitied and forgiven,
because he who acts in ignorance of any of these circumstances is
an involuntary agent.

16   Perhaps then it will be as well to specify the nature and number
of these circumstances. They are (1) the agent, (2) the act, (3) the
thing[10] that is affected by or is the sphere of the act; and
sometimes also (4) the instrument, for instance, a tool with which
the act is done, (5) the effect, for instance, saving a man's life, and

(6) the manner, for instance, gently or violently.

17   Now no one, unless mad, could be ignorant of all these circumstances together; nor yet, obviously, of (1) the agent – for a man must know who he is himself. But a man may be ignorant of (2) what he is doing, as for instance when people say 'it slipped out while they were speaking', or 'they were not aware that the matter was a secret', as Aeschylus said of the Mysteries[11]; or that 'they let it off when they only meant to show how it worked' as the prisoner pleaded in the catapult case. Again (3) a person might mistake his son for an enemy, as Merope does;[12] or (4) mistake a sharp spear for one with a button on it, or a heavy stone for a pumice-stone; or (5) one might kill a man by giving him medicine with the intention of saving his life; or (6) in loose wrestling[13] hit him a blow when meaning only to grip his hand.

18   Ignorance therefore being possible in respect of all these circumstances of the act, one who has acted in ignorance of any of them is held to have acted involuntarily, and especially so if ignorant of the most important of them; and the most important of the circumstances seem to be the nature of the act itself and the effect it will produce.

19   Such then is the nature of the ignorance that justifies our speaking of an act as involuntary, given the further condition that the agent feels sorrow and regret for having committed it.

20   An involuntary action being one done under compulsion or through ignorance, a voluntary act would seem to be an act of which the origin lies in the agent, who knows the particular

21   circumstances in which he is acting. For it is probably a mistake to say[14] that acts caused by anger or by desire are involuntary. In

22   the first place, (1) this will debar us from speaking of any of the

23   lower animals as acting voluntarily, or children either. Then (2) are none of our actions that are caused by desire or anger voluntary, or are the noble ones voluntary and the base involuntary? Surely this is an absurd distinction when one person

24   is the author of both. Yet perhaps it is strange to speak of acts aiming at things which it is right to aim at as involuntary; and it is right to feel anger at some things, and also to feel desire for some

25   things, for instance health, knowledge. Also (3) we think that involuntary actions are painful and actions that gratify desire

26   pleasant. And again (4) what difference is there in respect of their

involuntary character between wrong acts committed deliber-
27 ately and wrong acts done in anger? Both are to be avoided; and
also we think that the irrational feelings are just as much a part of
human nature as the reason, so that the actions done from anger
or desire also belong to the human being who does them. It is
therefore strange to class these actions as involuntary.

ii Having defined voluntary and involuntary action, we next
have to examine the nature of choice.[15] For this appears to be
intimately connected with virtue, and to afford a surer test of
character than do our actions.

2 Choice is manifestly a voluntary act. But the two terms are not
synonymous, the latter being the wider. Children and the lower
animals as well as men are capable of voluntary action, but not of
choice. Also sudden acts may be termed voluntary, but they
cannot be said to be done by choice.

3 Some identify choice with (1) desire, or (2) passion, or (3)
wish, or (4) some form of opinion. These views however appear
to be mistaken.

(1) The irrational animals do not exercise choice, but they do
4 feel desire, and also passion. Also a man of defective self-restraint
acts from desire but not from choice; and on the contrary a self-
5 restrained man acts from choice and not from desire. Again, desire
can run counter to choice, but not desire to desire.[16] And desire
has regard to an object as pleasant or painful, choice has not.[17]

6 (2) Still less is choice the same as passion. Acts done from
passion seem very far from being done of deliberate choice.

7 (3) Again, choice is certainly not a wish, though they appear
closely akin. Choice cannot have for its object impossibilities: if a
man were to say he chose something impossible he would be
thought a fool; but we can wish for things that are impossible,
8 for instance immortality. Also we may wish for what cannot be
secured by our own agency, for instance, that a particular actor[18]
or athlete may win; but no one chooses what does not rest with
himself, but only what he thinks can be attained by his own act.
9 Again, we wish rather for ends than for means, but choose the
means to our end; for example, we wish to be healthy, but
choose things to make us healthy; we wish to be happy, and that
is the word we use in this connection, but it would not be
proper to say that we choose to be happy; since, speaking

generally, choice seems to be concerned with things within our own control.

10   (4) Nor yet again can it be opinion. It seems that anything may be matter of opinion – we form opinions about what is eternal,[19] or impossible, just as much as about what is within our power. Also we distinguish opinion by its truth or falsehood, not by its being good or bad, but choice is distinguished rather as being

11   good or bad. Probably therefore nobody actually identifies choice with opinion in general. But neither is it the same as some particular opinion.[20] For it is our choice of good or evil that determines our character, not our opinion about good or evil.

12   And we choose to take or avoid some good or evil thing, but we opine what a thing is, or for whom it is advantageous, or how it is so:[21] we do not exactly form an opinion to take or avoid a

13   thing. Also we praise a choice rather for choosing the right thing, but an opinion for opining in the right way. And we choose only things that we absolutely know to be good, we opine things we

14   do not quite certainly know to be true. Nor do the same persons appear to excel both at choosing and at forming opinions: some people seem to form opinions better, but yet to choose the

15   wrong things from wickedness. That choice is preceded or accompanied by the formation of an opinion is immaterial, for that is not the point we are considering, but whether choice is the same thing as some form of opinion.

16   What then are the genus and differentia of choice, inasmuch as it is not any of the things above mentioned? It manifestly belongs to the genus voluntary action; but not every voluntary act is

17   chosen. Perhaps we may define it as voluntary action preceded by deliberation, since choice involves reasoning and some process of thought. Indeed previous deliberation seems to be implied by the very term *proaireton*, which denotes something *chosen before* other things.

iii   As for deliberation, do people deliberate about everything – are all things possible objects of deliberation – or are there some

2   things about which deliberation is impossible? The term 'object of deliberation' presumably must not be taken to include things about which a fool or a madman might deliberate, but to mean what a sensible person would deliberate about

3   Well then, nobody deliberates about things eternal,[22] such as

the order of the universe, or the incommensurability of the
4 diagonal and the side of a square. Nor yet about things that
change but follow a regular process, whether from necessity or
by nature[23] or through some other cause: such phenomena for
instance as the solstices and the sunrise. Nor about irregular
5 occurrences, such as droughts and rains. Nor about the results of
6 chance, such as finding a hidden treasure. The reason[24] why we
do not deliberate about these things is that none of them can be
7 effected by our agency. We deliberate about things that are in
our control and are attainable by action (which are in fact the
only things that still remain to be considered; for nature,
necessity, and chance, with the addition of intelligence and
human agency generally, exhaust the generally accepted list of
causes). But we do not deliberate about all human affairs without
exception either: for example, no Lacedaemonian deliberates
about the best form of government[25] for Scythia; but any
particular set of men deliberates about the things attainable by
8 their own actions. Also there is no room for deliberation about
matters fully ascertained and completely formulated as sciences;
such for instance as orthography, for we have no uncertainty as
to how a word ought to be spelt. We deliberate about things in
which our agency operates but does not always produce the same
results; for instance about questions of medicine and of business;
and we deliberate about navigation more than about athletic
training, because it has been less completely reduced to a science;
9 and similarly with other pursuits also. And we deliberate more
about the arts[26] than about the sciences, because we are more
uncertain about them.

10 Deliberation then is employed in matters which, though
subject to rules that generally hold good, are uncertain in their
issue; or where the issue is indeterminate,[27] and where, when the
matter is important, we take others into our deliberations,
distrusting our own capacity to decide.

11 And we deliberate not about ends, but about means. A doctor
does not deliberate whether he is to cure his patient, nor an
orator whether he is to convince his audience, nor a statesman
whether he is to secure good government, nor does anyone else
debate about the end of his profession or calling; they take some
12 end for granted, and consider how and by what means it can be

achieved. If they find that there are several means of achieving it, they proceed to consider which of these will attain it most easily and best. If there is only one means by which it can be accomplished, they ask how it is to be accomplished by that means, and by what means that means can itself be achieved, until they reach the first link in the chain of causes, which is the last in the order of discovery. (For when deliberating one seems in the procedure described to be pursuing an investigation or analysis that resembles the analysis of a figure in geometry[28] – indeed it appears that though not all investigation is deliberation, for example, mathematical investigation is not, yet all deliberation is investigation – and the last step in the analysis seems to be

13 the first step in the execution of the design.) Then, if they have come up against an impossibility, they abandon the project – for instance, if it requires money and money cannot be procured; but if on the other hand it proves to be something possible, they begin to act. By possible, I mean able to be performed by our agency – things we do through the agency of our friends counting in a sense as done by ourselves, since the origin of their action is in us.

14 (In practising an art)[29] the question is at one moment what tools to use, and at another how to use them; and similarly in other spheres, we have to consider sometimes what means to employ, and sometimes how exactly any given means are to be employed.

15 It appears therefore, as has been said, that a man is the origin of his actions, and that the province of deliberation is to discover actions within one's own power to perform; and all our actions

16 aim at ends other than themselves. It follows that we do not deliberate about ends, but about means. Nor yet do we deliberate about particular facts, for instance, Is this object a loaf? or, Is this loaf properly baked? for these are matters of direct perception. Deliberation must stop at the particular fact, or it will embark on a process *ad infinitum*.

17 The object of deliberation and the object of choice are the same, except that when a thing is chosen it has already been determined, since it is the thing already selected as the result of our deliberation that is chosen. For a man stops enquiring how he shall act as soon as he has carried back the origin of action to

himself, and to the dominant part[30] of himself, for it is this part
18 that chooses. This may be illustrated by the ancient constitutions
represented in Homer: the kings used to proclaim to the people
the measures they had chosen to adopt.

19 As then the object of choice is something within our power
which after deliberation we desire, choice will be a deliberate
desire of things in our power; for we first deliberate, then select,
and finally fix our desire according to the result of our
deliberation.

20 Let this serve as a description in outline of choice, and of the
nature of its objects, and the fact that it deals with means to ends.

iv Wishes, on the contrary, as was said above,[31] are for ends. But
while some hold that what is wished for[32] is the good, others
2 think it is what appears to be good. Those however who say that
what is wished for is the really good, are faced by the conclusion,
that what a man who chooses his end wrongly wishes for is not
really wished for at all; since if it is to be wished for, it must on
their showing be good, whereas in the case assumed it may so
3 happen that the man wishes for something bad. And those on the
other hand who say that what appears good is wished for, are
forced to admit that there is no such thing as that which is by
nature wished for, but that what each man thinks to be good is
wished for in his case; yet different, and it may be opposite,
things appear good to different people.

4 If therefore neither of these views is satisfactory, perhaps we
should say that what is wished for in the true and unqualified
sense is the good, but that what appears good to each person is
wished for by him; and accordingly that the good man wishes for
what is truly wished for, the bad man for anything as it may
happen (just as in the case of our bodies, a man of sound
constitution finds really healthy food best for his health, but some
other diet may be healthy for one who is delicate; and so with
things bitter[33] and sweet, hot, heavy, etc.). For the good man
judges everything correctly; what things truly are, that they seem
5 to him to be, in every department[34] – for special things are noble
and pleasant corresponding to each type of character, and perhaps
what chiefly distinguishes the good man is that he sees the truth
in each kind, being himself as it were the standard and measure of
the noble and pleasant. It appears to be pleasure that misleads the

6 mass of mankind; for it seems to them to be a good, though it is not, so they choose what is pleasant as good and shun pain as evil.

V   If then whereas we wish for our end, the means to our end are matters of deliberation and choice, it follows that actions dealing with these means are done by choice, and voluntary. But the activities in which the virtues are exercised deal with means.

2 Therefore virtue also depends on ourselves. And so also does vice. For where we are free to act we are also free to refrain from acting, and where we are able to say No we are also able to say Yes; if therefore we are responsible for doing a thing when to do it is right, we are also responsible for not doing it when not to do it is wrong, and if we are responsible for rightly not doing a

3 thing, we are also responsible for wrongly doing it. But if it is in our power to do and to refrain from doing right and wrong, and if, as we saw,[35] being good or bad is doing right or wrong, it consequently depends on us whether we are virtuous or vicious.

4   To say that

> None would be vile, and none would not be blest[36]

seems to be half false, though half true: it is true that no one is unwilling to be blessed, but not true that wickedness is involun-

5 tary; or else we must contradict what we just now[37] asserted, and say that man is not the originator and begetter of his actions as he

6 is of his children. But if it is manifest that a man is the author of his own actions, and if we are unable to trace our conduct back to any other origins than those within ourselves, then actions of which the origins are within us, themselves depend upon us, and are voluntary.

7   This conclusion seems to be attested both by men's behaviour in private life and by the practice of lawgivers; for they punish and exact redress from those who do evil (except when it is done under compulsion, or through ignorance for which the agent himself is not responsible), and honour those who do noble deeds, in order to encourage the one sort and to repress the other; but nobody tries to encourage us to do things that do not depend upon ourselves and are not voluntary, since it is no good our being persuaded not to feel heat or pain or hunger or the like, because we shall feel them all the same.

8   Indeed the fact that an offence was committed in ignorance is

itself made a ground for punishment, in cases where the offender is held to be responsible for his ignorance; for instance, the penalty is doubled if the offender was drunk,[38] because the origin of the offence was in the man himself, as he might have avoided getting drunk, which was the cause of his not knowing what he was doing. Also men are punished for offences committed through ignorance of some provision of the law which they

9 ought to have known, and might have known without difficulty; and so in other cases where ignorance is held to be due to negligence, on the ground that the offender need not have been ignorant, as he could have taken the trouble to ascertain the facts.

10 It may be objected that perhaps he is not the sort of man to take the trouble. Well, but men are themselves responsible for having become careless through living carelessly, as they are for being unjust or profligate if they do wrong or pass their time in drinking and dissipation. They acquire a particular quality by

11 constantly acting in a particular way. This is shown by the way in which men train themselves for some contest or pursuit: they

12 practise continually. Therefore only an utterly senseless person can fail to know that our characters are the result of our conduct;[39] but if a man knowingly acts in a way that will result in his becoming unjust, he must be said to be voluntarily unjust.

13 Again, though it is unreasonable to say that a man who acts unjustly or dissolutely does not wish to be unjust or dissolute,

14 nevertheless this by no means implies that he can stop being unjust and become just merely by wishing to do so; any more than a sick man can get well by wishing, although it may be the case that his illness is voluntary, in the sense of being due to intemperate living and neglect of the doctors' advice. At the outset then, it is true, he might have avoided the illness, but once he has let himself go he can do so no longer. When you have thrown a stone, you cannot afterwards bring it back again, but nevertheless you are responsible for having taken up the stone and flung it, for the origin of the act was within you. Similarly the unjust and profligate might at the outset have avoided becoming so, and therefore they are so voluntarily, although when they have become unjust and profligate it is no longer open to them not to be so.

15 And not only are vices of the soul voluntary, but in some cases

bodily defects are so as well, and we blame them accordingly. Though no one blames a man for being born ugly, we censure uncomeliness that is due to neglecting exercise and the care of the person. And so with infirmities and mutilations: though nobody would reproach, but rather pity, a person blind from birth, or owing to disease or accident, yet all would blame one
16 who had lost his sight from tippling or debauchery. We see then that bodily defects for which we are ourselves responsible are blamed, while those for which we are not responsible are not. This being so, it follows that we are responsible for blameworthy moral defects also.

17 But suppose somebody says: 'All men seek what seems to them good, but they are not responsible for its seeming good: each man's conception of his end is determined by his character, whatever that may be. Although therefore, on the hypothesis[40] that each man is in a sense responsible for his moral disposition, he will in a sense be responsible for his conception of the good, if on the contrary this hypothesis be untrue, no man is responsible for his own wrongdoing. He does wrong through ignorance of the right end, thinking that wrongdoing will procure him his greatest good; and his aim at his end[41] is not of his own choosing. A man needs to be born with moral vision, so to speak, whereby to discern correctly and choose what is truly good. A man of good natural disposition is a man well endowed by nature in this respect; for if a thing is the greatest and noblest of gifts, and is something which cannot be acquired or learnt from another, but which a man will possess in such form as it has been bestowed on him at birth, a good and noble natural endowment in this respect will constitute a good disposition in the full and true meaning of the term.'

18 Now if this theory be true, how will virtue be voluntary any more than vice? Both for the good man and the bad man alike, their view of their end is determined in the same manner, by nature or however it may be; and all their actions of whatever sort are guided by reference to their end as thus determined.

19 Whether then a man's view of his end, whatever it may be, is not given by nature but is partly due to himself, or whether, although his end is determined by nature, yet virtue is voluntary because the good man's actions to gain his end are voluntary, in either

case vice will be just as much voluntary as virtue; for the bad man equally with the good possesses spontaneity in his actions, even if
20 not in his choice of an end. If then, as is said, our virtues are voluntary (and in fact we are in a sense ourselves partly the cause of our moral dispositions, and it is our having a certain character that makes us set up an end of a certain kind), it follows that our vices are voluntary also; they are voluntary in the same manner as our virtues.

21 We have then now discussed in outline the virtues in general, having indicated their genus [namely, that it is a mean, and a disposition],[42] and having shown that they render us apt to do the same actions as those by which they are produced,[43] and to do them in the way in which right reason may enjoin;[44] and that they depend on ourselves and are voluntary.[45]

22 But[46] our dispositions are not voluntary in the same way as are our actions. Our actions we can control from beginning to end, and we are conscious of them at each stage.[47] With our dispositions on the other hand, though we can control their beginnings, each separate addition to them is imperceptible, as is the case with the growth of a disease; though they are voluntary in that we were free to employ our capacities in the one way or the other.

23 But to resume, let us now discuss the virtues severally, defining the nature of each, the class of objects to which it is related, and the way in which it is related to them. In so doing we shall also make it clear how many virtues there are.

vi Let us first take courage. We have already seen[48] that courage is the observance of the mean in respect of fear and confidence.
2 Now it is clear that the things we fear are fearful things, which means, broadly speaking, evil things; so that fear is sometimes
3 defined as the anticipation of evil. It is true then that we fear all evil things, for example, disgrace, poverty, disease, lack of friends, death; but it is not thought that courage is related to all these things, for there are some evils which it is right and noble to fear and base not to fear, for instance, disgrace. One who fears disgrace is an honourable man, with a due sense of shame; one who does not fear it is shameless: though some people apply the term courageous to such a man by analogy, because he bears some resemblance to the courageous man in that the courageous

man also is a fearless person.

4   Again, it is no doubt right not to fear poverty, or disease, or in general any evil not caused by vice and not due to ourselves. But one who is fearless in regard to these things is not courageous either (although the term is applied to him, too, by analogy); since some men who are cowards in war are liberal with money and face loss of fortune boldly.

5   Nor yet is a man cowardly if he fears insult to his wife and children, or envy, or the like; nor courageous if he shows a bold face when about to undergo a flogging.

6   What then are the fearful things in respect of which courage is displayed? I suppose those which are the greatest, since there is no one more brave in enduring danger than the courageous man. Now the most terrible thing of all is death; for it is the end, and when a man is dead, nothing, we think, either good or evil can

7   befall him any more. But even death, we should hold, does not in all circumstances give an opportunity for courage: for instance, we do not call a man courageous for facing death by drowning or

8   disease. What form of death then is a test of courage? Presumably that which is the noblest. Now the noblest form of death is death in battle, for it is encountered in the midst of the greatest and

9   most noble of dangers. And this conclusion is borne out by the principle on which public honours are bestowed in republics and under monarchies.

10   The courageous man, therefore, in the proper sense of the term, will be he who fearlessly confronts a noble death, or some sudden[49] peril that threatens death; and the perils of war answer

11   this description most fully. Not that the courageous man is not also fearless in a storm at sea (as also in illness), though not in the same way as sailors are fearless, for he thinks there is no hope of safety, and to die by drowning is revolting to him,[50] whereas

12   sailors keep up heart because of their experience. Also courage is shown in dangers where a man can defend himself by valour or die nobly, but neither is possible in disasters like shipwreck.

vii   Now although the same things are not fearful to everybody, there are some terrors which we pronounce beyond human endurance, and these of course are fearful to everyone in his senses. And the terrors that man can endure differ in magnitude and degree; as also do the situations inspiring confidence.[51] But

2   the courageous man is proof against fear so far as man may be. Hence although he will sometimes fear even terrors not beyond man's endurance, he will do so in the right way, and he will endure them as principle dictates, for the sake of what is noble;[52]

3 for that is the end at which virtue aims. On the other hand it is possible to fear such terrors too much, and too little; and also to

4 fear things that are not fearful as if they were fearful. Error arises either from fearing what one ought not to fear, or from fearing in the wrong manner, or at the wrong time, or the like; and similarly with regard to occasions for confidence.

5   The courageous man then is he that endures or fears the right things and for the right purpose and in the right manner and at the right time, and who shows confidence in a similar way. (For the courageous man feels and acts as the circumstances merit, and

6 as principle may dictate. And every activity aims at the end that corresponds to the disposition of which it is the manifestation. So it is therefore with the activity of the courageous man: his courage is noble; therefore its end is nobility, for a thing is defined by its end; therefore the courageous man endures the terrors and dares the deeds that manifest courage, for the sake of that which is noble.)

7   Of the characters that run to excess, on the other hand, he who exceeds in fearlessness has no name (this, as we remarked before,[53] is the case with many qualities), but we should call a man mad, or else insensitive to pain, if he feared nothing, 'earthquake nor billows',[54] as they say of the Kelts; he who exceeds in confidence [in the face of fearful things][55] is rash. The

8 rash man is generally thought to be an impostor, who pretends to courage which he does not possess; at least, he wishes to appear to feel towards fearful things as the courageous man actually does feel, and therefore he imitates him in the things in which he

9 can.[56] Hence most rash men really are cowards at heart, for they make a bold show in situations that inspire confidence, but do not endure terrors.

10   He that exceeds in fear[57] is a coward, for he fears the wrong things, and in the wrong manner, and so on with the rest of the list. He is also deficient in confidence, but his excessive fear in

11 face of pain is more apparent. The coward is therefore a despondent person, being afraid of everything; but the

courageous man is just the opposite, for confidence belongs to a sanguine temperament.

12   The coward, the rash man, and the courageous man are therefore concerned with the same objects, but are differently disposed towards them: the two former exceed and fall short, the last keeps the mean and the right disposition. The rash, moreover, are impetuous, and though eager before the danger comes they hang back at the critical moment; whereas the courageous are keen at the time of action but calm beforehand.

13   As has been said then, courage is the observance of the mean in relation to things that inspire confidence or fear, in the circumstances stated;[58] and it is confident and endures[59] because it is noble to do so or base not to do so. But to seek death in order to escape from poverty, or the pangs of love, or from pain or sorrow, is not the act of a courageous man, but rather of a coward; for it is weakness to fly from troubles, and the suicide does not endure death because it is noble to do so, but to escape evil.

viii   Such is the nature of courage; but the name is also applied to five divergent types of character.

(1) First, as most closely resembling true courage, comes the citizen's courage.[60] Citizen troops appear to endure dangers because of the legal penalties and the reproach attaching to cowardice, and the honours awarded to bravery; hence those races appear to be the bravest among which cowards are degraded and brave men held in honour. It is this citizen courage which inspires the heroes portrayed by Homer, like Diomedes and Hector:

> Polydamas will be the first to flout me;[61]

and Diomedes says

> Hector will make his boast at Troy hereafter:
> 'By me was Tydeus' son . . . '[62]

3   This type of courage most closely resembles the one described before, because it is prompted by a virtue, namely the sense of shame,[63] and by the desire for something noble, namely honour, and the wish to avoid the disgrace of being reproached.

4   The courage of troops forced into battle by their officers may

be classed as of the same type, though they are inferior inasmuch as their motive is not a sense of shame but fear, and the desire to avoid not disgrace but pain. Their masters compel them to be brave, after Hector's fashion:

> Let me see any skulking off the field –
> He shall not save his carcase from the dogs![64]

5 The same is done by commanders who draw up their troops in front of them and beat them if they give ground, or who form them in line with a trench or some other obstacle in the rear; all these are using compulsion. A man ought not to be brave because he is compelled to be, but because courage is noble.

6   (2) Again, experience of some particular form of danger is taken for a sort of courage; hence arose Socrates' notion that courage is knowledge.[65] This type of bravery is displayed by various people in various circumstances, and particularly in war by professional soldiers.[66] For war (as the saying is) is full of false alarms, a fact which these men have had most opportunity of observing; thus they appear courageous owing to others' 7 ignorance of the true situation. Also experience renders them the most efficient in inflicting loss on the enemy without sustaining it themselves, as they are skilled in the use of arms, and equipped 8 with the best ones both for attack and defence. So that they are like armed men fighting against unarmed, or trained athletes against amateurs; for even in athletic contests it is not the bravest men who are the best fighters, but those who are strongest and in 9 the best training. But professional soldiers prove cowards when the danger imposes too great a strain, and when they are at a disadvantage in numbers and equipment; for they are the first to run away, while citizen troops stand their ground and die fighting, as happened in the battle at the temple of Hermes.[67] This is because citizens think it disgraceful to run away, and prefer death to safety so procured; whereas professional soldiers were relying from the outset on superior strength, and when they discover they are outnumbered they take to flight, fearing death more than disgrace. But this is not true courage.

10   (3) Spirit or anger[68] is also classed with courage. Men emboldened by anger, like wild beasts which rush upon the hunter that has wounded them, are supposed to be courageous,

because the courageous also are high-spirited; for spirit is very impetuous in encountering danger. Hence Homer writes,[69] 'he put strength in their spirit', and 'roused their might and their spirit', and 'bitter wrath up through his nostrils welled', and 'his blood boiled'; for all such symptoms seem to indicate an
11 excitement and impulse of the spirit. Thus the real motive of courageous men is the nobility of courage, although spirit operates in them as well; but wild animals are emboldened by pain, for they turn to bay because they are wounded, or frightened – since if they are in a forest or a swamp[70] they do not attack. Therefore they are not to be considered courageous for rushing upon danger when spurred by pain and anger, and blind to the dangers that await them; since on that reckoning even asses would be brave when they are hungry, for no blows will make them stop grazing![71] (And adulterers also are led to do many daring things by lust.)[72]

12   But[73] the form of courage that is inspired by spirit seems to be the most natural, and when reinforced by deliberate choice and purpose it appears to be true courage. And human beings also feel pain when angry, and take pleasure in revenge. But those who fight for these motives, though valiant fighters, are not courageous; for the motive of their confidence is not honour, nor is it guided by principle, but it springs from feeling. However, they show some affinity to true courage.

13   (4) Nor yet again is the boldness of the sanguine the same thing as courage. The sanguine are confident in face of danger because they have won many victories over many foes before. They resemble the courageous, because both are confident, but whereas the courageous are confident for the reasons already explained,[74] the sanguine are so because they think they are
14 stronger than the enemy, and not likely to come to any harm. (A similar boldness is shown by those getting drunk, for this makes them sanguine for the time being.) When however things do not turn out as they expect, the merely sanguine run away, whereas the mark of the courageous man, as we have seen, is to endure things that are terrible to a human being and that seem so to him,
15 because it is noble to do so and base not to do so. Hence it is thought a sign of still greater courage to be fearless and undismayed in sudden alarms than in dangers that were foreseen.

Bravery in unforeseen danger springs more from character, as there is less time for preparation; one might resolve to face a danger one can foresee, from calculation and on principle, but only a fixed disposition of courage will enable one to face sudden peril.

16 (5) Those who face danger in ignorance also appear courageous; and they come very near to those whose bravery rests on a sanguine temperament, though inferior to them inasmuch as they lack self-confidence, which the sanguine possess. Hence the sanguine stand firm for a time; whereas those who have been deceived as to the danger, if they learn or suspect the true state of affairs, take to flight, as the Argives did when they encountered the Spartans and thought they were Sicyonians.[75]

17 We have now described the characteristics both of the courageous and of those who are thought to be courageous.

ix Courage is displayed with respect to confidence and fear, but not with respect to both equally: it is more particularly displayed in regard to objects of fear; for one who is unperturbed in the presence of terrors and comports himself rightly towards these is courageous in a fuller sense than one who does so in situations 2 that inspire confidence. In fact, as has been said,[76] men are sometimes called courageous for enduring pain. Hence courage itself is attended by pain; and it is justly praised, because it is 3 harder to endure pain than to abstain from pleasure. Not but what it would appear that the end corresponding[77] to the virtue of courage is really pleasant, only its pleasantness is obscured by the attendant circumstances. This is illustrated by the case of athletic contests: to boxers, for example, their end – the object they box for, the wreath and the honours of victory – is pleasant, but the blows they receive must hurt them, being men of flesh and blood, and also all the labour they undergo is painful; and these painful incidentals are so numerous that the final object, being a small thing, appears not to contain any pleasure at all. If 4 then the same is true of courage, the death or wounds that it may bring will be painful to the courageous man, and he will suffer them unwillingly; but he will endure them because it is noble to do so, or because it is base not to do so. And the more a man possesses all virtue, and the more happy he is, the more pain will death cause him; for to such a man life is worth most, and he stands to lose the greatest goods, and knows that this is so, and this must be painful. But he is none the less courageous on that account, perhaps indeed he is more so, because he prefers glory in war to the greatest prizes of life.

5   It is not true therefore of every virtue that its active exercise is essentially pleasant, save in so far as it attains its end.[78]

6   No doubt it is possible that such men as these do not make the best professional soldiers, but men who are less courageous, and have nothing of value besides life to lose; for these face danger readily, and will barter their lives for trifling gains.

7   Let this suffice as an account of courage: from what has been said it will not be difficult to form at all events a rough conception of its nature.

After courage let us speak of temperance; for these appear to be the virtues of the irrational parts of the soul.

X   Now we have said[79] that temperance is the observance of the mean in relation to pleasures (for it is concerned only in a lesser degree and in a different way with pains); and profligacy also is displayed in the same matters. Let us then now define the sort of pleasures to which these qualities are related.

2   Now we must make a distinction between pleasures of the body and pleasures of the soul. Take for instance ambition, or love of learning: the lover of honour or of learning takes pleasure in the thing he loves without his body being affected at all; the experience is purely mental. But we do not speak of men as either temperate or profligate in relation to the pleasures of ambition and of learning. Nor similarly can these terms be applied to the enjoyment of any of the other pleasures that are not bodily pleasures: those who love hearing marvellous tales and telling anecdotes, and who spend their days in trivial gossip, we call idle chatterers, but not profligates; nor do we call men profligate who feel excessive pain for the loss of fortune or friends.

3   Temperance therefore has to do with the pleasures of the body. But not with all even of these; for men who delight in the pleasures of the eye, in colours, forms and paintings, are not termed either temperate or profligate, although it would be held that these things also can be enjoyed in the right manner, or too

4   much, or too little. Similarly with the objects of hearing: no one

would term profligate those who take an excessive pleasure in music, or the theatre, nor temperate those who enjoy them as is

5　right. Nor yet does temperance apply to enjoyment of the sense of smell, unless accidentally;[80] we do not call those who are fond of the scent of fruit or roses or incense profligate, though we may be inclined so to style those who love perfumes and the smell of savoury dishes, for the profligate take pleasure in these odours

6　because they remind them of the objects of their desires. One may notice that other persons too like the smell of food when they are hungry; but to delight in things of this kind is a mark of the profligate, since they are the things on which the profligate's desires are set.[81]

7　Nor do the lower animals derive any pleasure from these senses, except accidentally.[82] Hounds do not take pleasure in scenting hares, but in eating them; the scent merely made them aware of the hare. The lion does not care about the lowing of the ox, but about devouring it, though the lowing tells him that the ox is near, and consequently he appears to take pleasure in the sound. Similarly he is not pleased by the sight of 'or stag or mountain goat',[83] but by the prospect of a meal.

8　Temperance and profligacy are therefore concerned with those pleasures which man shares with the lower animals, and which consequently appear slavish and bestial. These are the pleasures of

9　touch and taste. But even taste appears to play but a small part, if any, in temperance. For taste is concerned with discriminating flavours, as is done by winetasters, and cooks preparing savoury dishes; but it is not exactly the flavours that give pleasure, or at all events not to the profligate: it is actually enjoying the object that is pleasant, and this is done solely through the sense of touch, alike in eating and drinking and in what are called the pleasures

10　of sex. This is why a certain gourmand[84] wished that his throat might be longer than a crane's, showing that his pleasure lay in the sensation of contact.

11　Hence the sense to which profligacy is related is the most universal of the senses; and there appears to be good ground for the disrepute in which it is held, because it belongs to us not as human beings but as animals. Therefore it is bestial to revel in such pleasures, and to like them better than any others. We do not refer to the most refined of the pleasures of touch, such as the enjoyment of friction and warm baths in the gymnasia; the tactual pleasures of the profligate have to do with certain parts only, not with the whole of the body.

xi   Desires seem to be of two kinds, one common to all men, the other peculiar to special peoples, and adventitious. For instance, the desire for food is natural, since everyone desires solid or liquid nourishment, and sometimes both, when in need of them; and also sexual intercourse, as Homer says,[85] when young and lusty. But not everybody desires this or that particular sort of nourishment, any more than everyone desires the same particular portion of food;[86] hence a taste for this or that sort of food seems

2   to be an individual peculiarity. Not but what there is also something natural in such tastes; for different things are pleasant to different people, and there are some special delicacies which all men like better than ordinary food.[87]

3   In the case of the natural desires, then, few men err, and in one way only, that of excess in quantity; for to eat or drink to repletion of ordinary food and drink is to exceed what is natural in amount, since the natural desire is only to satisfy one's wants. Hence people who over-eat are called 'mad-bellies', meaning that they fill that organ beyond the right measure; it is persons of especially slavish nature that are liable to this form of excess.

4   But in regard to the pleasures peculiar to particular people, many men err, and err in many ways. For when people are said to be 'very fond of' so-and-so, it is either because they like things that it is not right to like, or like them more than most people do, or like them in a wrong manner; and the profligate exceed in all these ways. For they like some things that are wrong, and indeed abominable, and any such things that it is right to like they like more than is right, and more than most people.

5   It is clear then that excess in relation to pleasures is profligacy, and that it is blameworthy. As regards pains on the other hand, it is not with temperance as it is with courage: a man is not termed temperate for enduring pain and profligate for not enduring it, but profligate for feeling more pain than is right when he fails to get pleasures (in his case pleasure actually causing pain), and temperate for not feeling pain at the absence of pleasure [or at abstaining from it].

6   The profligate therefore desires all pleasures, or those that are the most pleasant, and is led by his desire to pursue these in preference to everything else. He consequently feels pain not only when he fails to get them, but also from his desire for them, since desire is accompanied by pain; paradoxical though it seems that pain should be caused by pleasure.

7   Men erring on the side of deficiency as regards pleasures, and taking less than a proper amount of enjoyment in them, scarcely occur; such insensibility is not human. Indeed, even the lower animals discriminate in food, and like some kinds and not others; and if there be a creature that finds nothing pleasant, and sees no difference between one thing and another, it must be very far removed from humanity. As men of this type scarcely occur, we have no special name for them.

8   The temperate man keeps a middle course in these matters. He takes no pleasure at all in the things that the profligate enjoys most, on the contrary, he positively dislikes them; nor in general does he find pleasure in wrong things, nor excessive pleasure in anything of this sort; nor does he feel pain or desire when they are lacking, or only in a moderate degree, not more than is right, nor at the wrong time, *et cetera*. But such pleasures as conduce to health and fitness he will try to obtain in a moderate and right degree; as also other pleasures so far us they are not detrimental to health and fitness, and not ignoble, nor beyond his means. The man who exceeds these limits cares more for such pleasures than they are worth. Not so the temperate man; he only cares for them as right principle enjoins.

xii   Profligacy seems to be more voluntary than cowardice. For the former is caused by pleasure, the latter by pain, and pleasure is a 2   thing we choose, pain a thing we avoid. Also pain makes us beside ourselves: it destroys the sufferer's nature; whereas pleasure has no such effect. Therefore profligacy is the more voluntary vice. And consequently it is the more reprehensible; since moreover it is easier to train oneself to resist the temptations of pleasure, because these occur frequently in life, and to practise resistance to them involves no danger, whereas the reverse is the case with the objects of fear.

3   On the other hand, the possession of a cowardly character

would seem to be more voluntary than particular manifestations of cowardice: for cowardliness in itself is not painful, but particular accesses of cowardice are so painful as to make a man beside himself, and cause him to throw away his arms or otherwise behave in an unseemly manner; so that cowardly

4   actions actually seem to be done under compulsion. But with the profligate on the contrary the particular acts are voluntary, for they are done with desire and appetite, but the character in general is less so, since no one desires to be a profligate .

5   The word profligacy[88] or wantonness we also apply to the naughtiness of children, which has some resemblance to the licentiousness of adults. Which of the two takes its name from the other is of no importance for the present enquiry, but it would seem clear that the state which comes later in life must be

6   named from the one which comes earlier. The metaphor appears apt enough, since it is that which desires what is disgraceful and whose appetites grow apace that needs chastisement or pruning,[89] and this description applies in the fullest degree to desire, as it does to the child. For children, like profligates, live at the prompting of desire; and the appetite for pleasure is strongest in childhood, so that if it be not disciplined and made obedient to

7   authority, it will make great headway. In an irrational being the appetite for pleasure is insatiable and undiscriminating, and the innate tendency is fostered by active gratification; indeed, if such gratification be great and intense it actually overpowers the reason. Hence our indulgences should be moderate and few, and

8   never opposed to principle – this is what we mean by 'well-disciplined' and 'chastened' – and the appetitive part of us should be ruled by principle, just as a boy should live in obedience to his

9   tutor. Hence in the temperate man the appetitive element must be in harmony with principle. For (1) the aim of both temperance and principle is that which is noble; and (2) the temperate man desires the right thing in the right way at the right time, which is what principle ordains.

10   Let this then be our account of temperance.

1 ἑκούσιον and ἀκούσιον are most conveniently rendered 'voluntary' and 'involuntary'; but the word ἀκούσιον suggests 'unwilling' or 'against the will', and to this meaning Aristotle limits it in § 13. There he introduces a third term, οὐχ ἑκούσιον, 'not voluntary' or 'not willing', to describe acts done in ignorance of their full circumstances and consequences, and so not willed in the full sense; but such acts when subsequently regretted by the agent are included in the class of ἀκούσια or unwilling acts, because had the agent not been in ignorance he would not have done them.

2 i.e., partly voluntary, partly involuntary.

3 which shows that the acts are regarded as voluntary.

4 i.e., some acts are so repulsive that a man's abhorrence of them must be stronger than any pressure that can be put on him to commit them; so that if he commits them he must be held to have chosen to do so.

5 In a play now lost, Eriphyle was bribed with a necklace to induce her husband Amphiaraus, king of Argos, to join the expedition of the Seven against Thebes. Foreseeing he would lose his life, he charged his sons to avenge his death upon their mother, invoking on them famine and childlessness if they disobeyed. The verse in question is preserved:

μάλιστα μέν μ' ἐπῆρ' ἐπισκήψας πατήρ.

Alcmaeon, fr. 69 (Nauck)

6 There is no such thing as an act which is not this particular act in these particular circumstances (Burnet).

7 See note 1.

8 i.e., choice of ends: see note 15.

9 'Things' seems to include persons; see example (3) in § 17.

10 See note 9.

11 Aeschylus was accused before the Areopagus of having divulged the Mysteries of Demeter in certain of his tragedies, but was acquitted. A phrase of his, 'It came to my mouth', became proverbial (Plato, Republic 563 c etc.), and he may have used it on this occasion.

12 in the lost Cresphontes of Euripides.

13 A style of wrestling in which the adversaries only gripped each other's hand's without crossing.

14 Plato, *Laws*, 683 b ff., coupled anger and appetite with ignorance as sources of wrong action.

15 The writer here examines the operation of the will, which is regarded as essentially an act of choosing between alternatives of conduct. The technical term employed, 'choice' or 'preference', has appeared in the formal definition of virtue (II, vi, 15). In the present passage (*cf.* § 9), it is viewed as directed to means: at the moment of action we select from among the alternative acts possible (or expressing it more loosely, among the various things here and now obtainable by our action) the one which we think will conduce to the end we wish. Elsewhere however (III, i, 15 and VI, xii, 8) it is used of the selection of ends, and it is almost equivalent to 'purpose'; while at VI, xiii, 8 it includes both ends and means (see also VII, ix, 1). The writer returns to the subject in VI, ii.

16 *i.e.*, you cannot feel two contradictory desires at once (though you can of course desire two incompatible things: you may want to eat your cake and have it but you cannot strictly speaking at the same time both desire to eat the cake and desire not to eat it). But you can desire to do a thing and choose not to do it.

17 but as good or bad.

18 Greek dramas were produced in competitions (and it is noteworthy that in the old comedy at Athens the play itself dramatised a contest or debate).

19 *cf.* iii, 3 and note 22.

20 *i.e.*, an opinion or belief that so-and-so is good, and is within our power to obtain.

21 perhaps to be emended 'how it is to be achieved'.

22 The term includes the notion of immutability.

23 Here and in § 7 'necessity' denotes natural law in the inanimate world, while 'nature' or 'growth' means natural law as governing animate creatures. Aristotle held that these agencies, and with them the operation of human intelligence and art, beside their designed results, produced by their interplay certain by-products in the shape of undesigned and irregular occurrences, which are referred to in the next section. These in the natural world he spoke of as due to τὸ αὐτόματον, or 'the spontaneous'; when due to the activity of man he ascribed them to fortune or chance. In § 7 chance is made to include 'the spontaneous'.

24 In the manuscripts the words 'The reason why . . . list of causes' come after 'But we do not deliberate . . . Scythia'.

NOTES TO BOOK THREE

25 or 'the best line in policy'.

26 A less well attested reading gives 'more about our opinions', and Aristotle does not usually distinguish sharply between the arts and crafts and the practical sciences (the theoretical sciences cannot here be meant, see §§ 3 and 4).

27 The text is probably corrupt, and perhaps should be altered to run 'and in which the right means to take are not definitely determined'.

28 The reference is to the analytical method of solving a problem: the figure required to be drawn is assumed to have been drawn, and then we analyse it and ask what conditions it implies, until we come down to something that we know how to draw already.

29 This clause seems implied by the context.

30 *i.e.*, the intellect or reason, which chooses a line of action for the individual, as the Homeric monarch chose a policy for his kingdom

31 ii, 9.

32 The inherent ambiguity of the Greek verbal adjective form causes some confusion in this chapter between what is and what ought to be wished for, the desired and the desirable.

33 *i.e.*, things really bitter, etc. seem so to a healthy man but not in some cases to an invalid.

34 *i.e.*, in each department of character and conduct.

35 ii, 11.

36 Possibly a verse of Solon. Doubtless πονηρός, translated 'vile' to suit the context here, in the original meant 'wretched'.

37 iii, 15.

38 An enactment of Pittacus, tyrant of Mitylene, *Politics*, II, *fin.*, 1274 b 19.

39 The words 'but if a man . . . unjust' in the manuscripts come after § 13, 'unjust or dissolute'.

40 This is Aristotle's view, which the imaginary objector challenges. It is not quite certain that his objection is meant to go as far as the end of the paragraph, as indicated by the quotation mark.

41 *i.e.*, the end he aims at.

42 This clause looks like an interpolation: ἕξις is the *genus* of virtue, II, v, *fin.*, vi, *init.*, μεσότης its *differentia*, II, vi, 15 and 17.

43 See II, ii, 8.

44 See II, ii, 2. This clause in the manuscripts follows the next one.

45 See v, 2 and 20.

46 This section some editors place before §21, but it is rather a footnote to §14; and the opening words of §23 imply that a digression has been made.

47 τὰ καθ' ἕκαστα seems to bear a somewhat different sense here from i, 15, ἡ καθ' ἕκαστα (ἄγνοια).

48 II, vii, 2.

49 or perhaps 'imminent', but *cf.* viii, 15.

50 *i.e.*, he resents it as inglorious.

51 In using τὰ θαρραλέα as the opposite of τά φοβερά Aristotle follows Plato, *Republic*, 450 e, *Protagoras*, 359 c, *Laches*, 195 b, etc.; but he is original in distinguishing confidence as regards the former from fearlessness as regards the latter, and so considering excessive fearlessness in grave dangers as a different vice from excessive confidence in dangers not really formidable.

52 *i.e.*, the rightness and fineness of the act itself, *cf.* § 13; viii, 5 and 14; ix, 4 and see I note 3 on p. 25. This amplification of the conception of virtue as aiming at the mean here appears for the first time: we now have the final as well as the formal cause of virtuous action.

53 II, vii, 2.

54 Apparently a verse quotation. *cf. Eudemian Ethics*, 1229 b 28, 'As the Kelts take up arms and march against the waves'; and *Strabo*, vii, p. 293, gives similar stories, partly on the authority of the fourth-century historian Ephorus. An echo survives in Shakespeare's metaphor 'to take arms against a sea of troubles'.

55 These words seem to be an interpolation: confidence is shown in face of θαρραλέα, not φοβερά.

56 *i.e.*, ἐν τοῖς θαρραλέοις, in situations not really formidable.

57 For symmetry this should have been 'he that is deficient in fearlessness'.

58 See vi, 10.

59 The manuscripts have 'it chooses and endures'.

60 'Political courage': Plato uses this phrase (*Republic*, 430 c) of patriotic courage, based on training and 'right opinion about what is terrible and what is not', and in contrast with the undisciplined courage of slaves and brute beasts. Elsewhere, on the other hand, he contrasts 'popular and citizen virtue' in general with the philosopher's virtue, which is based on knowledge.

61 *Iliad*, xxii, 100 (Hector) –

> Alas, should I retire within the gates,
> Polydamas . . .

62 *Iliad*, viii, 148 –

> By me was Tydeus's son routed in flight
> Back to the ships.

63 For this emotion see II, vii, 14 and IV, ix, 1, where it is said not to be, strictly speaking, a virtue.

64 *Iliad*, ii, 391, but the words are Agamemnon's and are slightly different in our text of Homer.

65 *i.e.*, knowledge of what is truly formidable and what is not (*cf.* note 60); but Socrates went on to show that this depended on knowledge of the good, with which he identified all virtue: see Plato's *Laches*.

66 *i.e.*, ξένοι, foreign mercenary troops, much employed in Greek warfare in Aristotle's time.

67 In Coronea, 353 BC; the Acropolis had been seized by Onomarchus the Phocian, and mercenaries, brought in to aid the citizens, ran away at the beginning of the battle.

68 θυμός means both 'spirit' or 'high spirit' and also its manifestation in anger.

69 *i.e.*, in describing courageous men, *Iliad*, xiv, 151 or xvi, 529, v, 470, *Odyssey*, xxiv, 318. The fourth phrase is not in our Homer, but occurs in Theocritus xx, 15.

70 *i.e.*, in a place where they can escape. The words 'or a swamp' are probably interpolated.

71 See *Iliad*, xi, 558.

72 This parenthetical note does not bear on the context.

73 This sentence should apparently come at the end of the section, 'but' being amended to 'for'.

74 *cf.* vii, 2–6.

75 This occurred in the battle at the Long Walls of Corinth, 392 BC. Spartan cavalry had dismounted and armed themselves with the shields of the routed Sicyonians, marked Σ (Xenophon, *Hellenica*, IV, iv, 10).

76 *cf.* vi, 4.

77 *cf.* vii, 6.

78 This qualifies what was said in II, iii, 1.

79 II, vii, 3.

80 *i.e.*, by association.

81 The text here is doubtful, and possibly the whole of §6 is an interpolation.

82 *i.e.*, by association.

83 *Iliad*, iii, 24.

84 Apparently a character of comedy, though later writers speak of him as a real person. Some manuscripts here insert his name, 'Hospitable, the son of Belch', *cf. Eudemian Ethics*, III, 1231 a 16, where the story recurs, and Aristophanes, *Frogs*, 934.

85 A reminiscence of *Iliad*, xxiv, 130.

86 The text should perhaps be amended to run 'nor desires the same

food always'.

87 Preferences are natural because (1) men's natures vary and therefore their tastes vary, (2) some preferences are universal.

88 ἀκολασία, literally 'the result of not being punished', seems to have been used of spoiled children as well as of vicious adults.

89 The primary meaning of κολάζειν, 'to punish'.

BOOK FOUR

The moral virtues *(continued)*

i   Liberality. Liberality in giving, for the nobility of giving. Liberality in getting. Liberality proportionate to resources. Prodigality. Meanness.

ii   Magnificence or munificence. Vulgarity. Paltriness.

iii   Greatness of soul. Smallness of soul. Vanity.

iv   Proper ambition.

v   Gentleness or good temper. Lack of spirit. Excess of anger, its various forms.

vi   Agreeableness. Obsequiousness and flattery. Surliness.

vii   Sincerity as regards one's own merits. Boastfulness. Self-depreciation.

viii   Wittiness. Buffoonery. Boorishness

ix   Modesty.

i Next let us speak of liberality. This virtue seems to be the observance of the mean in relation to wealth: we praise a man as liberal not in war, nor in matters in which we praise him as temperate, nor in judicial decisions, but in relation to giving and getting[1] wealth, and especially in giving; wealth meaning all those things whose value is measured by money.

2 Prodigality and meanness[2] on the other hand are both of them modes of excess and of deficiency in relation to wealth.

3 Meanness is always applied to those who care more than is proper about wealth, but prodigality is sometimes used with a wider connotation, since we call the unrestrained and those

4 who squander money on debauchery prodigal; and therefore prodigality is thought to be extremely wicked, because it is a

5 combination of vices. But this is not the proper application of the word: really it denotes the possessor of one particular vice, that of wasting one's substance; for he who is ruined by his own agency is a hopeless case indeed,[3] and to waste one's substance seems to be in a way to ruin oneself, inasmuch as wealth is the means of life. This then is the sense in which the term prodigality is here understood.

6 Now riches are an article of use; but articles of use can be used either well or ill, and he who uses a thing best is he who possesses the virtue related to that thing; therefore that man will use riches best who possesses the virtue related to wealth; and this is the

7 liberal man. But the use of wealth seems to consist in spending and in giving; getting wealth and keeping it are modes of acquisition rather than of use. Hence the liberal man is more concerned with giving to the right recipients than with getting wealth from the right sources and not getting it from the wrong ones. Virtue is displayed in doing good rather than in having good done to one, and in performing noble acts rather than in

8 avoiding base ones; but manifestly doing good and acting nobly go with giving, while having good done to one and avoiding base actions go with getting. Again, gratitude is bestowed on a

giver, not on one who refrains from taking; and still more is this
9 true of praise. Also it is easier not to take than to give: men are
more reluctant to give away what belongs to them than to refrain
10 from taking what belongs to someone else. Again, it is those who
give whom we call liberal; those who refrain from taking[4] are not
praised for liberality but rather for justice, and those who take[5]
11 are not praised at all And of all virtuous people the liberal are
perhaps the most beloved, because they are beneficial to others;
and they are so in that they give.

12   Acts of virtue are noble, and are performed for the sake of their
nobility; the liberal man therefore will give for the nobility of
giving. And he will give rightly, for he will give to the right
people, and the right amount, and at the right time, and fulfil all
13 the other conditions of right giving. Also he will give with
pleasure, or at all events without pain; for virtuous action is
14 pleasant, or painless – it certainly cannot be painful. One who
gives to the wrong people,[6] or not for the nobility of giving but
from some other motive, will not be called liberal, but by some
different title; nor will he who gives with pain, for he would
prefer the money to the noble deed, which is not the mark of a
liberal man.

15   Consequently the liberal man will not take money from a
wrong source either, since one who holds wealth in low esteem
16 is not the man to make improper gains. Nor yet will he be fond
of asking favours, for one who confers benefits does not readily
17 accept them. But he will acquire wealth from the proper source,
that is, from his own possessions, not because he thinks it is a
noble thing to do, but because it is a necessary condition of
having the means to give. He will not be careless of his property,
inasmuch as he wishes to employ it for the assistance of others.
He will not give indiscriminately, in order that he may be able to
give to the right persons and at the right time, and where it is
18 noble to do so. But the liberal man is certainly prone to go to
excess in giving, so as to leave himself the smaller share; for it is a
mark of a liberal nature to be regardless of self.

19   In crediting people with liberality their resources must be taken
into account; for the liberality of a gift does not depend on its
amount, but on the disposition of the giver, and a liberal
disposition gives according to its substance.[7] It is therefore

possible that the smaller giver may be the more liberal, if he give
20 from smaller means. Men who have inherited a fortune are
reputed to be more liberal than those who have made one, since
they have never known what it is to want; moreover everybody
is specially fond of a thing that is his own creation: parents and
poets show this. But it is not easy for a liberal man to be rich,
since he is not good either at getting money or at keeping it,
while he is profuse in spending it and values wealth not for its
21 own sake but as a means of giving. Hence people blame fortune
because the most deserving men are the least wealthy. But this is
really perfectly natural: you cannot have money, any more than
anything else, without taking pains to have it.

22   On the other hand, the liberal man will not give to the wrong
people, nor at the wrong time, and so forth, for this would not
be an act of liberality at all; and if he spent his money on the
wrong objects he would not have any to spend on the right ones.
23 In fact, as was said before, the liberal man is one who spends in
proportion to his means as well as on the right objects; while he
that exceeds his means is prodigal. This is why we do not call the
lavishness of princes prodigality; because we feel that however
much they spend and give away they can hardly exceed the limit
of their resources.

24   Liberality then being the observance of the mean in the giving
and getting of wealth, the liberal man will not only give and
spend the right amounts on the right objects alike in small matters
and in great, and feel pleasure in so doing, but will also take the
right amounts, and from the right sources. For as this virtue is a
mean both in giving and in getting, he will do both in the right
way. Right getting goes with right giving, wrong getting is
opposed to right giving; the two concordant practices therefore
may be found in the same person, but the two opposite ones
clearly cannot be.

25   If the liberal man should happen to spend in a manner contrary
to what is right and noble, he will feel pain, though in a
moderate degree and in the right manner; for it is a mark of
virtue to feel both pleasure and pain on the right occasions and in
26 the right manner. Also the liberal man is an easy person to deal
27 with in money matters; he can be cheated, because he does not
value money, and is more distressed if he has paid less than he

ought than he is annoyed if he has paid more: he does not agree with the saying of Simonides.[8]

28   The prodigal on the other hand errs in his feelings with regard to money as well as in his actions; he feels neither pleasure nor pain on the right occasions nor in the right manner. This will become clearer as we proceed.

29   We have said[9] then that prodigality and meanness are modes of excess and of deficiency, and this in two things, giving and getting – giving being taken to include spending. Prodigality exceeds in giving [without getting],[10] and is deficient in getting; meanness falls short in giving and goes to excess in getting, only not on the great scale. Now the two forms of prodigality are very

30   seldom found united in the same person, because it is not easy to give to everyone without receiving from anyone: the giver's means are soon exhausted, if he is a private citizen, and only such

31   persons are considered prodigal.[11] In fact, a man who is prodigal in both ways may be thought considerably superior to the mean man; for he is easily cured by age or by poverty, and is able to be brought to the due mean, because he possesses the essentials of the liberal character – he gives, and he refrains from taking, though he does neither in the proper way or rightly. Correct this by training, or otherwise reform him, and he will be liberal, for he will now give his money to the right objects, while he will not get it from the wrong sources. This is why he is felt to be not really bad in character; for to exceed in giving without getting is

32   foolish rather than evil or ignoble. The prodigal of this type therefore seems to be much superior to the mean man, both for the reasons stated, and because the former benefits many people, but the latter benefits nobody, not even himself.

33   But the majority of prodigal people, as has been said, besides giving wrongly, take from wrong sources; in respect of getting

34   they are in fact mean. And what makes them grasping is that they want to spend, but cannot do so freely because they soon come to the end of their resources, and so are compelled to obtain supplies from others. Moreover, being indifferent to nobility of conduct, they are careless how they get their money, and take it from anywhere; their desire is to give, and they do not mind

35   how or where they get the means of giving. Hence even their giving is not really liberal: their gifts are not noble, nor given for

the nobility of giving, nor in the right way; on the contrary, sometimes they make men rich who ought to be poor, and will not give anything to the worthy, while heaping gifts on flatterers and others who minister to their pleasures. Hence most prodigal men are also profligate; for as they spend their money freely, some of it is squandered in debauchery; and having no high moral standard they readily yield to the temptation of pleasure.

36 This then is what the prodigal comes to if he is not brought under discipline; but if he is taken in hand, he may attain the due
37 mean and the right scale of liberality. Meanness on the contrary is incurable; for we see that it can be caused by old age or any form of weakness. Also it is more ingrained in man's nature than prodigality; the mass of mankind are avaricious rather than open-
38 handed. Moreover meanness is a far-reaching vice, and one of varied aspect: it appears to take several shapes. For as it consists in two things, deficiency in giving and excess in getting, it is not found in its entirety in every case, but sometimes the two forms occur separately, some men going too far in getting, while others
39 fall short in giving. The characters described by such names as niggardly, close-fisted, and stingy all fall short in giving, but they do not covet the goods of others nor wish to take them. With some of them this is due to an honourable motive of a sort, namely a shrinking from base conduct – since some persons are thought, or at all events profess, to be careful of their money because they wish to avoid being forced at some time or other to do something base; to this class belong the skinflint[12] and similar characters, who get their names from an excessive reluctance to give. But some keep their hands off their neighbours' goods from fear; they calculate that it is not easy to take what belongs to others without others taking what belongs to oneself, and so they
40 'prefer (as they say) neither to take nor to give'. The other sort of people are those who exceed in respect of getting, taking from every source and all they can; such are those who follow degrading trades, brothel-keepers and all people of that sort, and petty usurers who lend money in small sums at a high rate of interest; all these take from wrong sources, and more than their
41 due. The common characteristic of all these seems to be sordid greed, since they all endure reproach for gain, and for a small
42 gain. Those who make improper gains from improper sources on

a great scale, for instance princes who sack cities and rob temples, are not termed mean, but rather wicked or impious or unjust.

43 But the dicer and the footpad or brigand are to be classed as mean, as showing sordid greed, for both ply their trade and endure reproach for gain, the robber risking his life for plunder, and the dicer making gain out of his friends, to whom one ought to give; hence both are guilty of sordid greed, trying as they do to get gain from wrong sources. And all similar modes of getting wealth are mean for the same reasons.

44 Meanness is naturally spoken of as the opposite of liberality; for not only is it a greater evil than prodigality, but also men more often err on the side of meanness than on that of prodigality as we defined it.[13]

45 Let this suffice as an account of liberality and of the vices which are opposed to it.

ii Next it would seem proper to discuss magnificence,[14] for this also appears to be a virtue concerned with wealth. It does not however, like liberality, extend to all actions dealing with wealth, but only refers to the spending of wealth; and in this sphere it surpasses liberality in point of magnitude, for, as its name itself implies, it consists in suitable expenditure on a great scale.

2 But this greatness of scale is relative. An amount of outlay that would be great for a person fitting out a galley for the navy would not be great for one equipping a state pilgrimage. The

3 suitability of the expenditure therefore is relative to the spender himself, and to the occasion or object. At the same time the term magnificent is not applied to one who spends adequate sums on objects of only small or moderate importance, like the man who said 'Oft gave I alms to homeless wayfarers';[15] it denotes someone who spends suitably on great objects. For though the magnificent man is liberal, the liberal man is not necessarily magnificent.

4 The defect corresponding to the magnificent disposition is called paltriness, and the excess vulgarity, want of taste or the like. The latter vices do not exceed by spending too great an amount on proper objects, but by making a great display on the wrong occasions and in the wrong way. We will however speak of them later.[16]

5 The magnificent man is an artist in expenditure: he can discern what is suitable, and spend great sums with good taste. (For as we

6 said at the outset,[17] a disposition is defined by the activities in
which it is displayed, and by the objects to which it is related.) So
the magnificent man's expenditure is suitable as well as great.
And consequently the objects he produces must also be great and
suitable; for so only will a great expenditure be suitable [to the
result][18] as well. Hence, as the object produced must be worthy
of the expenditure, so also must the expenditure be worthy of or
7 even exceed the object produced. Again, the motive of the
munificent man in such expenditure will be the nobility of the
8 action, this motive being characteristic of all the virtues.
Moreover he will spend gladly and lavishly, since nice calculation
9 is shabby; and he will think how he can carry out his project
most nobly and splendidly, rather than how much it will cost and
10 how it can be done most cheaply. The magnificent man will
therefore necessarily be also a liberal man. For the liberal man too
will spend the right amount in the right manner; and it is in the
amount and manner of his expenditure that the element 'great' in
the magnificent or 'greatly splendid'[19] man, that is to say his
greatness, is shown, these being the things in which liberality is
displayed. And the magnificent man from an equal outlay will
achieve a more magnificent result;[20] for the same standard of
excellence does not apply to an achievement as to a possession:
with possessions the thing worth the highest price is the most
honoured, for instance gold, but the achievement most honoured is one that is great and noble (since a great achievement
arouses the admiration of the spectator, and the quality of causing
admiration belongs to magnificence); and excellence in an
11 achievement involves greatness. Now there are some forms
of expenditure definitely entitled honourable, for instance
expenditure on the service of the gods – votive offerings, public
buildings, sacrifices – and the offices of religion generally; and
those public benefactions which are favourite objects of
ambition, for instance the duty, as it is esteemed in certain states,
of equipping a chorus splendidly or fitting out a ship of war, or
12 even of giving a banquet to the public. But in all these matters, as
has been said, the scale of expenditure must be judged with
reference to the person spending, that is, to his position and his
resources; for expenditure should be proportionate to means, and
13 suitable not only to the occasion but to the giver. Hence a poor

man cannot be magnificent, since he has not the means to make a great outlay suitably; the poor man who attempts magnificence is foolish, for he spends out of proportion to his means, and beyond what he ought, whereas an act displays virtue only when it is

14 done in the right way. But great public benefactions are suitable for those who have adequate resources derived from their own exertions or from their ancestors or connections, and for the high-born and famous and the like, since birth, fame and so on

15 all have an element of greatness and distinction. The magnificent man therefore is especially of this sort, and magnificence mostly finds an outlet in these public benefactions, as we have said, since these are the greatest forms of expenditure and the ones most honoured. But magnificence is also shown on those private occasions for expenditure which only happen once, for instance, a wedding or the like, and which arouse the interest of the general public, or of people of position; and also in welcoming foreign guests and in celebrating their departure, and in the complimentary interchange of presents; for the magnificent man does not spend money on himself but on public objects, and his

16 gifts have some resemblance to votive offerings. It is also characteristic of the magnificent man to furnish his house in a manner suitable to his wealth, since a fine house is a sort of distinction; and to prefer spending on permanent objects, because

17 these are the most noble; and to spend an amount that is appropriate to the particular occasion, for the same gifts are not suitable for the gods and for men, and the same expenditure is not appropriate to a sacrifice and a funeral. In fact, inasmuch as the greatness of any form of expenditure varies with its particular

18 kind, and, although the most magnificent expenditure absolutely is great expenditure on a great object, the most magnificent in a particular case is the amount that is great in that case, and since the greatness of the result achieved is not the same as the greatness of the expenditure (for the finest ball or oil-flask does not cost much or involve a very liberal outlay, though it makes a

19 magnificent present in the case of a child), it follows that it is the mark of the magnificent man, in expenditure of whatever kind, to produce a magnificent result (for that is a standard not easily exceeded), and a result proportionate to the cost.

20   Such then is the character of the magnificent man. His

counterpart on the side of excess, the vulgar man, exceeds, as has
been said, by spending beyond what is right. He spends a great
deal and makes a tasteless display on unimportant occasions: for
instance, he gives a dinner to his club on the scale of a wedding
banquet, and when equipping a chorus at the comedies he brings
it on in purple at its first entrance, as is done at Megara.[21]
Moreover, he does all this not from a noble motive but to show
off his wealth, and with the idea that this sort of thing makes
people admire him; and he spends little where he ought to spend
21 much and much where he ought to spend little. The paltry man
on the other hand will err on the side of deficiency in everything;
even when he is spending a great deal, he will spoil the effect for
a trifle, and by hesitating at every stage and considering how he
can spend least, and even so grudging what he spends and always
thinking he is doing things on a greater scale than is necessary.
22 These dispositions then are vices, but they do not bring serious
discredit, since they are not injurious to others, nor are they
excessively unseemly.

iii   Greatness of soul,[22] as the word itself implies, seems to be
related to great objects; let us first ascertain what sort of objects
2 these are. It will make no difference whether we examine the
quality itself or the person that displays the quality.

3   Now a person is thought to be great-souled if he claims much
and deserves much; he who claims much without deserving it is
foolish, but no one of moral excellence is foolish or senseless.
4 The great-souled man is then as we have described. He who
deserves little and claims little is modest or temperate, but not
5 great-souled, since to be great-souled involves greatness just as
handsomeness involves size: small people may be neat and well-
6 made, but not handsome. He that claims much but does not
deserve much is vain; though not everybody who claims more
7 than he deserves is vain.[23] He that claims less than he deserves is
small-souled, whether his deserts be great or only moderate, or
even though he deserves little, if he claims still less. The most
small-souled of all would seem to be the man who claims less
than he deserves when his deserts are great; for what would he
have done had he not deserved so much?

8   Though therefore in regard to the greatness of his claim the
great-souled man is an extreme,[24] by reason of its rightness he

stands at the mean point, for he claims what he deserves; while the vain and the small-souled err by excess and defect respectively.

9   If then the great-souled man claims and is worthy of great things and most of all the greatest things, greatness of soul must
10 be concerned with some one object especially. 'Worthy' is a term of relation: it denotes having a claim to goods external to oneself. Now the greatest external good we should assume to be the thing which we offer as a tribute to the gods, and which is most coveted by men of high station, and is the prize awarded for the noblest deeds; and such a thing is honour, for honour is clearly the greatest of external goods. Therefore the great-souled man is he who has the right disposition in relation to honours
11 and disgraces. And even without argument it is evident that honour is the object with which the great-souled are concerned, since it is honour above all else which great men claim and deserve.

12 The small-souled man[25] falls short both as judged by his own deserts and in comparison with the claim of the great-souled
13 man; the vain man on the other hand exceeds as judged by his own standard, but does not however exceed the great-souled man.[26]

14 And inasmuch as the great-souled man deserves most, he must be the best of men; for the better a man is the more he deserves, and he that is best deserves most. Therefore the truly great-souled man must be a good man. Indeed greatness in each of the virtues
15 would seem to go with greatness of soul. For instance, one cannot imagine the great-souled man running at full speed when retreating in battle,[27] nor acting dishonestly; since what motive for base conduct has a man to whom nothing is great?[28] Considering all the virtues in turn, we shall feel it quite ridiculous to picture the great-souled man as other than a good man. Moreover, if he were bad, he would not be worthy of honour, since honour is the prize of virtue, and the tribute that we pay to the good. Greatness of
16 soul seems therefore to be as it were a crowning ornament of the virtues: it enhances their greatness, and it cannot exist without them. Hence it is hard to be truly great-souled,[29] for greatness of soul is impossible without moral nobility.

17 Honour and dishonour then are the objects with which the great-souled man is especially concerned. Great honours accorded

by persons of worth will afford him pleasure in a moderate
degree: he will feel he is receiving only what belongs to him, or
even less, for no honour can be adequate to the merits of perfect
virtue, yet all the same he will deign to accept their honours,
because they have no greater tribute to offer him. Honour
rendered by common people and on trivial grounds he will
utterly despise, for this is not what he merits. He will also despise
dishonour, for no dishonour can justly attach to him. The great-
18 souled man then, as has been said, is especially concerned with
honour; but he will also observe due measure in respect to
wealth, power, and good and bad fortune in general, as they may
befall him; he will not rejoice overmuch in prosperity, nor grieve
overmuch at adversity. For he does not care much even about
honour, which is the greatest of external goods[30] (since power
and wealth are desirable only for the honour they bring, at least
their possessors wish to be honoured for their sake); he therefore
to whom even honour is a small thing will be indifferent to other
things as well. Hence great-souled men are thought to be
haughty.

19 But it is thought that the gifts of fortune also conduce to
greatness of soul; for the high-born and those who are powerful
or wealthy are esteemed worthy of honour, because they are
superior to their fellows, and that which is superior in something
good is always held in higher honour; so that even these gifts of
fortune make men more great-souled, because their possessors
20 are honoured by some people. But in reality only the good man
ought to be honoured, although he that has both virtue and
fortune is esteemed still more worthy of honour; whereas those
who possess the goods of fortune without virtue are not justified
in claiming high worth, and cannot correctly be styled great-
souled, since true worth and greatness of soul cannot exist
21 without complete virtue. It is true that even those who merely
possess the goods of fortune may be haughty and insolent;
because without virtue it is not easy to bear good fortune
becomingly, and such men, being unable to carry their prosperity, and thinking themselves superior to the rest of mankind,
despise other people, although their own conduct is no better
than another's. The fact is that they try to imitate the great-
souled man without being really like him, and only copy him in

what they can, reproducing his contempt for others but not his
22 virtuous conduct. For the great-souled man is justified in
despising other people – his estimates are correct; but most proud
men have no good ground for their pride.

23 The great-souled man does not run into danger for trifling
reasons, and is not a lover of danger, because there are few things
he values; but he will face danger in a great cause, and when so
doing will be ready to sacrifice his life, since he holds that life is
not worth having at every price.

24 He is fond of conferring benefits, but ashamed to receive them,
because the former is a mark of superiority and the latter of
inferiority. He returns a service done to him with interest, since
this will put the original benefactor into his debt in turn, and
25 make him the party benefited. The great-souled are thought to
have a good memory for any benefit they have conferred, but a
bad memory for those which they have received (since the
recipient of a benefit is the inferior of his benefactor, whereas
they desire to be superior); and to enjoy being reminded of the
former but to dislike being reminded of the latter: this is why the
poet makes Thetis[31] not specify her services to Zeus; nor did the
Spartans treating with the Athenians[32] recall the occasions when
Sparta had aided Athens, but those on which Athens had aided
Sparta.

26 It is also characteristic of the great-souled man never to ask
help from others, or only with reluctance, but to render aid
willingly; and to be haughty towards men of position and
fortune, but courteous towards those of moderate station,
because it is difficult and distinguished to be superior to the great,
but easy to outdo the lowly, and to adopt a high manner with the
former is not ill-bred, but it is vulgar to lord it over humble
27 people: it is like putting forth one's strength against the weak. He
will not compete for the common objects of ambition, or go
where other people take the first place; and he will be idle and
slow to act, except when pursuing some high honour or
achievement; and will not engage in many undertakings, but
28 only in such as are important and distinguished. He must be open
both in love and in hate, since concealment shows timidity; and
care more for the truth than for what people will think; and
speak and act openly, since as he despises other men he is

outspoken and frank, except when speaking with ironical self-
29 depreciation,[33] as he does to common people. He will be
incapable of living at the will of another, unless a friend, since to
do so is slavish, and hence flatterers are always servile, and
30 humble people flatterers. He is not prone to admiration, since
nothing is great to him. He does not bear a grudge, for it is not a
mark of greatness of soul to recall things against people, especially
the wrongs they have done you, but rather to overlook them.
31 He is no gossip, for he will not talk either about himself or about
another, as he neither wants to receive compliments nor to hear
other people run down (nor is he lavish of praise either); and so
he is not given to speaking evil himself, even of his enemies,
32 except when he deliberately intends to give offence. In troubles
that cannot be avoided or trifling mishaps he will never cry out
or ask for help, since to do so would imply that he took them to
33 heart. He likes to own beautiful and useless things, rather than
useful things that bring in a return, since the former show his
independence more.

34 Other traits generally attributed to the great-souled man are a
slow gait, a deep voice, and a deliberate utterance; to speak in
shrill tones and walk fast denotes an excitable and nervous
temperament, which does not belong to one who cares for few
things and thinks nothing great.

35 Such then being the great-souled man, the corresponding
character on the side of deficiency is the small-souled man, and
on that of excess the vain man. These also[34] are not thought to be
actually vicious, since they do no harm, but rather mistaken. The
small-souled man deprives himself of the good things that he
deserves; and his failure to claim good things makes it seem that
he has something bad about him [and also that he does not know
himself],[35] for (people argue), if he deserved any good, he would
try to obtain it. Not that such persons are considered foolish, but
rather too retiring; yet this estimate of them is thought to make
them still worse, for men's ambitions show what they are worth,
and if they hold aloof from noble enterprises and pursuits, and
forgo the good things of life, presumably they think they are not
worthy of them.

36 The vain on the other hand are foolish persons, who are
deficient in self-knowledge and expose their defect: they undertake

honourable responsibilities of which they are not worthy, and then are found out. They are ostentatious in dress, manner and so on. They want people to know how well off they are, and talk about it,[36] imagining that this will make them respected.

37   Smallness of soul is more opposed than vanity to greatness of soul, being both more prevalent and worse.

38   Greatness of soul then, as we have said, is concerned with great honours.

iv   It appears however that honour also,[37] as was said in the first part of this work, has a certain virtue concerned with it, which may be held to bear the same relation to greatness of soul that liberality bears to magnificence. This virtue as well as liberality is without the element of greatness, but causes us to be rightly disposed towards moderate and small honours as liberality does
2   towards moderate and small amounts of money; and just as there is a mean and also excess and deficiency in getting and in giving money, so also it is possible to pursue honour more or less than is right and also to seek it from the right source and in the right
3   way. We blame a man as ambitious if he seeks honour more than is right, or from wrong sources; we blame him as unambitious if he does not care about receiving honour even on noble grounds.
4   But at another time we praise the ambitious man as manly and a lover of what is noble, or praise the unambitious man as modest and temperate, as we said in the first part of this work.[38] The fact is that the expression 'fond of' so-and-so is ambiguous, and we do not always apply the word 'fond of honour' (ambitious) to the same thing; when we use it as a term of praise, we mean 'more fond of honour than most men', but when as a reproach, 'more than is right'. As the observance of the mean has no name, the two extremes dispute as it were for the unclaimed estate. But where there is excess and deficiency there must also be a mean.
5   Now men do seek honour both more and less than is right; it must therefore be possible also to do so rightly. It is therefore this nameless middle disposition in regard to honour that we really praise. Compared with ambition it appears unambitiousness, and compared with unambitiousness it appears ambition: compared
6   with both, it appears in a sense to be both. This seems to be true of the other virtues also; but in the present case the extremes appear to be opposed only to one another, because the middle

character has no name.

V   Gentleness is the observance of the mean in relation to anger. There is as a matter of fact no recognised name for the mean in this respect – indeed there can hardly be said to be names for the extremes either – so we apply the word gentleness to the mean 2 though really it inclines to the side of the defect. This has no name, but the excess may be called a sort of irascibility, for the emotion concerned is anger, though the causes producing it are many and various.

3   Now we praise a man who feels anger on the right grounds and against the right persons, and also in the right manner and at the right moment and for the right length of time. He may then be called gentle-tempered, if we take gentleness to be a praiseworthy quality (for 'gentle' really denotes a calm temper, not led by emotion but only becoming angry in such a manner, 4 for such causes and for such a length of time as principle may ordain; although the quality is thought rather to err on the side of defect, since the gentle-tempered man is not prompt to seek redress for injuries, but rather inclined to forgive them).

5   The defect, on the other hand, call it a sort of lack of spirit or what not, is blamed; since those who do not get angry at things at which it is right to be angry are considered foolish, and so are those who do not get angry in the right manner, at the right 6 time, and with the right people. It is thought that they do not feel or resent an injury, and that if a man is never angry he will not stand up for himself; and it is considered servile to put up with an insult to oneself or suffer one's friends to be insulted.

7   Excess also is possible in each of these ways, for one can be angry with the wrong people, for the wrong things, or more violently or more quickly or longer than is right; but not all these excesses of temper are found in the same person. This would be impossible, since evil destroys even itself, and when present in its 8 entirety becomes unbearable. There are then first the irascible, who get angry quickly and with the wrong people and for the wrong things and too violently, but whose anger is soon over. This last is the best point in their character, and it is due to the fact that they do not keep their anger in, but being quick-tempered display it openly by retaliating, and then have done 9 with it. The excessively quick-tempered are passionate; they fly

into a passion at everything and on all occasions: hence their
10 name. The bitter-tempered on the other hand are implacable,
and remain angry a long time, because they keep their wrath in;
whereas when a man retaliates there is an end of the matter: the
pain of resentment is replaced by the pleasure of obtaining
redress, and so his anger ceases. But if they do not retaliate, men
continue to labour under a sense of resentment – for as their
anger is concealed no one else tries to placate them either, and it
takes a long time to digest one's wrath within one. Bitterness is
the most troublesome form of bad temper both to a man himself
11 and to his nearest friends. Those who lose their temper at the
wrong things, and more and longer than they ought, and who
refuse to be reconciled without obtaining redress or retaliating,
we call harsh-tempered.

12   We consider the excess to be more opposed to gentleness than
the defect, because it occurs more frequently, human nature
being more prone to seek redress than to forgive; and because the
harsh-tempered are worse to live with than the unduly placable.

13   But what was said above[39] is also clear from what we are now
saying; it is not easy to define in what manner and with whom
and on what grounds and how long one ought to be angry, and
up to what point one does right in so doing and where error
begins. For he who transgresses the limit only a little is not held
blameworthy, whether he errs on the side of excess or defect; in
fact, we sometimes praise those deficient in anger and call them
gentle-tempered, and we sometimes praise those who are harsh-
tempered as manly, and fitted to command. It is therefore not
easy to pronounce on principle what degree and manner of error
is blameworthy, since this is a matter of the particular circum-
14 stances, and judgement rests with the faculty of perception. But
thus much at all events is clear, that the middle disposition is
praiseworthy, which leads us to be angry with the right people
for the right things in the right manner and so on, while the
various forms of excess and defect are blameworthy – when of
slight extent, but little so, when greater, more, and when
extreme, very blameworthy indeed. It is clear therefore that we
should strive to attain the middle disposition.

15   Let this be our account of the dispositions related to anger.

vi   In society and the common life and intercourse of conversation

2 and business, some men are considered to be obsequious; these are people who complaisantly approve of everything and never raise objections, but think it a duty to avoid giving pain to those with whom they come in contact. Those on the contrary who object to everything and do not care in the least what pain they cause, are

3 called surly or quarrelsome. Now it is clear that the dispositions described are blameworthy, and that the middle disposition between them is praiseworthy – that is, the tendency to acquiesce in the right things, and likewise to disapprove of the right things,

4 in the right manner. But to this no special name has been assigned, though it very closely resembles friendship;[40] for he who exemplifies this middle disposition is the sort of man we mean by the expression 'a good friend', only that includes an element of

5 affection. It differs from friendship in not possessing the emotional factor of affection for one's associates; since a man of this character takes everything in the right way not from personal liking or dislike, but from natural amiability. He will behave with the same propriety towards strangers and acquaintances alike, towards people with whom he is familiar and those with whom he is not – though preserving the shades of distinction proper to each class, since it is not appropriate to show the same regard or disregard for the feelings of friends and of strangers.

6 We have said then in general terms that he will behave in the right manner in society. We mean that in designing either to give pain or to contribute pleasure he will be guided by considerations

7 of honour and of expediency. For he seems to be concerned with pleasure and pain in social intercourse. He will disapprove of pleasures in which it is dishonourable or harmful to himself for him to join, preferring to give pain;[41] and he will also disapprove of and refuse to acquiesce in a pleasure that brings any considerable discredit or harm to the agent, if his opposition will not cause

8 much pain. And he will comport himself differently with men of high position and with ordinary people, with persons more and less well known to him, and similarly as regards other distinctions, assigning to each class the proper degree of deference, and, other things apart, preferring to join in the pleasures of his companions and being reluctant to give pain; but being guided by the consequences, that is to say, the effects on his and his friends' credit or interest, if these outweigh the pleasure he will give by

compliance. Also he will give a small amount of pain at the moment for the sake of a large amount of pleasure in the future.

9   Such is the middle character, although it has no name. The man who always joins in the pleasures of his companions, if he sets out to be pleasant for no ulterior motive, is obsequious; if he does so for the sake of getting something by it in the shape of money or money's worth, he is a flatterer. He that disapproves of everything is, as we said, surly or quarrelsome. As the mean has no name, the extremes appear to be opposite to each other.

vii   The observance of the mean[42] in relation to boastfulness has to do with almost the same things. It also is without a name; but it will be as well to discuss these unnamed excellences with the rest, since we shall the better understand the nature of the moral character if we examine its qualities one by one; and we shall also confirm our belief that the virtues are modes of observing the mean, if we notice how this holds good in every instance. Now we have treated of behaviour in society with relation to giving pleasure and pain. Let us now discuss truthfulness and falsehood similarly displayed in word and deed, and in one's personal pretensions.

2   As generally understood then, the boaster is a man who pretends to creditable qualities that he does not possess, or possesses in a lesser degree than he makes out, while conversely the self-depreciator disclaims or disparages good qualities that he
3   does possess; midway between them is the straightforward sort of
4   man who is sincere both in behaviour and in speech, and admits the truth about his own qualifications without either exaggeration or understatement. Each of these things may be done with
5   or without an ulterior motive; but when a man is acting without ulterior motive, his words, actions, and conduct always represent
6   his true character.[43] Falsehood is in itself base and reprehensible, and truth noble and praiseworthy; and similarly the sincere man who stands between the two extremes is praised, and the insincere of both kinds are blamed, more especially the boaster. Let us discuss each of the two, beginning with the truthful man.

7   We are speaking not of truthfulness in business relations, nor in matters where honesty and dishonesty are concerned (for these matters would come under a different virtue),[44] but of cases where a man is truthful both in speech and conduct when no

considerations of honesty come in, from an habitual sincerity of
8   disposition. Such sincerity may be esteemed a moral excellence;
for the lover of truth, who is truthful even when nothing
depends on it, will *a fortiori* be truthful when some interest is at
stake, since having all along avoided falsehood for its own sake,
he will assuredly avoid it when it is morally base; and this is a
9   disposition that we praise. The sincere man will diverge from the
truth, if at all, in the direction of understatement rather than
exaggeration; since this appears in better taste, as all excess is
offensive.

10   The man who pretends to more merit than he possesses for no
ulterior object seems, it is true, to be a person of inferior
character, since otherwise he would not take pleasure in false-
11   hood; but he appears to be more foolish than vicious. When, on
the other hand, a man exaggerates his own merits to gain some
object, if that object is glory or honour he is not very much to be
blamed [as is the boaster], but if he boasts to get money or things
12   that fetch money, this is more unseemly. (Boastfulness is not a
matter of potential capacity but of deliberate purpose; a man is a
boaster if he has a fixed disposition to boast – a boastful
character.) Similarly liars are divided into those who like lying for
13   its own sake and those who lie to get reputation or profit. Those
then who boast for the sake of reputation pretend to possess such
qualities as are praised and admired; those who do so for profit
pretend to accomplishments that are useful to their fellows and
also can be counterfeited without detection; for instance,[45]
proficiency in prophecy, philosophy, or medicine. Because these
arts have the two qualities specified they are the commonest
fields of pretence and bragging.

14   Self-depreciators, who understate their own merits, seem of a
more refined character, for we feel that the motive underlying
this form of insincerity is not gain but dislike of ostentation.
These also[46] mostly disown qualities held in high esteem, as
15   Socrates used to do. Those who disclaim merely trifling or
obvious distinctions are called affected humbugs, and are decid-
edly contemptible; and sometimes such mock humility seems to
be really boastfulness, like the dress of the Spartans,[47] for extreme
negligence in dress, as well as excessive attention to it, has a touch
16   of ostentation. But a moderate use of self-depreciation in matters

not too commonplace and obvious has a not ungraceful air.

17   The boaster seems to be the opposite of the sincere man, because boastfulness is worse than self-depreciation.

viii   But life also includes relaxation, and one form of relaxation is playful conversation. Here, too, we feel that there is a certain standard of good taste in social behaviour, and a certain propriety in the sort of things we say and in our manner of saying them, and also in the sort of things we allow to be said to us; and it will also concern us whether those in whose company we speak or to

2   whom we listen conform to the same rules of propriety. And it is clear that in these matters too it is possible either to exceed or to fall short of the mean.

3   Those then who go to excess in ridicule are thought to be buffoons and vulgar fellows, who itch to have their joke at all costs, and are more concerned to raise a laugh than to keep within the bounds of decorum and avoid giving pain to the object of their raillery. Those on the other hand who never by any chance say anything funny themselves and take offence at those who do, are considered boorish and morose. Those who jest with good taste are called witty[48] or versatile – that is to say, full of good turns; for such sallies seem to spring from the character, and we judge men's characters, like their bodies, by

4   their movements. But as matter for ridicule is always ready to hand, and as most men are only too fond of fun and raillery, even buffoons are called witty and pass for clever fellows; though it is clear from what has been said that wit is different, and widely

5   different, from buffoonery. The middle disposition is further characterised by the quality of tact, the possessor of which will say, and allow to be said to him, only the sort of things that are suitable to a virtuous man and a gentleman: since there is a certain propriety in what such a man will say and hear in jest, and the jesting of a gentleman differs from that of a person of servile nature, as does that of an educated from that of an uneducated

6   man. The difference may be seen by comparing the old and the modern comedies; the earlier dramatists found their fun in obscenity, the moderns prefer innuendo, which marks a great

7   advance in decorum. Can we then define proper raillery by saying that its jests are never unbecoming to gentlemen, or that it avoids giving pain or indeed actually gives pleasure to its object?

Or is it impossible to define anything so elusive? for tastes differ as
8 to what is offensive and what amusing. Whatever rule we lay
down, the same will apply to the things that a man should allow
to be said to him, since we feel that deeds which a man permits
9 to be ascribed to him he would not stop at actually doing. Hence
a man will draw the line at some jokes; for raillery is a sort of
vilification, and some forms of vilification are forbidden by law;
perhaps some forms of raillery ought to be prohibited also. The
10 cultivated gentleman will therefore regulate his wit, and will be as
it were a law to himself.

Such then is the middle character, whether he be called
'tactful' or 'witty'. The buffoon is one who cannot resist a joke;
he will not keep his tongue off himself or anyone else, if he can
raise a laugh, and will say things which a man of refinement
would never say, and some of which he would not even allow to
be said to him. The boor is of no use in playful conversation:
11 he contributes nothing and takes offence at everything, yet
relaxation and amusement seem to be a necessary element in life.

12 We have now discussed three modes of observing the mean in
our behaviour, all of which are concerned with conversation or
with common occupations of some sort. They differ in that one
is concerned with truthfulness and the others with being pleasant.
Of the two that deal with pleasure, one is displayed in our
amusements, and the other in the general intercourse of life.

ix　　Modesty cannot properly be described as a virtue, for it seems
to be a feeling rather than a disposition; at least it is defined as a
2 kind of fear of disrepute, and indeed in its effects it is akin to the
fear of danger; for people who are ashamed blush, while those in
fear of their lives turn pale; both therefore appear to be in a sense
bodily affections, and this indicates a feeling rather than a
disposition.

3　　The feeling of modesty is not suitable to every age, but only to
the young. We think it proper for the young to be modest,
because as they live by feeling they often err, and modesty may
keep them in check; and we praise young people when they are
modest, though no one would praise an older man for being
shamefaced, since we think he ought not to do anything of
4 which he need be ashamed. For indeed the virtuous man does
5 not feel shame, if shame is the feeling caused by base actions;

since one ought not to do base actions (the distinction between acts really shameful and those reputed to be so is immaterial, since one ought not to do either), and so one never ought to feel 6 shame. Shame is a mark of a base man, and springs from a character capable of doing a shameful act. And it is absurd that, because a man is of such a nature that he is ashamed if he does a shameful act, he should therefore think himself virtuous, since actions to cause shame must be voluntary, but a virtuous man 7 will never voluntarily do a base action. Modesty can only be virtuous conditionally – in the sense that a good man would be ashamed *if* he were to do so and so; but the virtues are not conditional. And though shamelessness and not shrinking from shameful actions is base, this does not prove that to be ashamed 8 when one does shameful acts is virtuous – any more than self-restraint is a virtue, and not rather a mixture of virtue and vice. But this will be explained later.[49] Let us now speak of justice.

NOTES TO BOOK FOUR

1 The word λαμβάνειν, the antithesis of 'give', varies in meaning with the context between 'get', 'receive' and 'take'.

2 See II, note 30 on p. 49.

3 ἄσωτος, 'prodigal', means literally 'not saved', 'in desperate case'.

4 *i.e.*, those who refrain from taking more than their due.

5 *i.e.*, those who take what is their due.

6 The manuscript text gives 'to the wrong people', but *cf.* § 12, line 25 ὀρθῶς.

7 or (accepting Bywater's emendation) 'and this is relative to his substance'.

8 Several parsimonious aphorisms, sincere or ironical, are ascribed to Simonides, but none exactly fits this allusion.

9 See § 2.

10 These words seem to be interpolated.

11 *cf.* § 23 above.

12 κυμινοπρίστης means literally 'one who saws cummin-seed in half'.

13 See § 5.

14 μεγαλοπρέπεια denotes munificence of a magnificent kind, the spending of money on a grand scale from the motive of public spirit. In discussing it Aristotle is thinking especially of the λητουργίαι or public services discharged at Athens, and in other Greek cities, by wealthy individuals; such as the refitting of a naval trireme, the equipment of a dramatic chorus, and the defraying of the cost of a θεωρία or delegation representing the state at one of the great Hellenic festivals. The word literally means 'great conspicuousness' or splendour, but in eliciting its connotation Aristotle brings in another meaning of the verb πρέπειν, 'to be fitting', and takes the noun to signify 'suitability on a great scale': and also he feels that the element 'great' denotes grandeur as well as mere magnitude.

15 *Odyssey*, xvii, 420; said by Odysseus pretending to be a beggar who formerly was well-to-do.

16 §§ 20 to 22.

17 *cf.* II, i, 7 *fin.*

18 These words are better omitted: 'suitable to the occasion' seems to be meant.

19 See note 14.

20 *sc.* than the vulgar man or the shabby man.

21 In the earlier scenes of the comedies of Aristophanes, the chorus appear in character as charcoal-burners, cavalrymen, wasps, clouds, etc., and take part in the action of the play as such. They seem to have stripped off their outer dress for the Parabasis, or interlude, in which they address the audience on behalf of the author (*Acharnians* 627, *Peace* 730). In the later scenes they tend to fall more into the position of spectators, like the chorus of tragedy, and the play usually ends with something in the nature of a triumphal procession, when purple robes (like the scarlet worn by the chorus at the end of the *Eumenides* of Aeschylus) would not be inappropriate, as they would be in the opening scenes. Megarian comedy is elsewhere associated with coarse buffoonery.

22 μεγαλοψυχία, *magnanimitas*, means lofty pride and self-esteem rather than magnanimity or high-mindedness (in the modern sense of the word).

23 The term χαῦνος does not apply to a man who deserves much but claims even more, nor to one who claims little but deserves even less.

24 *cf.* II, vi, 17.

25 §§ 12, 13 should properly follow § 8.

26 That is, the small-souled man claims less than he deserves and less than the great-souled man deserves and claims; the vain man claims more than he deserves, but not more than the great-souled man deserves and claims.

27 Literally 'fleeing swinging his arms at his side', *i.e.* deficient in the virtue of courage. If this be the meaning the phrase recalls by contrast the leisurely retirement of Socrates from the stricken field of Delium (Plato, *Symposium* 221 a). But the words have been taken with what follows as illustrating the lack of justice or honesty, and the whole translated either 'outstripping an opponent in a race by flinging the arms backward [which was considered unsportsmanlike], nor fouling', or else 'being prosecuted on a charge of blackmailing, nor cheating in business'. Emendation would give a buried verse-quotation, 'to swing his arms in flight nor in pursuit'.

28 *i.e.*, nothing is of much value in his eyes (*cf.* §§ 30, 34), so that gain, which is a motive to dishonesty with others, is no temptation to him.

29 An echo of a line of Simonides, ἀνδρ' ἀγαθὸν μὲν ἀλαθέως
    γενέσθαι χαλεπόν, cf. I, note 67 on p. 29.

30 The manuscript reading gives 'For even honour he does not feel to
    be of the greatest importance.'

31 An incorrect recollection of *Iliad*, i, 393 ff., 503 f.; there Achilles
    says that his mother has often reminded Zeus how she rescued him
    when the other gods wished to put him in chains, and Thetis goes
    to Zeus and reminds him of her services in general terms.

32 The reference is uncertain.

33 See II, note 31 on p. 49.

34 *cf.* ii, 22.

35 These words seem to be interpolated. The small-souled man does
    not claim his deserts, but he may know what they are; he is not
    charged with ignorance of self, as is the vain man, § 36.

36 A variant reading is 'talk about themselves'.

37 *i.e.*, honour as well as wealth is the object of both a major and a
    minor virtue: see II, vii, 8.

38 See II, vii, 8.

39 II, ix, 7-9, a passage closely repeated here.

40 At II, vii, 13 it was actually termed φιλία, friendliness.

41 *sc.* by refusing to participate.

42 See II, note 31 on p. 49.

43 This oddly contradicts the preceding words.

44 Justice, Book V.

45 The true text very probably is 'for example "physician or seer
    sage" '; a verse quotation.

46 Just as boastfulness is chiefly shown in pretending to qualities of
    value.

47 Aristotle regards the cheapness and simplicity of the Spartans' dress
    as an affectation; or perhaps the reference is to 'Laconisers' at
    Athens who affected Spartan manners.

48 εὐτράπελοι, lit. 'turning well', nimble-witted.

49 in Book VII.

BOOK FIVE

The moral virtues *(concluded)*

i In regard to justice[1] and injustice, we have to enquire what sort
of actions precisely they are concerned with, in what sense
justice is the observance of a mean, and what are the
2 extremes between which that which is just is a mean. Our
enquiry may follow the same procedure as our preceding
investigations.

3   Now we observe that everybody means by justice that moral
disposition which renders men apt to do just things, and which
causes them to act justly and to wish what is just; and similarly by
injustice that disposition which makes men act unjustly and wish
what is unjust. Let us then assume this definition to start with as
broadly correct.

4   The fact is that it is not the same with dispositions as with
sciences and faculties. It seems that the same faculty or science
deals with opposite things;[2] but a disposition or condition which
produces a certain result does not also produce the opposite
results; for example, health does not give rise to unhealthy
actions, but only to healthy ones: healthy walking means walking
as a healthy man would walk.[3]

5   Hence[4] sometimes the nature of one of two opposite dispositions is inferred from the other, sometimes dispositions are
known from the things in which they are found; for instance, if
we know what good bodily condition is, we know from this
what bad condition is as well, but we also know what good
condition is from bodies in good condition, and know what
bodies are in good condition from knowing what good condition is. Thus, supposing good condition is firmness of flesh, bad
condition must be flabbiness of flesh, and a diet productive of
good condition[5] must be a diet producing firmness of flesh.

6   Also, if one of two correlative groups of words is used in
several senses, it follows as a rule that the other is used in several
senses too: for example, if 'just' has more than one meaning, so
7 also has 'unjust' and 'injustice'. Now it appears that the terms
justice and injustice are used in several senses, but as their

equivocal uses are closely connected, the equivocation is not
detected; whereas in the case of widely different things called by
a common name, the equivocation is comparatively obvious: for
example (the difference being considerable when it is one of
external form), the equivocal use of the word *kleis* (key) to
denote both the bone[6] at the base of the neck and the instrument
with which we lock our doors.

8   Let us then ascertain in how many senses a man is said to be
'unjust'. Now the term 'unjust' is held to apply both to the man
who breaks the law and the man who takes more than his due,
the unfair[7] man. Hence it is clear that the law-abiding man and
the fair man will both be just. 'The just' therefore means that
which is lawful and that which is equal or fair, and 'the unjust'
means that which is illegal and that which is unequal or unfair.

9   Again, as the unjust man is one who takes the larger share, he
will be unjust in respect of good things; not all good things, but
those on which good and bad fortune depend. These though
always good in the absolute sense, are not always good for a
particular person. Yet these are the goods men pray for and
pursue, although they ought not to do so; they ought, while
choosing the things that are good for them, to pray that what is
good absolutely may also be good for them.

10   The unjust man does not however always choose the larger
share: of things that, speaking absolutely, are bad he chooses the
smaller share; but nevertheless he is thought to take more than his
due, because the lesser of two evils seems in a sense to be a good,
and taking more than one's due means taking more than one's
11 due of good. Let us call him 'unfair', for that is a comprehensive
term, and includes both taking too much of good things and too
little of bad things.[8]

12   Again, we saw that the law-breaker is unjust and the law-
abiding man just. It is therefore clear that all lawful things are just
in one sense of the word, for what is lawful is decided by
legislature, and the several decisions of the legislature we call rules
13 of justice. Now all the various pronouncements of the law aim
either at the common interest of all, or at the interest of a ruling
class determined either by excellence or in some other similar
way; so that in one of its senses the term 'just' is applied to
anything that produces and preserves the happiness, or the

component parts of the happiness, of the political community.

14   And the law prescribes certain conduct; the conduct of a brave man, for example not to desert one's post, not to run away, not to throw down one's arms; that of a temperate man, for example not to commit adultery or outrage; that of a gentle man, for example not to strike, not to speak evil; and so with actions exemplifying the rest of the virtues and vices, commanding these and forbidding those – rightly if the law has been rightly enacted, not so well if it has been made at random.

15   Justice then in this sense is perfect virtue, though with a qualification, namely that it is displayed towards others. This is why justice is often thought to be the chief of the virtues, and more sublime 'or than the evening or the morning star';[9] and we have the proverb –

In justice is all virtue found in sum.[10]

And justice is perfect virtue because it is the practice of perfect virtue; and perfect in a special degree,[11] because its possessor can practise his virtue towards others and not merely by himself; for there are many who can practise virtue in their own private
16   affairs but cannot do so in their relations with another. This is why we approve the saying of Bias, 'Office will show a man'; for in office one is brought into relation with others and becomes a member of a community.

17   The same reason, namely that it involves relationship with someone else, accounts for the view[12] that justice alone of the virtues is 'the good of others', because it does what is for the
18   advantage of another, either a ruler or an associate. As then the worst man is he who practises vice towards his friends as well as in regard to himself, so the best is not he who practises virtue in regard to himself but he who practises it towards others; for that is a difficult task.

19   Justice in this sense then is not a part of virtue, but the whole of virtue; and its opposite injustice is not a part of vice but the
20   whole of vice (the distinction between virtue and justice in this sense being clear from what has been said: they are the same quality of mind, but their essence is different;[13] what as displayed in relation to others is justice, as being simply a disposition of a certain kind is virtue).

ii What we are investigating, however, is the justice which is a part of virtue, since we hold that there is such a thing as justice in this sense; and similarly we are investigating injustice in the particular sense. The existence of the latter is proved by the
2 following considerations: (1) When a man displays the other vices – for instance, throws away his shield, from cowardice, or uses abusive language, from bad temper, or refuses to assist a friend with money, from meanness – though he acts unjustly, he is not taking more than his share of anything; whereas when a man takes more than his share, it is frequently not due to any of these vices, and certainly not to all of them, yet nevertheless the action does display some vice, since we blame it; in fact it displays
3 the vice of injustice. Therefore there is another sort of injustice, which is a part of injustice in the universal sense, and there is something unjust which is a part of the unjust in general, or
4 illegal. (2) Again, suppose two men to commit adultery, one for profit, and gaining by the act, the other from desire, and having to pay, and so losing by it: then the latter would be deemed to be a profligate rather than a man who takes more than his due, while the former would be deemed unjust, but not profligate; clearly therefore it is being done for profit that makes the action
5 unjust. (3) Again, whereas all other unjust acts are invariably ascribed to some particular vice – for example, adultery is put down to profligacy, desertion from the ranks to cowardice, assault to anger – an unjust act by which a man has profited is not attributed to any vice except injustice.

6 Hence it is manifest that there is another sort of injustice besides universal injustice, the former being a part of the latter. It is called by the same name because its definition falls in the same genus, both sorts of injustice being exhibited in a man's relation to others; but whereas injustice in the particular sense is concerned with honour or money or security, or whatever term we may employ to include all these things, its motive being the pleasure of gain, injustice in the universal sense is concerned with all the things that are the sphere of virtue.

7 Thus it is clear that there are more kinds of justice than one, and that the term has another meaning besides virtue as a whole. We have then to ascertain the nature and attributes of justice in this special sense.

8   Now we have distinguished two meanings of 'the unjust', namely the unlawful and the unequal or unfair, and two meanings of 'the just', namely the lawful and the equal or fair. Injustice then, in the sense previously mentioned, corresponds to

9 the meaning 'unlawful'; but since the unfair is not the same as the unlawful, but different from it, and related to it as part to whole (for not everything unlawful is unfair, though everything unfair is unlawful), so also the unjust and injustice in the particular sense are not the same as the unjust and injustice in the universal sense, but different from them, and related to them as part to whole; for injustice in this sense is a part of universal injustice, and similarly the justice we are now considering is a part of universal justice. We have therefore to discuss justice and injustice, and the just and unjust, in the particular sense .

10 We may then set aside that justice which is coextensive with virtue in general, being the practice of virtue in general towards someone else, and that injustice which is the practice of vice in general towards someone else. It is also clear how we should define what is just and unjust in the corresponding senses. For the actions that spring from virtue in general are in the main identical with the actions that are according to law, since the law enjoins conduct displaying the various particular virtues and forbids conduct displaying the various particular vices. Also the regulations laid down for the education that fits a man for social life are

11 the rules productive of virtue in general. As for the education of the individual as such, that makes a man simply a good man, the question whether this is the business of political science or of some other science must be determined later: for it would seem that to be a good man is not in every case the same thing as to be good citizen.[14]

12 Particular justice on the other hand, and that which is just in the sense corresponding to it, is divided into two kinds. One kind is exercised in the distribution of honour, wealth, and the other divisible assets of the community, which may be allotted

13 among its members in equal or unequal shares. The other kind is that which supplies a corrective principle in private transactions. This corrective justice again has two sub-divisions, corresponding to the two classes of private transactions, those which are voluntary and those which are involuntary.[15] Examples of

voluntary transactions are selling, buying, lending at interest, pledging, lending without interest, depositing, letting for hire; these transactions being termed voluntary because they are voluntarily entered upon.[16] Of involuntary transactions some are furtive, for instance, theft, adultery, poisoning, procuring, entice- ment of slaves, assassination, false witness; others are violent, for instance, assault, imprisonment, murder, robbery with violence, maiming, abusive language, contumelious treatment.

iii   Now since an unjust man is one who is unfair, and the unjust is the unequal, it is clear that corresponding to the unequal there is
2 a mean, namely that which is equal; for every action admitting of
3 more and less admits of the equal also. If then the unjust is the unequal, the just is the equal – a view that commends itself to all without proof; and since the equal is a mean, the just will be a
4 sort of mean too. Again, equality involves two terms at least. It accordingly follows not only (a) that the just is a mean and equal [and relative to something and just for certain persons],[17] but also (b) that, as a mean, it implies certain extremes between which it lies, namely the more and the less; (c) that, as equal, it implies two shares that are equal; and (d) that, as just, it implies certain
5 persons for whom it is just. It follows therefore that justice involves at least four terms, namely, two persons for whom it is
6 just and two shares which are just. And there will be the same equality between the shares as between the persons, since the ratio between the shares will be equal to the ratio between the persons; for if the persons are not equal, they will not have equal shares; it is when equals possess or are allotted unequal shares, or persons not equal equal shares, that quarrels and complaints arise.
7   This is also clear from the principle of 'assignment by desert'. All are agreed that justice in distributions must be based on desert of some sort, although they do not all mean the same sort of desert; democrats make the criterion free birth; those of oligarchical sympathies wealth, or in other cases birth; upholders
8 of aristocracy make it virtue. Justice is therefore a sort of proportion; for proportion is not a property of numerical quantity only, but of quantity in general, proportion being equality of ratios, and involving four terms at least.
9   (That a discrete proportion[18] has four terms is plain, but so also has a continuous proportion, since it treats one term as two, and

repeats it: for example,[19] as the line representing term one is to the line representing term two, so is the line representing term two to the line representing term three; here the line representing term two is mentioned twice, so that if it be counted twice, there will be four proportionals.)

10   Thus the just also involves four terms at least, and the ratio between the first pair of terms is the same as that between the second pair. For the two lines representing the persons and shares 11 are similarly divided;[20] then, as the first term is to the second, so is the third to the fourth; and hence, by alternation, as the first is to the third, so is the second to the fourth; and therefore also, as the first is to the second, so is the sum of the first and third to the sum of the second and fourth. Now this is the combination effected by a distribution of shares, and the combination is a just one, if persons and shares are added together in this way. The 12 principle of distributive justice, therefore, is the conjunction of the first term of a proportion with the third and of the second with the fourth; and the just in this sense is a mean between two extremes that are disproportionate,[21] since the proportionate is a mean, and the just is the proportionate.

13   (This kind of proportion is termed by mathematicians geometrical proportion;[22] for a geometrical proportion is one in which the sum of the first and third terms will bear the same ratio to the sum of the second and fourth as one term of either pair 14 bears to the other term. Distributive justice is not a continuous proportion, for its second and third terms, a recipient and a share, do not constitute a single term.)

The just in this sense is therefore the proportionate, and the unjust is that which violates proportion. The unjust may therefore be either too much or too little; and this is what we 15 find in fact, for when injustice is done, the doer has too much and the sufferer too little of the good in question; though *vice versa* in the case of an evil, because a lesser evil in comparison 16 with a greater counts as a good, since the lesser of two evils is more desirable than the greater, but what is desirable is good, and the more desirable it is, the greater good it is.

17   This then is one kind of justice.

iv   The remaining kind is corrective justice, which operates in private transactions, both voluntary and involuntary. This justice

2 is of a different sort from the preceding. For justice in distributing common property always conforms with the proportion we have described (since when a distribution is made from the common stock, it will follow the same ratio as that between the amounts which the several persons have contributed to the common stock); and the injustice opposed to justice of this kind is a

3 violation of this proportion. But the just in private transactions, although it is the equal in a sense (and the unjust the unequal), is not the equal according to geometrical but according to arithmetical proportion.[23] For it makes no difference[24] whether a good man has defrauded a bad man or a bad one a good one, nor whether it is a good or a bad man that has committed adultery; the law looks only at the nature of the damage, treating the parties as equal, and merely asking whether one has done and the other suffered injustice, whether one inflicted and the other has

4 sustained damage. Hence the unjust being here the unequal, the judge endeavours to equalise it: inasmuch as when one man has received and the other has inflicted a blow, or one has killed and the other been killed, the line[25] representing the suffering and doing of the deed is divided into unequal parts, but the judge endeavours to make them equal by the penalty or loss[26] he

5 imposes, taking away the gain. (For the term 'gain' is used in a general way to apply to such cases, even though it is not strictly

6 appropriate to some of them, for example to a person who strikes another, nor is 'loss' appropriate to the victim in this case; but at all events the results are called 'loss' and 'gain' respectively when the amount of the damage sustained comes to be estimated.) Thus, while the equal is a mean between more and less, gain and loss are at once both more and less in contrary ways, more good and less evil being gain and more evil and less good loss; and as the equal, which we pronounce to be just, is, as we said, a mean between them, it follows that justice in rectification[27] will be the mean between loss and gain.

7   This is why when disputes occur men have recourse to a judge. To go to a judge is to go to justice, for the ideal judge is so to speak justice personified. Also, men require a judge to be a

middle term or *medium* – indeed in some places judges are called *mediators* – for they think that if they get the mean they will get what is just. Thus the just is a sort of mean, inasmuch as the judge is a medium between the litigants.

8　　Now the judge restores equality: if we represent the matter by a line divided into two unequal parts, he takes away from the greater segment that portion by which it exceeds one-half of the whole line, and adds it to the lesser segment. When the whole has been divided into two halves, people then say that they 'have

9　their own', having got what is equal.[28] This is indeed the origin of the word *dikaion* (just): it means *dicha* (in half), as if one were to pronounce it *dichaion;* and a *dikast* (judge) is a *dichast* (halver). The equal is a mean by way of arithmetical proportion between

10　the greater and the less. For when of two equals[29] a part is taken from the one and added to the other, the latter will exceed the former by twice that part, since if it had been taken from the one but not added to the other, the latter would exceed the former by once the part in question only. Therefore the latter will exceed the mean by once the part, and the mean will exceed the

11　former, from which the part was taken, by once that part. This process then will enable us to ascertain what we ought to take away from the party that has too much and what to add to the one that has too little: we must add to the one that has too little the amount whereby the mean between them exceeds him, and take away from the greatest[30] of the three the amount by which

12　the mean is exceeded by him. Let the lines[31] AA', BB', CC' be equal to one another; let the segment AE be taken away from the line AA', and let the segment CD be added to the line CC', so that the whole line DCC' exceeds the line EA' by CD+CF; then DCC' will exceed BB' by CD.[32]

13　　The terms 'loss' and 'gain' in these cases are borrowed from the operations of voluntary exchange. There, to have more than one's own is called gaining, and to have less than one had at the outset is called losing, as for instance in buying and selling, and all

14　other transactions sanctioned by law;[33] while if the result of the transaction is neither an increase nor a decrease, but exactly what the parties had of themselves, they say they 'have their own' and have neither lost nor gained. Hence justice in involuntary transactions is a mean between gain and loss in a sense: it is to have after the transaction an amount equal to the amount one had before it.

v   The view is also held by some that simple reciprocity is justice. This was the doctrine of the Pythagoreans, who defined the just simply as 'suffering reciprocally with another'.[34]

2   Reciprocity however does not coincide either with distribu-
3   tive or with corrective justice, although people mean to identify it with the latter when they quote the rule of Rhadamanthys –

> An a man suffer even that which he did
> Right justice will be done.

4   For in many cases reciprocity is at variance with justice: for example, if an officer strikes a man, it is wrong for the man to strike him back; and if a man strikes an officer, it is not enough for the officer to strike him, but he ought to be punished as well.
5   Again, it makes a great difference whether an act was done with
6   or without the consent of the other party.[35] But in the interchange of services justice in the form of reciprocity is the bond that maintains the association: reciprocity, that is, on the basis of proportion, not on the basis of equality. The very existence of the state depends on proportionate reciprocity; for men demand that they shall be able to requite evil with evil – if they cannot, they feel they are in the position of slaves; and to repay good with good – failing which, no exchange takes place,
7   and it is exchange that binds them together. This is why we set up a shrine of the Graces in a public place, to remind men to return a kindness; for that is a special characteristic of grace, since it is a duty not only to repay a service done one, but another time to take the initiative in doing a service oneself.

8   Now proportionate requital is effected by diagonal conjunction. For example, let A be a builder, B a shoemaker, C a house, and D a shoe. It is required that the builder shall receive from the shoemaker a portion of the product of his labour, and give him a portion of the product of his own. Now[36] if proportionate equality between the products be first established, and then reciprocation take place, the requirement indicated will have been achieved; but if this is not done, the bargain is not equal, and intercourse does not continue. For it may happen that the product of one of the parties is worth more than that of the

9   other, and in that case therefore they have to be equalised. This holds good with the other arts as well; for they would have passed out of existence if the active element did not produce, and did not receive the equivalent in quantity and quality of what the passive element receives.[37] For an association for interchange of services is not formed between two physicians, but between a physician and a farmer, and generally between persons who are different, and who may be unequal, though in that case they

10   have to be equalised. Hence all commodities exchanged must be able to be compared in some way. It is to meet this requirement that men have introduced money; money constitutes in a manner a middle term, for it is a measure of all things, and so of their superior or inferior value, that is to say, how many shoes are equivalent to a house or to a given quantity of food. As therefore a builder is to a shoemaker,[38] so must such and such a number of shoes be to a house [or to a given quantity of food];[39] for without this reciprocal proportion, there can be no exchange and no association; and it cannot be secured unless the commodities in question be equal in a sense.

11   It is therefore necessary that all commodities shall be measured by some one standard, as was said before. And this standard is in reality demand, which is what holds everything together, since if men cease to have wants or if their wants alter, exchange will go on no longer, or will be on different lines. But demand has come to be conventionally represented by money; this is why money is called *nomisma* (customary currency), because it does not exist by nature but by custom (*nomos*), and can be altered and rendered useless[40] at will.

12   There will therefore be reciprocal proportion when the products have been equated, so that as farmer is to shoemaker,[41] so may the shoemaker's product be to the farmer's product. And when they exchange their products they must reduce them to the form of a proportion, otherwise one of the two extremes will have both the excesses;[42] whereas when they have their own[43] they then are equal, and can form an association together, because equality in this sense can be established in their case (farmer A, food C, shoemaker B, shoemaker's product equalised D);[44] whereas if it were impossible for reciprocal proportion to be effected in this way, there could be no association between them.

13   That it is demand which, by serving as a single standard, holds such an association together, is shown by the fact that, when there is no demand for mutual service on the part of both or at least of one of the parties, no exchange takes place between them [as when someone needs something that one has oneself, for instance, the state offering a licence to export corn in exchange for wine].[45] This inequality of demand has therefore to be equalised.

14   Now money serves us as a guarantee of exchange in the future: supposing we need nothing at the moment, it ensures that exchange shall be possible when a need arises, for it meets the requirement of something we can produce in payment so as to obtain the thing we need. Money, it is true, is liable to the same fluctuation of demand as other commodities, for its purchasing power varies at different times; but it tends to be comparatively constant. Hence the proper thing is for all commodities to have their prices fixed; this will ensure that exchange, and consequently association, shall always be possible. Money then serves as a measure which makes things commensurable and so reduces them to equality. If there were no exchange there would be no association, and there can be no exchange without equality, and no equality without commensurability. Though therefore it is impossible for things so different to become commensurable in the strict sense, our demand furnishes a sufficiently accurate

15   common measure for practical purposes. There must therefore be some one standard, and this accepted by agreement (which is why it is called *nomisma*, customary currency); for such a standard makes all things commensurable, since all things can be measured by money. Let A be a house, B ten minae and C a bedstead. Then $A = B/2$ (supposing the house to be worth, or equal to, five minae), and C (the bedstead) $= B/10$; it is now clear how many

16   bedsteads are equal to one house, namely five. It is clear that before money existed this is how the rate of exchange was actually stated – five beds for a house – since there is no real difference between that and the price of five beds for a house.

17   We have now stated what justice and injustice are in principle. From the definition given, it is plain that just conduct is a mean between doing and suffering injustice, for the former is to have too much and the latter to have too little. And justice is a mode

of observing the mean, though not in the same way as the other virtues are, but because it is related to a mean, while injustice is related to the extremes. Also, justice is that quality in virtue of which a man is said to be disposed to do by deliberate choice that which is just, and, when distributing things between himself and another, or between two others, not to give too much to himself and too little to his neighbour of what is desirable, and too little to himself and too much to his neighbour of what is harmful, but to each what is proportionately equal; and similarly when he is
18 distributing between two other persons. Injustice on the contrary is similarly related to that which is unjust, which is a disproportionate excess or deficiency of something beneficial or harmful. Hence injustice is excess and defect, in the sense that it results in excess and defect: namely, in the offender's own case, an excess of anything that is generally speaking beneficial and a deficiency of anything harmful, and in the case of others,[46] though the result as a whole is the same, the deviation from proportion may be in either direction as the case may be.

Of the injustice done, the smaller part is the suffering and the larger part the doing of injustice.

19 So much may he said about the nature of justice and injustice, and of the just and the unjust regarded universally.

vi But[47] seeing that a man may commit injustice without actually being unjust, what is it that distinguishes those unjust acts the commission of which renders a man actually unjust under one of the various forms of injustice, for example, a thief or an adulterer or a brigand? Or shall we rather say that the distinction does not lie in the quality of the act? For a man may have intercourse with a woman knowing who she is, yet not from the motive of
2 deliberate choice, but under the influence of passion; in such a case, though he has committed injustice, he is not an unjust man: for instance, he is not a thief, though guilty of theft, not an adulterer, though he has committed adultery, and so forth.

3 The relation of reciprocity to justice has been stated already.

4 But we must not forget that the subject of our investigation is at once justice in the absolute sense and political justice. Political justice means justice as between free and (actually or proportionately) equal persons, living a common life for the purpose of satisfying their needs. Hence between people not free and equal

political justice cannot exist, but only a sort of justice in a metaphorical sense. For justice can only exist between those whose mutual relations are regulated by law, and law exists among those between whom there is a possibility of injustice, for the administration of the law means the discrimination of what is just and what is unjust. Persons therefore between whom injustice can exist can act unjustly towards each other (although unjust action does not necessarily involve injustice): to act unjustly meaning to assign oneself too large a share of things generally good and too small a share of things generally evil. This

5 is why we do not permit a man to rule, but the law, because a man rules in his own interest, and becomes a tyrant; but the function of a ruler is to be the guardian of justice, and if of justice,

6 then of equality. A just ruler seems to make nothing out of his office; for he does not allot to himself a larger share of things generally good, unless it be proportionate to his merits; so that he labours for others, which accounts for the saying mentioned

7 above,[48] that 'justice is the good of others'. Consequently some recompense has to be given him, in the shape of honour and dignity. It is those whom such rewards do not satisfy who make themselves tyrants.

8 Justice between master and slave and between father and child is not the same as absolute and political justice, but only analogous to them. For there is no such thing as injustice in the absolute sense towards what is one's own; and a chattel,[49] or a child till it reaches a certain age and becomes independent, is, as it were, a part of oneself, and no one chooses to harm himself;

9 hence there can be no injustice towards them, and therefore nothing just or unjust in the political sense. For these, as we saw, are embodied in law, and exist between persons whose relations are naturally regulated by law, that is, persons who share equally in ruling and being ruled. Hence justice exists in a fuller degree between husband and wife than between father and children, or master and slaves; in fact, justice between husband and wife is domestic justice in the real sense, though this too is different from political justice.

vii Political justice is of two kinds, one natural, the other conventional. A rule of justice is natural that has the same validity everywhere, and does not depend on our accepting it or not. A rule is conventional that in the first instance may be settled in one way or the other indifferently, though having once been settled it is not indifferent: for example, that the ransom for a prisoner shall be a mina, that a sacrifice shall consist of a goat and not of two sheep; and any regulations enacted for particular cases, for instance the sacrifice in honour of Brasidas,[50] and ordinances in

2   the nature of special decrees. Some people think that all rules of justice are merely conventional, because whereas a law of nature is immutable and has the same validity everywhere, as fire burns both here and in Persia, rules of justice are seen to vary. That

3   rules of justice vary is not absolutely true, but only with qualifications. Among the gods indeed it is perhaps not true at all; but in our world,[51] although there is such a thing as natural justice, all rules of justice are variable. But nevertheless there is such a thing as natural justice as well as justice not ordained by

4   nature; and it is easy[52] to see which rules of justice, though not absolute, are natural, and which are not natural but legal and conventional, both sorts alike being variable. The same distinction will hold good in all other matters; for instance, the right hand is naturally stronger than the left, yet it is possible for any man to make himself ambidextrous.

5   The rules of justice based on convention and expediency are like standard measures. Corn and wine measures are not equal in all places, but are larger in wholesale and smaller in retail markets. Similarly the rules of justice ordained not by nature but by man are not the same in all places, since forms of government are not the same, though in all places there is only one form of government that is natural, namely, the best form.

6   The several rules of justice and of law are related to the actions conforming with them as universals to particulars, for the actions done are many, while each rule or law is one, being universal.

7   There is a difference between 'that which is unjust' and 'unjust conduct', and between 'that which is just' and 'just conduct'. Nature or ordinance pronounces a thing unjust: when that thing is done, it is 'unjust conduct'; till it is done, it is only 'unjust'. And similarly with 'just conduct', *dikaioma* (or more correctly, the general term is *dikaiopragema*, *dikaioma* denoting the rectification of an act of injustice).

We shall have later[53] to consider the several rules of justice and of law, and to enumerate their various kinds and describe them and the things with which they deal.

viii   Such being an account of just and unjust actions, it is their voluntary performance that constitutes just and unjust conduct. If a man does them involuntarily, he cannot be said to act justly, or unjustly, except incidentally, in the sense that he does an act
2 which happens to be just or unjust. Whether therefore an action is or is not an act of injustice, or of justice, depends on its voluntary or involuntary character. When it is voluntary, the agent is blamed, and only in that case is the action an act of injustice; so that it is possible for an act to be unjust without being an act of injustice, if the qualification of voluntariness be
3 absent. By a voluntary action, as has been said before,[54] I mean any action within the agent's own control which he performs knowingly, that is, without being in ignorance of the person affected, the instrument employed, and the result (for example, he must know whom he strikes, and with what weapon, and the effect of the blow); and in each of these respects both accident[55] and compulsion must be excluded. For instance, if A took hold of B's hand and with it struck C, B would not be a voluntary agent, since the act would not be in his own control. Or again, a man may strike his father without knowing that it is his father, though aware that he is striking some person, and perhaps that it is one or other of the persons present;[56] and ignorance may be similarly defined with reference to the result, and to the circumstances of the action generally. An involuntary act is therefore an act done in ignorance, or else one that though not done in ignorance is not in the agent's control, or is done under compulsion; since there are many natural processes too that we perform or undergo knowingly, though none of them is either voluntary or involuntary;[57] for example, growing old, and dying.
4 Also an act may be either just or unjust incidentally. A man may restore a deposit unwillingly and from fear of consequences, and we must not then say that he does a just act, nor that he acts justly, except incidentally; and similarly a man who under compulsion and against his will fails to restore a deposit can only be said to act unjustly or do what is unjust incidentally.
5 Again voluntary acts are divided into acts done by choice and those done not by choice, the former being those done after

deliberation and the latter those done without previous deliberation.

6 There are then three ways[58] in which a man may injure his fellow. An injury done in ignorance is an error, the person affected or the act or the instrument or the result being other than the agent supposed; for example, he did not think to hit, or not with this missile, or not this person, or not with this result, but it happened that either the result was other than he expected (for instance he did not mean to inflict a wound but only a

7 prick), or the person, or the missile. When then the injury happens contrary to reasonable expectation, it is (1) a misadventure. When, though not contrary to reasonable expectation, it is done without evil intent, it is (2) a culpable error; for an error is culpable when the cause of one's ignorance lies in oneself, but

8 only a misadventure when the cause lies outside oneself. When an injury is done knowingly but not deliberately, it is (3) an act of injustice or wrong; such, for instance, are injuries done through anger, or any other unavoidable or natural passion to which men are liable; since in committing these injuries and errors a man acts unjustly, and his action is an act of injustice, but he is not *ipso facto* unjust or wicked, for the injury was not done out of wickedness. When however an injury is done from choice, the doer is unjust

9 and wicked. Hence acts due to sudden anger are rightly held not to be done of malice aforethought, for it is the man who gave the provocation that began it, not he who does the deed in a fit of

10 passion. And moreover the issue is not one of fact, but of justification (since it is apparent injustice that arouses anger); the fact of the injury is not disputed (as it is in cases of contract, where one or the other of the parties must be a knave, unless they dispute the facts out of forgetfulness). They agree as to the facts but dispute on which side justice lies; so that one thinks he has been unjustly treated and the other does not. On the other hand, one who does an injury intentionally is not acting in

11 ignorance;[59] but if a man does an injury of set purpose, he is guilty of injustice, and injustice of the sort that renders the doer an unjust man, if it be an act that violates proportion or equality. Similarly one who acts justly on purpose is a just man; but he acts justly only if he acts voluntarily.

12 Of involuntary actions some are pardonable and some are not.

Errors not merely committed in ignorance but caused by ignorance are pardonable; those committed in ignorance, but caused not by that ignorance but by unnatural or inhuman passion, are unpardonable.

ix   But it may perhaps be doubted whether our discussion of suffering and doing injustice has been sufficiently definite; and in the first place, whether the matter really is as Euripides has put it in the strange lines – [60]

> I killed my mother – that's the tale in brief !
> Were you both willing, or unwilling both?

Is it really possible to suffer injustice[61] voluntarily, or on the contrary is suffering injustice always involuntary, just as acting unjustly is always voluntary? And again, is suffering injustice always voluntary, or always involuntary, or sometimes one and 2 sometimes the other? And similarly with being treated justly (acting justly being always voluntary). Thus it would be reasonable to suppose that both being treated unjustly and being treated justly are similarly opposed to acting unjustly and acting justly respectively: that either both are voluntary or both involuntary. But it would seem paradoxical to assert that even being treated justly is always voluntary; for people are sometimes treated justly 3 against their will. The fact is that the further question might be raised, must a man who has had an unjust thing done to him always be said to have been treated unjustly, or does the same thing hold good of suffering as of doing something unjust? One may be a party to a just act, whether as its agent or its object, incidentally.[62] And the same clearly is true of an unjust act: doing what is unjust is not identical with acting unjustly, nor yet is suffering what is unjust identical with being treated unjustly, and the same is true of acting and being treated justly; for it is impossible to be treated unjustly unless the other acts unjustly, or to be treated justly unless he acts justly.

4   But if to act unjustly is simply to do harm to someone voluntarily, and voluntarily means knowing the person affected, the instrument, and the manner of injury, it will follow both that the man of defective self-restraint, inasmuch as he voluntarily harms himself, voluntarily suffers injustice, and also that it is possible for a man to act unjustly towards himself (for the

5 possibility of this is also a debated question). Moreover, lack of self-restraint may make a person voluntarily submit to being harmed by another; which again would prove that it is possible to suffer injustice voluntarily. But perhaps this definition of acting unjustly is incorrect, and we should add to the words 'to do harm knowing the person affected, the instrument and the manner' the

6 further qualification 'against that person's wish'. If so, though a man can be harmed and can have an unjust thing done to him voluntarily, no one can suffer injustice voluntarily, because no one can wish to be harmed: even the unrestrained man does not, but acts contrary to his wish, since no one wishes for a thing that he does not think to be good, and the unrestrained man does

7 what he thinks he ought not to do. One who gives away what is his own – as Homer[63] says that Glaucus gave to Diomedes

> golden arms for bronze,
> An hundred beeves' worth for the worth of nine –

cannot be said to suffer injustice; for giving rests with oneself, suffering injustice does not – there has to be another person who acts unjustly.

8 It is clear then that it is not possible to suffer injustice voluntarily.

There still remain two of the questions that we proposed to discuss: (1) Is it ever he who gives the unduly large share, or is it always he who receives it, that is guilty of the injustice? and (2) Can one act unjustly towards oneself?

9 If the former alternative is possible, that is, if it may be the giver and not the receiver of too large a share who acts unjustly, then when a man knowingly and voluntarily assigns a larger share to another than to himself – as modest people are thought to do, for an equitable man is apt to take less than his due – this is a case of acting unjustly towards oneself. But perhaps this also requires qualification. For the man who gave himself the smaller share may possibly have got a larger share of some other good thing, for instance glory, or intrinsic moral nobility. Also the inference may be refuted by referring to our definition of acting unjustly: in the case supposed, the distributor has nothing done to him against his wish; therefore he does not suffer injustice merely because he gets the smaller share: at most he only suffers damage.

10 And it is clear that the giver as well as the receiver of an undue share may be acting unjustly, and that the receiver is not doing so in all cases. For the charge of injustice attaches, not to a man of whom it can be said that he does what is unjust, but to one of whom it can be said that he does this voluntarily, that is to say one from whom the action originates; and the origin of the act in this case lies in the giver and not in the receiver of the share.

11 Again, 'to do a thing' has more than one meaning. In a certain sense a murder is done by the inanimate instrument, or by the murderer's hand, or by a slave acting under orders. But though these do what is unjust, they cannot be said to act unjustly.[64]

12 Again, although if a judge has given an unfair judgement in ignorance, he is not guilty of injustice, nor is the judgement unjust, in the legal sense of justice (though the judgement is unjust in one sense, for legal justice is different from justice in the primary sense), yet if he knowingly gives an unjust judgement, he is himself taking more than his share, either of favour or of

13 vengeance. Hence a judge who gives an unjust judgement for these motives takes more than his due just as much as if he shared the proceeds of the injustice; for even a judge who assigns a piece of land on that condition does not receive land but money.

14 Men think that it is in their power to act unjustly, and therefore that it is easy to be just. But really this is not so. It is easy to lie with one's neighbour's wife or strike a bystander or slip some money into a man's hand, and it is in one's power to do these things or not, but to do them as a result of a certain disposition of mind is not easy, and is not in one's power.

15 Similarly men suppose it requires no special wisdom to know what is just and what is unjust, because it is not difficult to understand the things about which the law pronounces. But the actions prescribed by law are only accidentally just actions. *How* an action must be performed, *how* a distribution must be made to be a just action or a just distribution – to know this is a harder task than to know what medical treatment will produce health. Even in medicine, though it is easy to know what honey, wine and hellebore, cautery and surgery are, to know how and to whom and when to apply them so as to effect a cure is no less an

16 undertaking than to be a physician. And for this very reason[65] men think that the just man may act unjustly no less than justly,

because the just man is not less but rather more able than another
to do any particular unjust thing: for example, he *can* lie with a
woman, or strike a blow, and a brave man *can* throw away his
shield, and *can* wheel to the right or left and run away. But to be
a coward and to be guilty of injustice consists not in doing these
things (except accidentally), but in doing them from a certain
disposition of mind; just as to be a physician and cure one's
patients is not a matter of employing or not employing surgery or
drugs, but of doing so in a certain manner.

17   Claims of justice exist between persons who share in things
generally speaking good, and who can have too large a share or
too small a share of them. There are persons who cannot have
too large a share of these goods: doubtless, for example, the gods.
And there are those who can derive no benefit from any share of
them: namely, the incurably vicious; to them all the things
generally good are harmful. But for others they are beneficial
within limits; and this is the case with ordinary mortals.

X   We have next to speak of equity and the equitable, and of their
relation to justice and to what is just respectively. For upon
examination it appears that justice and equity are neither
absolutely identical nor generically different. Sometimes, it is
true, we praise equity and the equitable man, so much so that we
even apply the word 'equitable'[66] as a term of approval to other
things besides what is just, and use it as the equivalent of 'good',
denoting by 'more equitable' merely that a thing is better. Yet at
other times, when we think the matter out, it seems strange that
the equitable should be praiseworthy if it is something other than
the just. If they are different, either the just or the equitable is not
good; if both are good, they are the same thing.

2   These then are the considerations, more or less, from which
the difficulty as to the equitable arises. Yet they are all in a
manner correct, and not really inconsistent. For equity, while
superior to one sort of justice, is itself just: it is not superior to
justice as being generically different from it. Justice and equity are
therefore the same thing, and both are good, though equity is the
better.

3   The source of the difficulty is that equity, though just, is not
4 legal justice, but a rectification of legal justice. The reason for this
is that law is always a general statement, yet there are cases which

it is not possible to cover in a general statement. In matters therefore where, while it is necessary to speak in general terms, it is not possible to do so correctly, the law takes into consideration the majority of cases, although it is not unaware of the error this involves. And this does not make it a wrong law; for the error is not in the law nor in the lawgiver, but in the nature of the case:

5 the material of conduct is essentially irregular. When therefore the law lays down a general rule, and thereafter a case arises which is an exception to the rule, it is then right, where the lawgiver's pronouncement because of its absoluteness is defective and erroneous, to rectify the defect by deciding as the lawgiver would himself decide if he were present on the occasion, and would have enacted if he had been cognisant of the case in

6 question. Hence, while the equitable is just, and is superior to one sort of justice, it is not superior to absolute justice, but only to the error due to its absolute statement. This is the essential nature of the equitable: it is a rectification of law where law is defective because of its generality. In fact this is the reason why things are not all determined by law: it is because there are some cases for which it is impossible to lay down a law, so that a special

7 ordinance becomes necessary. For what is itself indefinite can only be measured by an indefinite standard, like the leaden rule[67] used by Lesbian builders; just as that rule is not rigid but can be bent to the shape of the stone, so a special ordinance is made to fit the circumstances of the case.

8 It is now plain what the equitable is, and that it is just, and that it is superior to one sort of justice. And from this it is clear what the equitable man is: he is one who by choice and habit does what is equitable, and who does not stand on his rights unduly, but is content to receive a smaller share although he has the law on his side. And the disposition described is equity; it is a special kind of justice, not a different quality altogether.

xi The foregoing discussion has indicated the answer to the question; is it possible or not for a man to commit injustice against himself? (1) One class of just actions consists of those acts, in accordance with any virtue, which are ordained by law.[68] For instance, the law does not sanction suicide (and what[69] it does not

2 expressly sanction, it forbids). Further, when a man voluntarily (which means with knowledge of the person affected and the

instrument employed) does an injury (not in retaliation) that is against the law, he commits injustice. But he who kills himself in a fit of passion, voluntarily does an injury (against the right

3   principle)[70] which the law does not allow. Therefore the suicide commits injustice; but against whom? It seems to be against the state rather than against himself; for he suffers voluntarily, and nobody suffers injustice voluntarily . This is why the state exacts a penalty; suicide is punished by certain marks of dishonour,[71] as being an offence against the state.

4   (2) Moreover, it is not possible to act unjustly towards oneself in the sense in which a man is unjust who is a doer of injustice only and not universally wicked. (This case is distinct from the former, because injustice in one sense is a special form of wickedness, like cowardice, and does not imply universal wickedness; hence it is necessary further to show that a man cannot commit injustice against himself in this sense either.) For (a) if it were, it would be possible for the same thing to have been taken away from and added to the same thing at the same time. But this is impossible: justice and injustice always necessarily

5   imply more than one person. Again (b) an act of injustice must be vóluntary and done from choice, and also unprovoked; we do not think that a man acts unjustly if having suffered he retaliates, and gives what he got. But when a man injures himself, he both does and suffers the same thing at the same time. Again (c) if a man could act unjustly towards himself, it would be possible to

6   suffer injustice voluntarily. Furthermore (d) no one is guilty of injustice without committing some particular unjust act; but a man cannot commit adultery with his own wife, or burglary on his own premises, or theft of his own property.

(3) And generally, the question, can a man act unjustly towards himself ? is solved by our decision upon the question, can a man suffer injustice voluntarily?

7   (It is further manifest that, though both to suffer and to do injustice are evils – for the former is to have less and the latter to have more than the mean, corresponding to what is health-giving in medicine and conducive to fitness in athletic training – nevertheless to do injustice is the worse evil, for it is reprehensible, implying vice in the agent, and vice utter and absolute – or nearly so, for it is true that not every wrong act

voluntarily committed implies vice; whereas to suffer injustice
8 does not necessarily imply vice or injustice in the victim. Thus in
itself to suffer injustice is the lesser evil, though accidentally it
may be the greater. With this however science is not concerned;
science pronounces pleurisy a more serious disorder than a sprain,
in spite of the fact that in certain circumstances a sprain may be
accidentally worse than pleurisy, as for instance if it should
happen that owing to a sprain you fell and in consequence were
taken by the enemy and killed.)

9 In a metaphorical and analogical sense however there is such a
thing as justice, not towards oneself but between different parts of
one's nature; not, it is true, justice in the full sense of the term,
but such justice as subsists between master and slave, or between
the head of a household and his wife and children. For in the
discourses on this question[72] a distinction is set up between the
rational and irrational parts of the soul; and this is what leads
people to suppose that there is such a thing as injustice towards
oneself, because these parts of the self may be thwarted in their
respective desires, so that there may be a sort of justice between
them, such as exists between ruler and subject.

10 So much may be said in description of justice and of the other
moral virtues.

NOTES TO BOOK FIVE

1 In what follows δικαιοσύνη is found to possess both the wider meaning of righteousness in general, covering all right conduct in relation to others, and the narrower sense of the virtue of right conduct in relation to others where gain or loss (whether to the agent or to other parties) is involved. δικαιοσύνη in this narrower sense is the special moral virtue which is the subject of Book V; it would be described in English sometimes as justice, sometimes as honesty or uprightness. The related adjectives and verbs have various connotations connected with the various meanings of δικαιοσύνη both in its wider and in its narrower usage. For instance, τά δίκαια means sometimes 'just acts' in the English sense, sometimes any acts in conformity with the law, sometimes 'rights' or 'claims', *i.e.*, any consideration which by law, equity, or custom, certain persons have a right to expect from certain others. Or again ἀδικεῖν means not only to act unjustly, or dishonestly, but also to do, or have done, any wrongful injury to another, or any wrongful or illegal act, and so, as a legal term, to be guilty of a breach of the law.

   In translating, however, if the connection of all these various meanings in the writer's mind is to be represented it seems necessary to keep the words 'justice', 'injustice', etc. throughout, in spite of their occasional unsuitability to the context.

2 For instance, medicine studies both health and disease.

3 i.e., it does not also mean walking lame.

4 because a faculty or science is the same for opposite things.

5 Literally 'that which has to do with good condition': the word here slightly shifts its meaning, for just above it meant 'that which is in good condition'.

6 the clavicle (*clavis*, a key), or collar-bone.

7 The word ἴσος means both 'equal' and 'equitable' or 'fair'.

8 Here some manuscripts add 'Also a law-breaker, for this, lawbreaking or else unfairness, includes all injustice and is a common term for all injustice.'

9 According to a scholiast, this is a quotation, slightly altered, from the lost play *Melanippe* of Euripides (fr. 490 Dindorf).

10 Theognis 147.

11 In the manuscripts the words 'in a special degree' follow 'perfect' in the line before.

12 put into the mouth of the sophist Thrasymachus in Plato's *Republic*, 343 c.

13 *cf*. VI, viii, 1.

14 This topic is discussed in *Politics*, III. Under certain forms of government the good man in the moral sense may not be a good citizen, that is, a citizen who will help to maintain the constitution.

15 'Involuntary' here means lacking the consent of one of the parties.

16 In chapter iv below, the writer gives no illustration of the operation of corrective justice in voluntary transactions, but he is clearly thinking of actions at law for damages resulting from breach of contract. See note 33.

17 These words appear to be an interpolation.

18 A 'discrete proportion' means one in which the two ratios are disconnected, being between different terms, whereas in a 'continuous proportion' they have one term in common.

19 Here the lecturer displayed a diagram.

20 Here was another diagram (one would expect the sentence to run 'Let two lines representing . . . have been similarly divided'). Two segments, A and B, of one line represented two persons, two segments, C and D, of another their shares. It is shown that, if A : B :: C : D, then A + C: B + D :: A : B, *i.e.*, if the shares are proportioned to the persons, their relative condition after receiving them will be the same as it was before.

21 *i.e.*, A's just share lies between too large a share and too small a one, too large and too small here meaning more or less than is proportionate to A's claim. *cf*. II, note 16 on p. 48 and II, vi, 7.

22 We call this a proportion simply: *cf*. iv, 3 and note 23.

23 That is, two pairs of terms (e.g. 1, 3; 7, 9), of which the second term exceeds the first by the same amount as the fourth exceeds the third. We do not call this a proportion at all, but, if also the third term exceeds the second by the same amount (e.g. 1, 3, 5, 7), an arithmetical progression.

24 For corrective justice the merits of the parties are immaterial.

25 Again a diagram is employed, *cf*. iii, 9 and 10, and below, § 8.

26 $\zeta\eta\mu\acute{\iota}\alpha$ has both senses.

27 A slightly different term is here introduced, but apparently without difference of meaning.

28 In the manuscripts this sentence follows the next one.

29 If $a = b$, then $(b + n) - (a - n) = 2n$, and $(b + n) - a = n$, and

$$(b + n) - \frac{(b + n) + (a - n)}{2} = n = \frac{(b + n) + (a - n)}{2} - (a - n).$$

Aristotle, of course, represented the quantities by lines, not algebraically.

30 *i.e.*, the party that has too much.

31

A	E		A'
B			B'
D C	F		C'

The writer intends both CD and CF to be equal to AE.

32 The manuscripts here insert the sentence that appears again at v, 9 *init.*

33 Literally 'where the law gives immunity', that is, does not give redress for inequality resulting from the contract. Should inequality result from a breach of the contract, this would of course be a case for the intervention of corrective justice in voluntary transactions (ii, *fin.*).

34 That is, retaliation: A shall have done to him what he has done to B.

35 Literally 'whether the act was voluntary or involuntary'; see note 15.

36 The relative value of the units of the two products must be ascertained, say one house must be taken as worth *n* shoes. Then the four terms are  and cross-conjunction gives totals A + *n*D, B + C, which are in 'arithmetical proportion' (see note 23) with the two first terms, *i.e.* the difference between each pair is the same; the builder and the shoemaker after the transaction are by an equal amount richer than they were before they began to make the articles.

37 This sentence also appeared in the manuscripts at iv, 12, where it made no sense. If genuine here, the phrases 'active element' and 'passive element' seem to mean producer and consumer. Even so, it is probable that there is some corruption.

38 It is uncertain whether this merely refers to the difference in value (or perhaps in labour used in production) between the unit products of different trades, or whether it introduces the further conception that different kinds of producers have different social values and deserve different rates of reward.

39 Apparently interpolated from the last sentence.

40 ἄχρηστον also connotes 'worthless', but an obsolete coin retains some value as metal.

41 See note 38.

42 That is, 'after any unfair exchange one party has too much by just the amount by which the other has too little. I ought to have given you ten shillings more or something worth that. Then I have ten

shillings too much, and you have ten too little; these two tens are my two "excesses"; in respect of the exchange, I am better off than you by twice ten' (Richards). *cf.* iv, 10–12.

43 For this proverbial phrase see iv, 8 and 14.

44 or 'shoemaker's product D multiplied to equivalence with C' (Blunt).

45 The clauses bracketed make neither grammar nor sense and have justly been suspected as interpolated.

46 That is, when A distributes unjustly not between himself and B but between B and C, the result for either B or C may be either excess or defect, either too large a share or too small of something beneficial (and either too small a share or too large of something harmful).

47 §§ 1 and 2 are an irrelevant fragment which Jackson would insert in viii, 8; § 3 he would transpose to the beginning of chapter x; § 4 continues the end of chapter v.

48 See note 12.

49 *i.e.*, a slave.

50 The Spartan Brasidas detached Amphipolis from the Athenian empire 424 BC, and fell defending it against Cleon 422. He was worshipped as a hero by the city, 'with games and yearly sacrifices' (Thucydides V, xi).

51 The order of the following sentences seems confused.

52 Perhaps Aristotle wrote 'though it is not easy'.

53 Possibly a reference to an intended (or now lost) book of the *Politics* on laws (Ross).

54 III, i, 19.

55 *i.e.*, mistake, ignorance: as in the illustration, it is an accident that the person struck is the striker's father.

56 *sc.*, of whom he knows his father to be one.

57 'Involuntary' is certainly corrupt: perhaps Aristotle wrote 'in our control'.

58 The three sorts of injury are ἀτύχημα, ἁμάρτημα, and ἀδίκημα. The second term is introduced first, in its wider sense of a mistake which leads to an offence against someone else (the word connotes both things). It is then subdivided into two: ἀτύχημα, accident or misadventure, an offence due to mistake and not reasonably to be expected, and ἁμάρτημα in the narrow sense, a similar offence that ought to have been foreseen. The third term, ἀδίκημα, a wrong, is subdivided into wrongs done in a passion, which do not prove wickedness, and wrongs done deliberately, which do.

59 In the manuscripts this clause stands before the preceding one.

60 Apparently from a dialogue between Alcmaeon and (possibly) Phegeus

in the lost play of Euripides named after the former: *cf.* III, i, 8.

61 *i.e.*, to suffer wrong: for the wide sense of ἀδικεῖν see note 1 above.

62 *cf.* viii, l.

63 *Iliad*, vi, 236.

64 It is not clear whether this is meant to apply, in certain circumstances, to the distributor, or to the receiver, or to both.

65 *i.e.*, that acting unjustly is in our own power, §14.

66 ἐπιεικές in some contexts means 'suitable' or 'reasonable'.

67 Explained either as used in building with polygonal stones (but this was not peculiar to Lesbos), or in making the Lesbian form of moulding, which had a double curve.

68 The argument seems to be, that suicide does not prove the possibility of a man's committing 'injustice', in the wider sense of any illegal injury, against himself. Suicide is an act of injustice in this sense, since it is the voluntary infliction of bodily harm not in retaliation and therefore contrary to law; but it is an offence not against oneself but against the state, since it is punished as such.

69 or perhaps, 'and any form of homicide that it does not expressly permit'.

70 *i.e.*, the principle of retaliation.

71 At Athens a suicide's hand was buried apart from the body; Aeschines, *Ctesiphon* 244.

72 Plato's *Republic*, and the writings of Plato's followers: *cf.* I, xiii, 9.

BOOK SIX

The intellectual virtues

i We have already said[1] that it is right to choose the mean and to avoid excess and deficiency, and that the mean is prescribed by the right principle. Let us now analyse the latter notion.

In the case of each of the moral qualities or dispositions that have been discussed, as with all the other virtues also, there is a certain mark to aim at, on which the man who knows the principle involved fixes his gaze, and increases or relaxes the tension[2] accordingly; there is a certain standard determining those modes of observing the mean which we define as lying between excess and defect, being in conformity with the right principle.

2 This bare statement however, although true, is not at all enlightening. In all departments of human endeavour that have been reduced to a science, it is true to say that effort ought to be exerted and relaxed neither too much nor too little, but to the medium amount, and as the right principle decides. Yet a person knowing this truth will be no wiser than before: for example, he will not know what medicines to take merely from being told to take everything that medical science or a medical expert would

3 prescribe. Hence with respect to the qualities of the soul also, it is not enough merely to have established the truth of the above formula; we also have to define exactly what the right principle is, and what is the standard that determines it.[3]

4 Now we have divided the virtues of the soul into two groups, the virtues of the character and the virtues of the intellect. The former, the moral virtues, we have already discussed. Our account of the latter must be prefaced by some remarks about psychology.

5 It has been said before[4] that the soul has two parts, one rational and the other irrational. Let us now similarly divide the rational part, and let it be assumed that there are two rational faculties, one whereby we contemplate those things whose first principles are invariable, and one whereby we contemplate those things which admit of variation: since, on the assumption that knowledge is based on a likeness or affinity of some sort between

subject and object, the parts of the soul adapted to the cognition of objects that are of different kinds must themselves differ in
6 kind. These two rational faculties may be designated the scientific faculty and the calculative faculty respectively; since calculation is the same as deliberation, and deliberation is never exercised about things that are invariable, so that the calculative faculty is a separate part of the rational half of the soul.

7 We have therefore to ascertain what disposition of each of these faculties is the best, for that will be the special virtue of each.

ii But the virtue of a faculty is related to the special function which that faculty performs. Now there are three elements in the soul which control action and the attainment of truth: namely, sensation, intellect,[5] and desire.

2 Of these, sensation never originates action, as is shown by the fact that animals have sensation but are not capable of action.[6]

[7]Pursuit and avoidance in the sphere of desire correspond to affirmation and denial in the sphere of the intellect. Hence inasmuch as moral virtue is a disposition of the mind in regard to choice,[8] and choice is deliberate desire,[9] it follows that, if the choice is to be good, both the principle must be true and the desire right, and that desire must pursue the same things as
3 principle affirms. We are here speaking of practical thinking, and of the attainment of truth in regard to action; with speculative thought, which is not concerned with action or production, right and wrong functioning consist in the attainment of truth and falsehood respectively. The attainment of truth is indeed the function of every part of the intellect, but that of the practical intelligence is the attainment of truth corresponding to right desire.[10]

4 Now the cause of action (the efficient, not the final cause) is choice,[11] and the cause of choice is desire and reasoning directed to some end. Hence choice necessarily involves both intellect or thought and a certain disposition of character [for doing well and the reverse in the sphere of action necessarily involve thought and character].[12]

5 Thought by itself however moves nothing, but only thought directed to an end, and dealing with action. This indeed is the moving cause of productive activity[13] also, since he who makes

something always has some further end in view: the act of making is not an end in itself, it is only a means, and belongs to something else. Whereas a thing done is an end in itself: since doing well (welfare[14]) is the end, and it is at this that desire aims.

Hence choice may be called either thought related to desire or desire related to thought; and man, as an originator of action, is a union of desire and intellect.

6   (Choice is not concerned with anything that has happened already: for example, no one chooses to have sacked Troy; for neither does one deliberate about what has happened in the past, but about what still lies in the future and may happen or not; what has happened cannot be made not to have happened. Hence Agathon is right in saying

> This only is denied even to God,
> The power to make what has been done undone.)

The attainment of truth is then the function of both the intellectual parts of the soul. Therefore their respective virtues are those dispositions which will best qualify them to attain truth.

iii   Let us then discuss these virtues afresh, going more deeply into the matter.

Let it be assumed that there are five qualities through which the mind achieves truth in affirmation or denial, namely art or technical skill,[15] scientific knowledge, prudence, wisdom, and intelligence. Conception and opinion are capable of error.

2   The nature of scientific knowledge (employing the term in its exact sense and disregarding its analogous uses) may be made clear as follows. We all conceive that a thing which we know scientifically cannot vary; when a thing that can vary is beyond the range of our observation, we do not know whether it exists or not. An object of scientific knowledge, therefore, exists of necessity. It is therefore eternal, for everything existing of absolute necessity is eternal; and what is eternal does not come into existence or perish. Again, it is held that all scientific knowledge can be communicated by teaching, and that what is scientifically known must be learnt. But all teaching starts from facts previously known, as we state in the *Analytics*,[16] since it proceeds either by way of induction, or else by way of deduction. Now induction supplies a first principle or universal,

deduction works *from* universals; therefore there are first principles from which deduction starts, which cannot be proved by
4   deduction; therefore they are reached by induction. Scientific
knowledge, therefore, is the quality whereby we demonstrate,[17]
with the further qualifications included in our definition of it in
the *Analytics*,[18] namely, that a man knows a thing scientifically
when he possesses a conviction arrived at in a certain way, and
when the first principles on which that conviction rests are
known to him with certainty – for unless he is more certain of his
first principles than of the conclusion drawn from them he will
only possess the knowledge in question accidentally.[19] Let this
stand as our definition of scientific knowledge.

iv   The class of things that admit of variation includes both things
2   made and actions done. But making is different from doing (a
distinction we may accept from extraneous discourses[20]). Hence
the rational quality concerned with doing is different from the
rational quality concerned with making. Nor is one of them a
part of the other, for doing is not a form of making, nor making a
3   form of doing. Now architectural skill, for instance, is an art, and
it is also a rational quality concerned with making; nor is there
any art which is not a rational quality concerned with making,
nor any such quality which is not an art. It follows that an art is
the same thing as a rational quality, concerned with making, that
4   reasons truly. All art deals with bringing something into existence; and to pursue an art means to study how to bring into
existence a thing which may either exist or not, and the efficient
cause of which lies in the maker and not in the thing made; for
art does not deal with things that exist or come into existence of
necessity, or according to nature, since these have their efficient
5   cause in themselves. But as doing and making are distinct, it
follows that art, being concerned with making, is not concerned
with doing. And in a sense art deals with the same objects as
chance, as Agathon says:

Chance is beloved of art, and art of chance.

6   Art, therefore, as has been said, is a rational quality, concerned
with making, that reasons truly. Its opposite, lack of art, is a
rational quality, concerned with making, that reasons falsely.
Both deal with that which admits of variation.

V   We may arrive at a definition of prudence by considering who are the persons whom we call prudent. Now it is held to be the mark of a prudent man to be able to deliberate well about what is good and advantageous for himself, not in some one department, for instance what is good for his health or strength, but what is
2 advantageous as a means to the good life in general. This is proved by the fact that we also speak of people as prudent or wise in some particular thing, when they calculate well with a view to attaining some particular end of value (other than those ends which are the object of an art); so that the prudent man in general will be the man who is good at deliberating in general.

3   But no one deliberates about things that cannot vary, nor about things not within his power to do. Hence inasmuch as scientific knowledge involves demonstration, whereas things whose fundamental principles are variable are not capable of demonstration, because everything about them is variable, and inasmuch as one cannot deliberate about things that are of necessity, it follows that prudence is not the same as science. Nor can it be the same as art. It is not science, because matters of conduct admit of variation; and not art, because doing and making are generically different,[21] since making aims at an end different from the act of making, whereas in doing the end cannot be other than the act itself: doing well[22] is in itself the end.
4 It remains therefore that it is a truth-attaining rational quality, concerned with action in relation to things that are good and bad for human beings.

5   Hence men like Pericles are deemed prudent, because they possess a faculty of discerning what things are good for themselves and for mankind; and that is our conception of an expert in domestic economy or political science.

   (This also accounts for the word temperance,[23] which signifies
6 'preserving prudence'. And temperance does in fact preserve our belief as to our own good; for pleasure and pain do not destroy or pervert all beliefs, for instance, the belief that the three angles of a triangle are, or are not, together equal to two right angles, but only beliefs concerning action. The first principles of action are the end to which our acts are means; but a man corrupted by a love of pleasure or fear of pain, entirely fails to discern any first principle,[24] and cannot see that he ought to choose and do

everything as a means to this end, and for its sake; for vice tends to destroy the sense of principle.[25])

It therefore follows that prudence is a truth-attaining rational quality, concerned with action in relation to the things that are good for human beings.

7   Moreover, we can speak of excellence in art,[26] but not of excellence in prudence. Also in art voluntary error is not so bad as involuntary, whereas in the sphere of prudence it is worse, as it is in the sphere of the virtues. It is therefore clear that prudence is an excellence or virtue, and not an art.

8   Of the two parts of the soul possessed of reason, prudence must be the virtue of one, namely, the part that forms opinions;[27] for opinion deals with that which can vary, and so does prudence. But yet prudence is not a rational quality merely, as is shown by the fact that a purely rational faculty can be forgotten, whereas a failure in prudence is not a mere lapse of memory.[28]

vi   Scientific knowledge is a mode of conception dealing with universals and things that are of necessity; and demonstrated truths and all scientific knowledge (since this involves reasoning) are derived from first principles. Consequently the first principles from which scientific truths are derived cannot themselves be reached by science; nor yet are they apprehended by art, nor by prudence. To be matter of scientific knowledge a truth must be demonstrated by deduction from other truths; while art and prudence are concerned only with things that admit of variation. Nor is wisdom the knowledge of first principles either:[29] for the philosopher has to arrive at some things by demonstration.[30]

2   If then the qualities whereby we attain truth,[31] and are never led into falsehood, whether about things invariable or things variable, are scientific knowledge, prudence, wisdom, and intelligence, and if the quality which enables us to apprehend first principles cannot be any one among three of these, namely scientific knowledge, prudence, and wisdom, it remains that first principles must be apprehended by intelligence.[32]

vii   The term wisdom is employed in the arts to denote those men who are the most perfect masters of their art; for instance, it is applied to Pheidias as a sculptor and to Polycleitus as a statuary. In this use then wisdom merely signifies artistic excellence. But we
2   also think that some people are wise in general and not in one

department, not 'wise in something else',[33] as Homer says in the *Margites*:

> Neither a delver nor a ploughman him
> The gods had made, nor wise in aught beside.

Hence it is clear that wisdom must be the most perfect of the
3 modes of knowledge. The wise man therefore must not only know the conclusions that follow from his first principles, but also have a true conception of those principles themselves. Hence wisdom must be a combination of intelligence and scientific knowledge:[34] it must be a consummated knowledge[35] of the most exalted[36] objects.

For it is absurd to think that political science or prudence is the loftiest kind of knowledge, inasmuch as man is not the highest
4 thing in the world. And as 'wholesome' and 'good' mean one thing for men and another for fishes, whereas 'white' and 'straight' mean the same thing always, so everybody would denote the same thing by 'wise', but not by 'prudent'; for each kind of beings will describe as prudent, and will entrust itself to, one who can discern its own particular welfare; hence even some of the lower animals are said to be prudent, namely those which display a capacity for forethought as regards their own lives.

It is also clear that wisdom cannot be the same thing as political science; for if we are to call knowledge of our own interests wisdom, there will be a number of different kinds of wisdom, one for each species: there cannot be a single such wisdom dealing with the good of all living things, any more than there is one art of medicine for all existing things. It may be argued that man is superior to the other animals, but this makes no difference: since there exist other things far more divine in their nature than man, for instance, to mention the most visible, the things[37] of which the celestial system is composed.

5 These considerations therefore show that wisdom is both scientific knowledge and intuitive intelligence as regards the things of the most exalted[38] nature. This is why people say that men like Anaxagoras and Thales[39] 'may be wise but are not prudent', when they see them display ignorance of their own interests; and while admitting them to possess a knowledge that is rare, marvellous, difficult and even superhuman, they yet declare

this knowledge to be useless, because these sages do not seek to
6 know the things that are good for human beings. Prudence on
the other hand is concerned with the affairs of men, and with
things that can be the object of deliberation. For we say that to
deliberate well is the most characteristic function of the prudent
man; but no one deliberates about things that cannot vary nor yet
about variable things that are not a means to some end, and that
end a good attainable by action; and a good deliberator in general
is a man who can arrive by calculation at the best of the goods
attainable by man.

7 Nor is prudence a knowledge of general principles only: it
must also take account of particular facts, since it is concerned
with action, and action deals with particular things. This is why
men who are ignorant of general principles are sometimes more
successful in action than others who know them: for instance,[40] if
a man knows that light meat is easily digested and therefore
wholesome, but does not know what kinds of meat are light, he
will not be so likely to restore you to health as a man who merely
knows that chicken is wholesome; and in other matters men of
experience are more successful than theorists. And prudence is
concerned with action, so one requires both forms of it, or
indeed knowledge of particular facts even more than knowledge
of general principles. Here too however there must be some
supreme directing faculty.[41]

viii Prudence is indeed the same quality of mind as political
2 science, though their essence is different.[42] Of prudence as
regards the state, one kind, as supreme and directive, is called
legislative science;[43] the other, as dealing with particular occurrences, has the name, political science, that really belongs to both
kinds. The latter is concerned with action and deliberation (for a
parliamentary enactment is a thing to be done, being the last
step[44] in a deliberative process), and this is why it is only those
persons who deal with particular facts who are spoken of as
'taking part in politics', because it is only they who perform
3 actions, like the workmen in an industry.[45] Prudence also is
commonly understood to mean especially that kind of wisdom
which is concerned with oneself, the individual; and this is given
the name, prudence, which really belongs to all the kinds, while
the others are distinguished as domestic economy, legislature, and

political science, the latter being subdivided into deliberative
4 science and judicial science. Now knowledge of one's own
interest will certainly be one kind of prudence; though it is very
different from the other kinds, and people think that the man
who knows and minds his own business is prudent, and that
politicians are busybodies: thus Euripides writes –

> Would that be prudent? when I might have lived
> A quiet life, a cipher in the crowd,
> Sharing the common fortune . . .
> Restless, aspiring, busy men of action . . . [46]

For people seek their own good, and suppose that it is right to do
so. Hence this belief has caused the word 'prudent' to mean
those who are wise in their own interest. Yet probably as a
matter of fact a man cannot pursue his own welfare without
domestic economy and even politics. Moreover, even the proper
conduct of one's own affairs is a difficult problem, and requires
consideration.

5   A further proof of what has been said[47] is, that although the
young may be experts in geometry and mathematics and similar
branches of knowledge, we do not consider that a young man
can have prudence. The reason is that prudence includes a
knowledge of particular facts, and this is derived from experi-
6 ence, which a young man does not possess; for experience is the
fruit of years.[48] (One might indeed further enquire why it is that,
though a boy may be a mathematician, he cannot be a
metaphysician or a natural philosopher.[49] Perhaps the answer is
that mathematics deals with abstractions, whereas the first principles of metaphysics and natural philosophy are derived from
experience: the young can only repeat them without conviction
of their truth,[50] whereas the formal concepts of mathematics are
7 easily understood.) Again, in deliberation there is a double
possibility of error: you may go wrong either in your general
principle or in your particular fact: for instance, either in asserting
that all heavy water is unwholesome, or that the particular water
in question is heavy.

8   And it is clear that prudence is not the same as scientific
knowledge: for as has been said, it apprehends ultimate particular
things, since the thing to be done is an ultimate particular thing.[51]

9 Prudence then stands opposite to intelligence; for intelligence[52] apprehends definitions, which cannot be proved by reasoning, while prudence deals with the ultimate particular thing, which cannot be apprehended by scientific knowledge, but only by perception: not the perception of the special senses,[53] but the sort of intuition whereby we perceive that the ultimate figure in mathematics is a triangle;[54] for there, too, there will be a stop.[55] But the term perception applies in a fuller sense to mathematical intuition than to prudence; the practical intuition of the latter belongs to a different species.[56]

ix [57]We ought also to ascertain the nature of deliberative excellence, and to discover whether it is a species of knowledge, or of opinion, or skill in conjecture, or something different from these in kind.

2 Now it is not knowledge: for men do not investigate matters about which they know, whereas deliberative excellence is one form of deliberation, and deliberating implies investigating and calculating. But deliberation is not the same as investigation: it is the investigation of a particular subject.[58]

Nor yet is it skill in conjecture: for this operates without conscious calculation, and rapidly, whereas deliberating takes a long time, and there is a saying that execution should be swift but

3 deliberation slow. Again, deliberative excellence is not the same as quickness of mind,[59] which is a form of skill in conjecture .

Nor yet is deliberative excellence any form of opinion.

But inasmuch as a bad deliberator makes mistakes and a good deliberator deliberates correctly, it is clear that deliberative excellence is some form of correctness; though it is not correctness of knowledge, nor of opinion. Correctness cannot be predicated of knowledge,[60] any more than can error, and correctness of opinion is truth; and also any matter about which one has an opinion has been settled already; [then again deliberative excellence necessarily involves conscious calculation. It remains therefore that deliberative excellence is correctness in thinking, for thought has not reached the stage of affirmation;][61] for opinion has passed beyond the stage of investigation and is a form of affirmation, whereas a man deliberating, whether he deliberates well or badly, is investigating and calculating something.

4   But deliberative excellence is a form of correctness in deliberation [so that we have first to investigate what deliberation is, and what object it deals with].[62] However, 'correctness' in this connection is ambiguous, and plainly it is not every kind of correctness in deliberation that constitutes deliberative excellence. A man of deficient self-restraint or a bad man may as a result of calculation arrive at the object he proposes as the right thing to do, so that he will have deliberated correctly, although he will have gained something extremely evil; whereas to have deliberated well is felt to be a good thing. Therefore it is this kind of correctness in deliberation that is deliberative excellence, namely being correct in the sense of arriving at something good.[63]

5   But it is possible to arrive at a good conclusion, as well as at a bad one, by a false process of reasoning; one may arrive at what is the right thing to do, but not arrive at it on the right grounds, but by means of a wrong middle term. This quality then, which leads one to arrive at the right conclusion, but not on the right grounds, is still not deliberative excellence.

6   Again, one man may arrive at the right conclusion by prolonged deliberation, while another may do so quickly. The former case also then does not amount to deliberative excellence; this is correctness of deliberation as regards what is advantageous, arriving at the right conclusion on the right grounds at the right time.[64]

7   Again, a man can be said to have deliberated well[65] either generally, or in reference to a particular end. Deliberative excellence in general is therefore that which leads to correct results with reference to the end in general, while correctness of deliberation with a view to some particular end is deliberative excellence of some special kind.

If therefore to have deliberated well is a characteristic of prudent men, deliberative excellence must be correctness of deliberation with regard to what is expedient as a means to the end, a true conception of which[66] constitutes prudence.

x   Understanding, or good understanding, the quality in virtue of which we call men 'persons of understanding' or 'of good understanding', is not the same thing as scientific knowledge in general (nor yet is it the same as opinion, for in that case everybody would have understanding), nor is it any one of the

particular sciences, as medicine is the science of what pertains to
2 health and geometry the science concerned with magnitudes. For
understanding does not deal with the things that exist for ever
and are immutable, nor yet with all of the things that come into
existence, but with those about which one may be in doubt and
may deliberate. Hence it is concerned with the same objects as
prudence. Understanding is not however the same thing as
prudence; for prudence issues commands, since its end is a
statement of what we ought to do or not to do, whereas
understanding merely makes judgements. (For understanding is
the same as good understanding; a 'man of understanding' means
a man of good understanding.)[67]

3   Thus understanding does not mean either the possession or the
acquisition of prudence; but when we employ the faculty of
opinion to *judge* what another person says about matters that are
in the sphere of prudence, we are said to *understand* (that is, to
judge rightly, for *right* judgement is the same as *good* understanding), in the same way as *learning* a thing is termed *understanding* it
4 when it means employing the faculty of scientific knowledge. In
fact, the use of the term understanding to denote the quality that
makes men 'persons of good understanding' is derived from
understanding as shown in learning; in fact we often use 'to learn'
in the sense of 'to understand'.[68]

xi   The quality termed consideration[69] in virtue of which men are
said to be considerate, or to show consideration for others
(forgiveness), is the faculty of judging correctly what is equitable.
This is indicated by our saying that the equitable man is specially
considerate for others (forgiving), and that it is equitable to show
consideration for others (forgiveness) in certain cases; but
consideration for others is that consideration which judges rightly
what is equitable, judging *rightly* meaning judging what is *truly*
equitable.

2   All these qualities, it is reasonable to say, refer to the same
thing; indeed we attribute considerateness, understanding,
prudence, and intelligence to the same persons when we say of
people that they 'are old enough to show consideration and
intelligence',[70] and are prudent and understanding persons. For
all these faculties deal with ultimate and particular things; and a
man has understanding and is considerate, or considerate for

others, when he is a good judge of the matters in regard to which prudence is displayed;[71] because equitable actions are common to
3 all good men[72] in their behaviour towards others, while on the other hand all matters of conduct belong to the class of particular and ultimate things (since the prudent man admittedly has to take cognisance of these things), and understanding and consideration
4 deal with matters of conduct, which are ultimate. Also intelligence apprehends the ultimates in both aspects – since ultimates as well as primary definitions[73] are grasped by intelligence and not reached by reasoning: in demonstrations intelligence apprehends the immutable and primary definitions, in practical inferences[74] it apprehends the ultimate and contingent fact, and the minor premise, since these are the first principles from which the end is inferred, as general rules are based on particular cases; hence we must have perception of particulars, and this immediate perception is intelligence.[75]

5 This is why it is thought that these qualities are a natural gift, and that a man is considerate, understanding and intelligent by
6 nature, though no one is a wise man by nature. That this is so is indicated by our thinking of them as going with certain ages: we say that at such and such an age a man must have got intelligence and considerateness, which implies that they come by nature.

[Hence intelligence is both a beginning and an end, for these things are both the starting-point and the subject matter of demonstration.][76]

Consequently the unproved assertions and opinions of experienced and elderly people, or of prudent men, are as much deserving of attention as those which they support by proof; for experience has given them an eye for things, and so they see correctly.

7 We have now discussed the nature and respective spheres of prudence and wisdom, and have shown that each is the virtue of a different part of the soul.

xii But the further question may be raised, what is the use of these intellectual virtues? Wisdom does not consider the means to human happiness at all, for it does not ask how anything comes into existence. Prudence, it must be granted, does do this; but what do we need it for? seeing that it studies that which is just and noble and good for man, but these are the things that a good man does by nature. Knowing about them does not make us any more capable of doing them, since the virtues are qualities of character; just as is the case with the knowledge of what is healthy and vigorous – using these words to mean not productive of health and vigour but resulting from them: we are not rendered any more capable of healthy and vigorous action by knowing the science of medicine or of physical training.

2   If on the other hand we are to say that prudence is useful not in helping us to act virtuously but in helping us to become virtuous, then it is of no use to those who are virtuous already. Nor is it of any use either to those who are not, since we may just as well take the advice of others who possess prudence as possess prudence ourselves. We may be content to do as we do in regard to our health; we want to be healthy, yet we do not learn medicine.

3   Moreover it would seem strange if prudence, which is inferior to wisdom, is nevertheless to have greater authority than wisdom: yet the faculty that creates a thing[77] governs and gives orders to it.

Let us now therefore discuss these difficulties, which so far have only been stated.

4   First then let us assert that wisdom and prudence, being as they are the virtues of the two parts of the intellect respectively, are necessarily desirable in themselves, even if neither produces any effect.

5   Secondly, they do in fact produce an effect: wisdom produces happiness, not in the sense in which medicine produces health, but in the sense in which healthiness is the cause of health. For wisdom is a part of virtue as a whole, and therefore by its possession, or rather by its exercise, renders a man happy.

6   Also prudence as well as moral virtue determines the complete performance of man's proper function: virtue ensures the rightness of the end we aim at, prudence ensures the rightness of the means we adopt to gain that end.

(The fourth part[78] of the soul on the other hand, the nutritive faculty, has no virtue contributing to the proper function of man, since it has no power to act or not to act.)[79]

7   But we must go a little deeper into the objection that prudence does not render men more capable of performing noble and just actions. Let us start with the following consideration. As some

people, we maintain, perform just acts and yet are not just men (for instance, those who do what the law enjoins but do it unwillingly, or in ignorance, or for some ulterior object, and not for the sake of the actions themselves, although they are as a matter of fact doing what they ought to do and all that a good man should), on the other hand, it appears, there is a state of mind in which a man may do these various acts with the result that he really is a good man: I mean when he does them from choice, and

8 for the sake of the acts themselves. Now rightness in our choice of an end is secured by virtue;[80] but to do the actions that must in the nature of things be done in order to attain the end we have chosen, is not a matter for virtue but for a different faculty.

We must dwell on this point to make it more clear. There is a

9 certain faculty called cleverness, which is the capacity for doing the things aforesaid that conduce to the aim we propose, and so attaining that aim. If the aim is noble, this is a praiseworthy faculty: if base, it is mere knavery; this is how we come to speak

10 of both prudent men and knaves as clever. Now this faculty is not identical with prudence, but prudence implies it. But that eye of the soul of which we spoke[81] cannot acquire the quality of prudence without possessing virtue. This we have said before, and it is manifestly true. For deductive inferences about matters of conduct always have a major premise of the form 'Since the end or supreme good is so and so' (whatever it may be, since we may take it as anything we like for the sake of the argument); but the supreme good only appears good to the good man: vice perverts the mind and causes it to hold false views about the first principles of conduct. Hence it is clear that we cannot be prudent without being good.

xiii We have therefore also to reconsider the nature of virtue. The fact is that the case of virtue is closely analogous to that of prudence in relation to cleverness. Prudence and cleverness are not the same, but they are similar; and natural virtue is related in the same way to virtue in the true sense. All are agreed that the various moral qualities are in a sense bestowed by nature: we are just, and capable of temperance, and brave, and possessed of the other virtues from the moment of our birth. But nevertheless we expect to find that true goodness is something different, and that the virtues in the true sense come to belong to us in another way.

For even children and wild animals possess the natural dispositions, yet without intelligence these may manifestly be harmful.
This at all events appears to be a matter of observation, that just as
a man of powerful frame who has lost his sight meets with heavy
falls when he moves about, because he cannot see, so it also
2 happens in the moral sphere; whereas if a man of good natural
disposition acquires intelligence,[82] then he excels in conduct, and
the disposition which previously only resembled virtue, will now
be virtue in the true sense. Hence just as with the faculty of
forming opinions[83] there are two qualities, cleverness and
prudence, so also in the moral part of the soul there are two
qualities, natural virtue and true virtue; and true virtue cannot
3 exist without prudence. Hence some people maintain that all the
virtues are forms of prudence; and Socrates' line of enquiry was
right in one way, though wrong in another; he was mistaken in
thinking that all the virtues are forms of prudence, but right in
4 saying that they cannot exist without prudence. A proof of this is
that everyone, even at the present day, in defining virtue, after
saying what disposition it is[84] and specifying the things with
which it is concerned, adds that it is a disposition determined by
the right principle; and the right principle is the principle
determined by prudence. It appears therefore that everybody in
some sense divines that virtue is a disposition of this nature,
5 namely regulated by prudence. This formula however requires a
slight modification. Virtue is not merely a disposition conforming
to right principle, but one co-operating with right principle; and
prudence is right principle[85] in matters of conduct. Socrates then
thought that the virtues *are* principles, for he said that they are all
of them forms of knowledge. We on the other hand say that the
virtues *co-operate with* principle.

6   These considerations therefore show that it is not possible to be
good in the true sense without prudence, nor to be prudent
without moral virtue.

(Moreover, this might supply an answer to the dialectical
argument that might be put forward to prove that the virtues can
exist in isolation from each other, on the ground that the same
man does not possess the greatest natural capacity for all of them,
so that he may have already attained one when he has not yet
attained another. In regard to the natural virtues this is possible;

but it is not possible in regard to those virtues which entitle a man to be called good without qualification. For if a man have the one virtue of prudence he will also have all the moral virtues together with it.)

7   It is therefore clear[86] that, even if prudence had no bearing on conduct, it would still be needed, because it is the virtue of that part of the intellect to which it belongs; and also that our choice of actions will not be right without prudence any more than without moral virtue, since, while moral virtue enables us to achieve[87] the end, prudence makes us adopt the right means to the end.

8   But nevertheless it is not really the case that prudence is in authority[88] over wisdom, or over the higher part of the intellect, any more than medical science is in authority over health. Medical science does not control health, but studies how to procure it; hence it issues orders *in the interests of* health, but not *to* health. And again, one might as well say that political science governs the gods, because it gives orders about everything[89] in the state.

1   *cf.* II, vi, especially § 15.

2   The words denote tightening and loosening a bowstring, and also tuning a lyre. The former image is suggested by the preceding words, but the latter perhaps is a better metaphor for that avoidance of the too much and the too little which, according to Aristotle, constitutes right conduct.

3   Book VI thus purports to explain further the definition of moral virtue (II, vi, 15), while at the same time (§ 4) continuing the analysis of the definition of happiness (I, vii, 15) by examining the intellectual virtues.

4   I, xiii, 9.

5   νοῦς here bears its usual philosophic sense of the intellect or rational part of the 'soul', as a whole, whose function is διάνοια, thought in general. In chapter vi it is given a special and restricted meaning, and this in chapter xi is related to the popular use of the word to denote 'good sense' or practical intelligence.

6   πρᾶξις means rational action/conduct. The movements of animals, Aristotle appears to think, are mere reactions to the stimuli of sensation.

7   The passage would be clearer if this paragraph and § 5, 'Thought by itself . . . desire aims', came lower down, after the verse-quotation in § 6.

8   II, vi, 15.

9   III, iii, 19.

10   *i.e.*, truth about the means to the attainment of the rightly desired end.

11   *cf.* III, note 15 on p. 78. Here again προαίρεσις seems to mean choice of means, not of ends.

12   This clause must be rejected as superfluous and logically unsound: the nature of action is explained by that of 'choice', not *vice versa*.

13   For this distinction between making and doing, production and action or conduct, see I, i, 2, 5.

14   See I, note 7 on p. 25.

15   τέχνη, art, as appears below, stands for εὐτεχνία and means here craftsmanship of any kind; it includes skill in fine art, but is not limited to it.

16 See *Posterior Analytics* I, 71 a 1 ff.

17 Demonstration in Aristotle means proof by deduction.

18 See *Posterior Analytics* I, 71 b 9 ff.

19 *i.e.*, the conviction may happen to be true, but he will not hold it as scientific knowledge in the proper sense of the term.

20 See I, note 77 on p. 30.

21 The words 'since . . . itself the end' in the manuscripts follow § 4 'for human beings'.

22 See I, note 7 on p. 25.

23 σωφροσύνη, the quality of the σώφρων (σῶς-φρήν) or 'sound-minded' man, Aristotle derives from σώζειν and φρόνησις. *cf.* VIII, viii, 4.

24 or 'to be one corrupted by pleasure or pain this end does not seem to be a first principle at all'.

25 *i.e.*, to destroy our perception of the true end of life, which constitutes the major premise of the practical syllogism.

26 τέχνη, art, is here (as in vii, 1) used in a neutral sense, of a systematic procedure for making something, or a body of principles for such a procedure – one may be good at it or bad; whereas φρόνησις, prudence or practical wisdom, itself denotes an excellence, not a neutral sphere in which one may excel or the reverse. Elsewhere in this book τέχνη has the positive sense of artistic excellence or technical skill.

27 called in i, 6 the calculative faculty.

28 A loss of prudence is felt to involve a moral lapse, which shows that it is not a purely intellectual quality.

29 *i.e.*, not exclusively: see vii, 3.

30 See note 17.

31 *cf* iii, 1. Art is here omitted from the list.

32 νοῦς now receives its special sense (see note 5) of a particular virtue of the intellect: that faculty of rational intuition whereby it correctly apprehends (by process of induction, see iii, 3) undemonstrable first principles. It is thus a part of σοφία (vii, 3, 5).

33 The sense rather requires 'wise in some particular thing', but the expression is assimilated to the quotation.

34 See vi, 1 and 2.

35 literally 'knowledge having as it were a head', a phrase copied from Plato, *Gorgias*, 505 d.

36 See §§ 4, 5, and, for the technical sense of τίμιος, I, xii.

37 This means, apparently, the sun, stars, and planets, elsewhere referred to by Aristotle as 'the divine bodies that move through the heaven', 'the visible divine things', 'the heaven and the most divine

of visible things' (*Metaphysics* 1074 a 30, 1026 a 18, *Physics* 196 a 33).

38 See note 36.

39 Thales was the first of the Seven Wise Men: Anaxagoras belonged to a later generation.

40 The words 'for instance . . . chicken is wholesome' in the manuscripts come after 'theorists'.

41 *i.e.*, πολιτική, political science or statesmanship (*cf.* I, i–ii), the relation of which to prudence is next considered.

42 *cf.* v, i, 20. Political wisdom is not a special sort of prudence but a special application of it, for though the term 'prudence' is in ordinary usage confined to practical wisdom in one's private affairs, it really extends to the affairs of one's family and of the community.

43 In the Greek city-state legislature was not regarded as the normal function of parliament, but of a founder or reformer of the constitution, or of a special legislative commission.

44 *cf.* III, iii, 12.

45 in contrast with the law-giver and the master–craftsman respectively.

46 From the lost *Philoctetes* of Euripides, frr. 785, 786 Dindorf. The third line went on

> with the wisest . . .
> For there is naught so foolish as a man!
> Restless, aspiring, busy men of action
> We honour and esteem as men of mark . . .

47 The reference seems to be to vii, 7, where it is stated that prudence takes cognisance of particular facts. The intervening passage, examining the relation of prudence to political science, emphasises its other aspect, the apprehension of general principles.

48 The Greek looks like a buried verse quotation.

49 The three divisions of the subject matter of wisdom.

50 Immelmann's emendation gives 'can only take them on credit from others'.

51 *cf.* § 2 above, vii, 7, and III, iii, 12.

52 See notes 32 and 76. Definitions are the first principles of science.

53 Literally 'of the objects peculiar to the special senses'. Shape was one of the 'common sensibles', perceived through the medium of more than one of the special senses, by the 'common sense'.

54 A triangle is the last form into which a rectilinear figure can be divided: two straight lines cannot enclose a space.

55 That is, we reach the limit of analysis just as much when we descend to particulars as when we ascend to first principles or

definitions. Or the words may mean 'in mathematics as in problems of conduct there is a point where analysis must stop'.

56 The intuition of particular facts which is a part of prudence also belongs to the genus perception, but it is intellectual, not sensuous. The Greek may however conceivably mean, 'But the intuition of the ultimate particular in problems of conduct approximates more to sensation than to prudence, though it is a different species from the perception of the separate senses.'

57 In the manuscripts the chapter begins with the sentence 'But deliberation', etc., here transferred to the middle of § 2.

58 *i.e.*, matters of conduct.

59 ἀγχίνοια appears from the *Posterior Analytics*, I, xxxiii, 89 b 10, to denote the faculty of guessing immediately the 'middle term' or fact which explains the relation observed between two objects.

60 *i.e.*, correct knowledge is a redundant expression; knowledge *means* correct notions; erroneous notions are not knowledge.

61 The two sentences bracketed interrupt the argument. The first seems to belong to § 2, though it does not fit in there exactly. The second is altogether irrelevant, and employs the term διάνοια of the intellect as enquiring, not as contemplating the results of enquiry, a Platonic use not found elsewhere in Aristotle: 'correctness in thinking' here is in fact equivalent to 'correctness in deliberation' in § 4.

62 The sentence bracketed interrupts the argument; and no examination of deliberation follows.

63 No distinction seems to be made between arriving at the right conclusion of a practical syllogism, *i.e.* inferring correctly what is to be done as a means to some end, and actually achieving that end by action.

64 At the right time, because deliberation must neither be so prolonged as to miss the opportunity for action, nor so rapid as to be merely skilful conjecture; see § 2.

65 *i.e.*, to be well-counselled, to know what steps to take: *cf.* § 4.

66 The antecedent of 'which' is probably not 'the end' but 'what is expedient as a means to the end', since it is indicated below that prudence deals with means, not ends. The difference therefore between deliberative excellence and prudence seems to be that the former is the intellectual quality displayed in the process of correctly investigating a problem of conduct, the latter the more permanent and fixed quality of the mind possessing and contemplating the results of such investigations. Or perhaps more strictly both these qualities are included in prudence, of which deliberative excellence is therefore one aspect or species.

67 This parenthesis would come better in the first section, after the words 'of good understanding'. It merely points out that the qualification 'good' need not be repeated.

68 μανθάνειν is idiomatically used of understanding what another person says.

69 The writer here strains the meaning of words by connecting under one sense (1) γνώμη, judgement in general or good judgement in particular, and its derivatives (2) εὐγνώμων, 'well-judging' in the sense of considerate and kindly, and (3) συγγνώμη, literally 'judgement with' or on the side of others, and hence, sympathy, lenience, forgiveness.

70 *i.e.*, 'have reached years of discretion'; *cf.* § 6 and VIII, xii, 2.

71 This has been proved for 'understanding' and 'the sensible man' in chapter x; it is extended to 'considerateness' in the words that follow: considerateness judges correctly what is equitable, equity is an element in all virtuous conduct towards others, and all virtuous conduct is determined by prudence.

72 *i.e.*, the possessors of each of the moral virtues.

73 See viii, 9.

74 The substantive to be understood may be προτάσεσι, 'propositions'; but the reference seems to be not to the practical syllogism in the ordinary sense (see VII, iii, 9), but to the establishment of ethical ἀρχαί by induction, which is the proper method of ethics (I, iv, 5-7).

75 Here the intuitive element in prudence, as well as in wisdom (chapters v and vi), is termed intelligence: at viii, 9 it was called merely prudence, in contrast with intelligence, which was limited to intuition of the first principles of science. Here then νοῦς approximates to its popular sense (see note 5).

76 This sentence seems irrelevant here. It might come in after § 4.

77 See xiii, 8, where it is implied that prudence stands in the same relation to wisdom as medicine to health: it provides the conditions for its development.

78 The other three are the scientific, calculative, and appetitive parts, see i, 5 and 6, whose virtues have now been considered in Books II-VI. Sensation is here omitted, since it is not peculiar to man: *cf.* I, vii, 12.

79 Digestion and growth function automatically, not voluntarily; so they form no part of conduct.

80 *i.e.*, moral virtue.

81 See xi, 6 and *cf.* I, vi, 12.

82 νοῦς here means φρόνησις as a whole: see note 75.

83 See note 27.

84 *See* the definition of moral virtue, II, vi, 15.

85 *i.e.*, prudence is the knowledge of right principle, the presence of the ὀρθὸς λόγος in the ψυχή of the φρόνιμος (see II, ii, 2 and vi, 15).

86 The writer recapitulates the solution reached in the last two chapters of the difficulty stated in xii, 1.

87 At xii, 6 Aristotle says more precisely that virtue 'makes the end right', *i.e.*, makes us choose the right end; strictly speaking, to *achieve* the end requires also prudence in the choice of the right means.

88 This is the solution of the difficulty stated in xii, 3.

89 including religious observances.

BOOK SEVEN

Relation of intellect and desire: weakness of will

Pleasure (*cf.* X, i–v)

i Let us next begin a fresh part of the subject by laying down that the states of moral character to be avoided are of three kinds – vice, unrestraint, and bestiality.[1] The opposite dispositions in the case of two of the three are obvious: one we call virtue, the other self-restraint. As the opposite of bestiality it will be most suitable to speak of superhuman virtue, or goodness on a heroic or divine scale; just as Homer[2] has represented Priam as saying of Hector, on account of his surpassing valour –

> nor seemed to be
> The son of mortal man, but of a god.

2 Hence if, as men say, surpassing virtue changes men into gods, the disposition opposed to bestiality will clearly be some quality more than human; for there is no such thing as virtue in the case of a god, any more than there is vice or virtue in the case of a beast: divine goodness is something more exalted than virtue, and
3 bestial badness is different in kind from vice. And inasmuch as it is rare for a man to be divine, in the sense in which that word is commonly used by the Spartans as a term of extreme admiration – 'Yon mon's divine', they say – , so a bestial character is rare among human beings; it is found most frequently among barbarians, and some cases also occur as a result of disease or arrested development. We sometimes also use 'bestial' as a term of opprobrium for a surpassing degree of human vice.[3]

4 But the nature of the bestial disposition will have to be touched on later; and of vice we have spoken already. We must however discuss unrestraint and softness or luxury, and also self-restraint and endurance. Neither of these two classes of character is to be conceived as identical with virtue and vice, nor yet as different in kind from them.

5 Our proper course with this subject as with others will be to present the various views about it, and then, after first reviewing the difficulties they involve, finally to establish if possible all or, if not all, the greater part and the most important of the opinions

generally held with respect to these states of mind; since if the discrepancies can be solved, and a residuum of current opinion left standing, the true view will have been sufficiently established.[4]

6   Now the following opinions are held: (a) that self-restraint and endurance are good and praiseworthy dispositions, unrestraint and softness bad and blameworthy; (b) that the self-restrained man is the man who abides by the results of his calculations, the unrestrained, one who readily abandons the conclusion he has reached; (c) that the unrestrained man does things that he knows to be evil, under the influence of passion, whereas the self-restrained man, knowing that his desires are evil, refuses to follow them on principle; (d) that the temperate man is always self-restrained and enduring; but that the converse is invariably the case some deny, although others affirm it: the latter identify the unrestrained with the profligate and the profligate with the unrestrained promiscuously, the former distinguish between

7   them. (e) Sometimes it is said that the prudent man cannot be unrestrained, sometimes that some prudent and clever men are unrestrained. (f) Again, men are spoken of as unrestrained in anger, and in the pursuit of honour and of gain. These then are the opinions advanced.

ii   The difficulties that may be raised are the following. (c) How can a man fail in self-restraint when believing correctly that what he does is wrong? Some people say that he cannot do so when he *knows* the act to be wrong; since, as Socrates held, it would be strange if, when a man possessed knowledge, some other thing should overpower it, and 'drag it about like a slave'.[5] In fact Socrates used to combat the view[6] altogether, implying that there is no such thing as unrestraint, since no one, he held, acts contrary to what is best, believing what he does to be bad, but

2   only through ignorance. Now this theory is manifestly at variance with plain facts; and we ought to investigate the state of mind in question more closely. If failure of self-restraint is caused by ignorance, we must examine what sort of ignorance it is. For it is clear that the man who fails in self-restraint does not think the action right before he comes under the influence of passion.

3   But some thinkers accept the doctrine in a modified form. They allow that nothing is more powerful than knowledge, but they do not allow that no one acts contrary to what he *opines* to be the

better course; and they therefore maintain that the unrestrained man when he succumbs to the temptations of pleasure possesses

4 not knowledge but only opinion. And yet if it is really opinion and not knowledge – not a strong belief that offers resistance but only a weak one (like that of persons in two minds about something) – we could forgive a man for not keeping to his opinions in opposition to strong desires; but we do not forgive

5 vice, nor any other blameworthy quality. (e) Is it then when desire is opposed by prudence that we blame a man for yielding? for prudence is extremely strong. But this is strange, for it means that the same person can be at once prudent and unrestrained; yet no one could possibly maintain that the prudent man is capable of doing voluntarily the basest actions. And furthermore it has already been shown[7] that prudence displays itself in action (for it is concerned with ultimate particulars), and implies the possession of the other virtues as well.

6 Again (d) if self-restraint implies having strong and evil desires, the temperate man cannot be self-restrained, nor thez self-restrained man temperate; for the temperate man does not have excessive or evil desires. But a self-restrained man must necessarily have strong and evil desires; since if a man's desires are good, the disposition that prevents him from obeying them will be evil, and so self-restraint will not always be good; while if his desires are weak and not evil, there is nothing to be proud of in resisting them; nor is it anything remarkable if they are evil and weak.

7 Again (a, b) if self-restraint makes a man steadfast in *all* his opinions, it may be bad, namely, if it makes him persist even in a false opinion. And if unrestraint makes him liable to abandon *any* opinion, in some cases unrestraint will be good. Take the instance of Neoptolemus in the *Philoctetes*[8] of Sophocles. Neoptolemus abandons a resolution that he has been persuaded by Odysseus to adopt, because of the pain that it gives him to tell a lie: in this case inconstancy is praiseworthy.

8 Again (a, c) there is the difficulty raised by the argument of the sophists. The sophists wish to show their cleverness by entrapping their adversary into a paradox, and when they are successful, the resultant chain of reasoning ends in a deadlock: the mind is fettered, being unwilling to stand still because it cannot approve the conclusion reached, yet unable to go forward because it

9 cannot untie the knot of the argument. Now one of their arguments proves that folly combined with unrestraint is a virtue. It runs as follows: if a man is foolish and also unrestrained, owing to his unrestraint he does the opposite of what he believes that he ought to do; but he believes[9] that good things are bad, and that he ought not to do them; therefore he will do good things and not bad ones.

10 Again (b, d) one who does and pursues what is pleasant from conviction and choice,[10] might be held to be a better man than one who acts in the same way not from calculation but from unrestraint, because he is more easy to cure, since he may be persuaded to alter his conviction; whereas the unrestrained man comes under the proverb that says 'when water chokes you, what are you to drink to wash it down?' Had he been convinced that what he does is right, a change of conviction might have caused him to desist; but as it is he is convinced that he ought to do one thing and nevertheless does another thing.[11]

11 Again (f) if self-restraint and unrestraint can be displayed with reference to anything, what is the meaning of the epithet 'unrestrained' without qualification? No one has every form of unrestraint, yet we speak of some men as simply 'unrestrained'.

12 Such, more or less, are the difficulties that arise. Part of the conflicting opinions we have to clear out of the way, but part to leave standing; for to solve a difficulty is to find the answer to a problem.[12]

iii We have then to consider, first (1) whether men fail in self-restraint knowing what they do is wrong, or not knowing, and if knowing, knowing in what sense; and next (2) what are to be set down as the objects with which self-restraint and unrestraint are concerned: I mean, are they concerned with pleasure and pain of all sorts, or only with certain special pleasures and pains? and (3) is self-restraint the same as endurance or distinct from it? and so on with (4) the other questions akin to this subject.

2 A starting-point for our investigation is to ask[13] whether the *differentia*[14] of the self-restrained man and the unrestrained is constituted by their objects, or by their dispositions: I mean, whether a man is called unrestrained solely because he fails to restrain himself with reference to certain things, or rather because he has a certain disposition, or rather for both reasons combined.

A second question is, can self-restraint and unrestraint be displayed in regard to everything, or not? When a man is said to be 'unrestrained' without further qualification, it does not mean that he is so in relation to everything, but to those things in regard to which a man can be profligate; and also it does not mean merely that he is concerned with these things (for in that case unrestraint would be the same thing as profligacy), but that he is concerned with them in a particular manner. The profligate yields to his appetites from choice, considering it right always to pursue the pleasure that offers, whereas the man of defective self-restraint does not think so, but pursues it all the same.

3 (i) Now the suggestion that it is not knowledge but true opinion, against which unrestrained men act, is of no importance for our argument. Some men hold their opinions with absolute certainty, and take them for positive knowledge; so that if

4 weakness of conviction be the criterion for deciding that men who act against their conception of what is right must be said to *opine* rather than to *know* the right, there will really be no difference in this respect between opinion and knowledge; since some men are just as firmly convinced of what they opine as others are of what they know: witness Heraclitus.[15]

5 (i) But the word *know* is used in two senses. A man who has knowledge but is not exercising it is said to know, and so is a man who is actually exercising his knowledge. It will make a difference whether a man does wrong having the knowledge that it is wrong but not consciously thinking of his knowledge, or with the knowledge consciously present to his mind. The latter would be felt to be surprising; but it is not surprising that a man should do what he knows to be wrong if he is not conscious of the knowledge at the time.

6 (ii) Again, reasoning on matters of conduct employs premises of two forms.[16] Now it is quite possible for a man to act against knowledge when he knows both premises but is only exercising his knowledge of the universal premise and not of the particular; for action has to do with particular things. Moreover, there is a distinction as regards the universal term: one universal is predicated of the man himself, the other of the thing; for example, he may know and be conscious of the knowledge that dry food is good for every man and that he himself is a man, or

even that food of a certain kind is dry, but either not possess or not be actualising the knowledge whether the particular food before him is food of that kind. Now clearly the distinction between these two ways of knowing will make all the difference in the world. It will not seem at all strange that the unrestrained man should 'know' in one way, but it would be astonishing if he knew in another way.

7   (iii) Again, it is possible for men to 'have knowledge' in yet another way besides those just discussed; for even in the state of having knowledge without exercising it we can observe a distinction: a man may in a sense both have it and not have it: for instance, when he is asleep, or mad, or drunk. But persons under the influence of passion are in the same condition; for it is evident that anger, sexual desire, and certain other passions, actually alter the state of the body, and in some cases even cause madness. It is clear therefore that we must pronounce the unrestrained to 'have knowledge' only in the same way as men
8   who are asleep or mad or drunk. Their using the language of knowledge[17] is no proof that they possess it. Persons in the states mentioned[18] repeat propositions of geometry and verses of Empedocles; students who have just begun a subject reel off its formulae, though they do not yet know their meaning, for knowledge has to become part of the tissue of the mind, and this takes time. Hence we must conceive that men who fail in self-restraint talk in the same way as actors speaking a part.

9   (iv) Again, one may also study the cause of unrestraint scientifically,[19] thus: In a practical syllogism, the major premise is an opinion, while the minor premise deals with particular things, which are the province of perception. Now when the two premises are combined, just as in theoretic reasoning the mind is compelled to *affirm* the resulting conclusion, so in the case of practical premises you are forced at once to *do* it. For example, given the premises 'All sweet things ought to be tasted' and 'Yonder thing is sweet' – a particular instance of the general class – you are bound, if able and not prevented, immediately to
10   taste the thing. When therefore there is present in the mind on the one hand a universal judgement forbidding you to taste and on the other hand a universal judgement saying 'All sweet things are pleasant', and a minor premise 'Yonder thing is sweet' (and it

is this minor premise that is active),[20] and when desire is present at the same time, then, though the former universal judgement says 'Avoid that thing', the desire leads you to it (since desire can put the various parts of the body in motion). Thus it comes about that when men fail in self-restraint, they act in a sense under the influence of a principle or opinion, but an opinion not in itself

11 but only accidentally opposed to the right principle (for it is the desire, and not the opinion, that is really opposed). Hence the lower animals cannot be called unrestrained, if only for the reason that they have no power of forming universal concepts, but only mental images and memories of particular things.

12 If we ask how the unrestrained man's ignorance is dissipated and he returns to a state of knowledge, the explanation is the same as in the case of drunkenness and sleep, and is not peculiar to failure of self-restraint. We must go for it to physiology.

13 But inasmuch as the last premise, which originates action, is an opinion as to some object of sense, and it is this opinion which the unrestrained man when under the influence of passion either does not possess, or only possesses in a way which as we saw does not amount to knowing it but only makes him repeat it as the drunken man repeats the maxims of Empedocles, and since the ultimate term is not a universal, and is not deemed to be an object of scientific knowledge in the same way as a universal term is, we do seem to be led to the conclusion[21] which Socrates

14 sought to establish. For the knowledge which is present when failure of self-restraint[22] occurs is not what is held to be knowledge in the true sense, nor is it true knowledge which is dragged about by passion, but knowledge derived from sense-perception.

So much for the question whether failure of self-restraint can go with knowledge or not, and with knowledge in what sense.

iv (2) We must next discuss whether any man can be called 'unrestrained' without qualification, or whether it must always be in relation to certain particular things, and if so, to what sort of things. Now it is plain that men are self-restrained and enduring,

2 unrestrained and soft, in regard to pleasures and pains. But the things that give pleasure are of two kinds: some are necessary,[23] others are desirable in themselves but admit of excess. The necessary sources of pleasures are those connected with the body:

I mean such as the functions of nutrition and sex, in fact those bodily functions which we have indicated[24] as the sphere of profligacy and temperance. The other sources of pleasure are not necessary, but are desirable in themselves: I mean for example victory, honour, wealth, and the other good and pleasant things of the same sort. Now those who against the right principle within them exceed in regard to the latter class of pleasant things, we do not call unrestrained simply, but with a qualification – unrestrained as to money, gain, honour or anger[25] – not merely 'unrestrained'; because we regard them as distinct from the unrestrained in the strict sense, and only so called by analogy, like our familiar example[26] of Man the Olympic winner, whose special definition is not very different[27] from the general definition of 'man', though nevertheless he is really quite distinct from men in general.[28] (That such persons are only called unrestrained by analogy is proved by our blaming unrestraint, whether unqualified or with reference to some particular bodily pleasure, as a vice and not merely an error, whereas we do not regard

3 those unrestrained in regard to money, etc. as guilty of vice.) But of those who exceed in relation to the bodily enjoyments with regard to which we speak of men as temperate or profligate, he who pursues excessive pleasure, and avoids the extremes[29] of bodily pains such as hunger, heat, cold, and the various pains of touch and taste, not from choice but against his own choice and reason, is described as unrestrained not with a qualification – unrestrained as regards these pleasures and pains – as is one who

4 yields to anger, but just simply as unrestrained. (A proof that 'unrestrained' unqualified denotes unrestraint as regards bodily pleasures and pains, is that we speak of men as 'soft' who yield to these, but not those who yield to anger or the like.) And hence we class the unrestrained man with the profligate (and the self-restrained with the temperate)[30], but not those who yield to anger or the like, because unrestraint and profligacy are related to the same pleasures and pains. But as a matter of fact, although they are related to the same things, they are not related to them in the same way; the profligate acts from choice, the unrestrained man does not. Hence we should pronounce a man who pursues excessive pleasures and avoids moderate pains when he feels only weak desires or none at all, to be more profligate than one who

does so owing to intense desires; for what would the former do if he possessed the ardent desires of youth, and felt violent pain when debarred from the 'necessary' pleasures?

5 And inasmuch as some desires and pleasures relate to things that are noble and good in kind (for some pleasant things are desirable by nature, others the opposite, while others again are neutral – compare the classification we gave above[31]): for instance money, gain, victory, honour: and inasmuch as in relation to all these naturally desirable things, as well as to the neutral ones, men are not blamed merely for regarding or desiring or liking them, but for doing so in a certain way, namely to excess (hence those[32] who yield to or pursue, contrary to principle, anything naturally noble and good, for example those who care too much for honour, or for their children and their parents – for parents and children are good things and people are praised who care for them, but nevertheless it is possible even in their case to go to excess, by vying even with the gods like Niobe,[33] or as Satyrus did,[34] who was nicknamed the filial for his devotion to his father, for he was thought to carry it to the point of infatuation –): well then, there cannot be any actual vice in relation to these things, because, as has been said, each of them is in itself desirable by nature, although excessive devotion to them

6 is bad and to be avoided. And similarly there cannot be unrestraint either, since that is not merely to be avoided, but actually blameworthy; though people do use the term in these matters with a qualification – 'unrestraint in' whatever it may be – because the affection does resemble unrestraint proper; just as they speak of someone as a bad doctor or bad actor whom they would not call simply 'bad'. As therefore we do not call bad doctors and actors bad men, because neither kind of incapacity is actually a vice, but only resembles vice by analogy, so in the former case it is clear that only self-restraint and lack of restraint in regard to the same things as are the objects of temperance and profligacy are to be deemed self-restraint and unrestraint proper, and that these terms are applied to anger only by analogy; and so we add a qualification, 'unrestrained in anger', just as we say 'unrestrained in the pursuit of honour' or 'gain'.

v Besides those things however which are naturally pleasant, of which some are pleasant generally and others pleasant to particular races of animals and of men, there are other things, not naturally pleasant, which become pleasant either as a result of arrested development or from habit, or in some cases owing to natural depravity. Now corresponding to each of these kinds of unnatural pleasures we may observe a related disposition of 2 character. I mean bestial characters, like the creature in woman's form[35] that is said to rip up pregnant females and devour their offspring, or certain savage tribes on the coasts of the Black Sea, who are alleged to delight in raw meat or in human flesh, and others among whom each in turn provides a child for the 3 common banquet;[36] or the reported depravity of Phalaris.[37] These are instances of bestiality. Other unnatural propensities are due to disease, and sometimes to insanity, as in the case of the madman that offered up his mother to the gods and partook of the sacrifice, or the one that ate his fellow slave's liver. Other morbid propensities are acquired by habit, for instance, plucking out the hair, biting the nails, eating cinders and earth, and also sexual perversion. These practices result in some cases from natural disposition, and in others from habit, as with those who 4 have been abused from childhood. When nature is responsible, no one would describe such persons as showing unrestraint, any more than one would apply that term to women because they are passive and not active in sexual intercourse; nor should we class as unrestraint a morbid state brought about by habitual indulgence.

5 Now these various morbid dispositions in themselves do not fall within the limits of vice, nor yet does bestiality; and to conquer or yield to them does not constitute unrestraint[38] in the strict sense, but only the state so called by analogy; just as a man who cannot control his anger must be described as 'unrestrained in' that passion, not 'unrestrained'.

(Indeed folly, cowardice, profligacy, and ill-temper, whenever 6 they run to excess, are either bestial or morbid conditions. One so constituted by nature as to be frightened by everything, even the sound of a mouse, shows the cowardice of a lower animal; the man who was afraid of a weasel was a case of disease. So with folly: people irrational by nature and living solely by sensation, like certain remote tribes of barbarians, belong to the bestial class; those who lose their reason owing to some disease, such as epilepsy, or through insanity, to the morbid.)

7   With these unnatural propensities it is possible in some cases merely to have the disposition and not to yield to it: I mean, for instance, Phalaris[39] might have had the desire to eat a child, or to practise unnatural vice, and refrained; or it is possible not merely

8 to possess but to yield to the propensity. As therefore with vice, that natural to man is called simply vice, whereas the other kind[40] is termed not simply vice, but vice with the qualifying epithet bestial or morbid; similarly with unrestraint, it is clear that the bestial and morbid kinds are distinct from unrestraint proper, and that the name without qualification belongs only to that kind of unrestraint which is co-extensive with profligacy of the human sort.

9   It is clear then that self-restraint and unrestraint relate only to the objects to which temperance and profligacy are related, and that unrestraint in relation to anything else is of another kind, which is only so called metaphorically and with a qualification.

vi   Let us now consider the point that unrestraint in anger[41] is less disgraceful than unrestraint in the desires.

Now it appears that anger does to some extent hear reason, but hears it wrong, just as hasty servants hurry out of the room before they have heard the whole of what you are saying, and so mistake your order, and as watch-dogs bark at a mere knock at the door, without waiting to see if it is a friend. Similarly anger, owing to the heat and swiftness of its nature, hears, but does not hear the order given, and rushes off to take vengeance. When reason or imagination suggests that an insult or slight has been received, anger flares up at once, but after reasoning as it were that you ought to make war on anybody who insults you. Desire on the other hand, at a mere hint from [the reason or][42] the senses that a thing is pleasant, rushes off to enjoy it. Hence anger follows reason in a manner, but desire does not. Therefore yielding to desire is more disgraceful than yielding to anger, for he that fails to restrain his anger is in a way controlled by reason, but the other[43] is controlled not by reason but by desire.

2   Again, when impulses are natural, it is more excusable to follow them, since even with the desires it is more excusable to follow those that are common to all men, and in so far as they are common. But anger and bad temper are more natural than desire

for excessive and unnecessary pleasures; witness the man who was had up for beating his father and who said in his defence, 'Well, my father used to beat his father, and he used to beat his, and (pointing to his little boy) so will my son here beat me when he grows up; it runs in our family'; and the man who, when his son was throwing him out of the house, used to beg him to stop when he got to the door, 'because he only used to drag his father as far as that'.[44]

3   Again, the craftier men are, the more unjust they are. Now the hot-tempered man is not crafty, nor is anger, but open; whereas desire is crafty, as they say of Aphrodite:

Weaver of wiles in Cyprus born [45]

and Homer writes of her 'broidered girdle'

Cajolery[46] that cheats the wisest wits.

As therefore unrestraint in desire is more unjust as well as more disgraceful than unrestraint as regards anger, unrestraint in desire is unrestraint in the strict sense, and is even in a certain sense vice.

4   Again, a wanton outrage[47] gives pleasure to the doer, never pain, whereas an act done in anger always causes him a feeling of pain. If then things are unjust in proportion to the justice of the anger they arouse in the victim, unrestraint arising from desire is more unjust than that arising from anger; for anger contains no element of wanton insolence.

5   It is clear therefore that unrestraint in one's desires is more disgraceful than unrestraint in anger, and that it is in relation to bodily desires and pleasures that self-restraint and unrestraint are really manifested.

6   But we must distinguish among the bodily desires and pleasures themselves. As was said at the beginning,[48] some of these are human and natural both in kind and degree, some bestial, and some due to arrested development or disease. Now it is only with the first class that temperance and profligacy are concerned; hence we do not use the terms temperate or profligate of the lower animals, except metaphorically, of certain entire species distinguished from the rest by their exceptionally lascivious, mischievous, or omnivorous habits; for animals have neither the faculty of choice nor of calculation: they are aberrations from

7 nature,[49] like men who are insane. Bestiality[50] is less [evil] than
   vice, though more horrible: for [in a bestial man as in an animal]
   the highest part [i.e. the intellect] is not corrupted, as it is in a
   man [who is wicked in a human way], but entirely lacking. So
   that it is like comparing an inanimate with an animate thing, and
   asking which is the more evil; for the badness of a thing which
   has no originating principle – and intelligence is such a principle –
   is always less capable of mischief. (It is therefore like comparing
   injustice with an unjust man: one is worse in one way and the
   other in another).[51] For a bad man can do ten thousand times
   more harm than an animal [or a bestial man].

vii   (3) But in relation to the pleasures and pains of touch and taste,
   and the corresponding desires and acts of avoidance, which have
   already[52] been defined as the sphere in which profligacy and
   temperance are displayed, it is possible on the one hand to have
   such a disposition as to succumb even to those temptations to
   which most men are superior, or on the other hand to conquer
   even those to which most men succumb. These two dispositions,
   when manifested in relation to pleasure, constitute unrestraint
   and restraint respectively; when in relation to pain, softness and
   endurance. The disposition of the great majority of men lies
   between the two, though they incline rather to the worse
   extremes.

2   And inasmuch as some pleasures are necessary and others not,
   and the former are only necessary within certain limits, excessive
   indulgence in them not being necessary, nor yet deficient
   indulgence[53] either, and inasmuch as the same holds good also of
   desires and of pains, one who pursues excessive pleasures, or
   pursues things[54] to excess and from choice, for their own sakes
   and not for the sake of some ulterior consequence, is a profligate;
   for a man of this character is certain to feel no regret for his
   excesses afterwards, and this being so, he is incurable,[55] since
   there is no cure for one who does not regret his error. The man
   deficient in the enjoyment of pleasures is the opposite of the
   profligate; and the middle character is the temperate man. And
   similarly, he who avoids bodily pains not because his will is
3 overpowered but of deliberate choice, is also profligate. (Those
   on the other hand who yield not from choice, are prompted
   either by the pleasure of indulgence, or by the impulse to avoid

the pain of unsatisfied desire. Hence there is a difference between deliberate and non-deliberate indulgence. Everyone would think a man worse if he did something disgraceful when he felt only a slight desire, or none at all, than if he acted from a strong desire, or if he struck another in cold blood than if he did so in anger; for what would he have done had his passions been aroused? Hence the profligate man is worse than the unrestrained.)

Of the dispositions described above, the deliberate avoidance of pain is rather a kind[56] of softness; the deliberate pursuit of pleasure is profligacy in the strict sense.

4   Self-restraint is the opposite of unrestraint, endurance of softness; for endurance means only successful resistance, whereas restraint implies mastery, which is a different matter: victory is more glorious than the mere avoidance of defeat. Hence self-

5 restraint is a more valuable quality than endurance. One who is deficient in resistance to pains that most men withstand with success, is soft or luxurious (for luxury is a kind of softness): such a man lets his cloak trail on the ground to escape the fatigue and trouble of lifting it, or feigns sickness, not seeing that to counterfeit

6 misery is to be miserable. The same holds good of self-restraint and unrestraint. It is not surprising that a man should be overcome by violent and excessive pleasures or pains: indeed it is excusable if he succumbs after a struggle, like Philoctetes in Theodectes when bitten by the viper, or Kerkyon in the *Alope* of Karkinos, or as men who try to restrain their laughter explode in one great guffaw, as happened to Xenophantus.[57] But we are surprised when a man is overcome by pleasures and pains which most men are able to withstand, except when his failure to resist is due to some innate tendency, or to disease: instances of the former being the hereditary effeminacy[58] of the royal family of Scythia, and the inferior endurance of the female sex as compared with the male.

7   People too fond of amusement are thought to be profligate, but really they are soft; for amusement is rest, and therefore a slackening of effort, and addiction to amusement is a form of excessive slackness.[59]

8   But there are two forms of unrestraint, impetuousness and weakness. The weak deliberate, but then are prevented by passion from keeping to their resolution; the impetuous are led by passion because they do not stop to deliberate: since some

people withstand the attacks of passion, whether pleasant or painful, by feeling or seeing them coming, and rousing themselves, that is, their reasoning faculty, in advance, just as one is proof against tickling if one has just been tickled already.[60] It is the quick and the excitable who are most liable to the impetuous form of unrestraint, because the former are too hasty and the latter too vehement to wait for reason, being prone to follow their imagination.

viii (4) The profligate, as we said,[61] does not feel remorse, for he abides by his choice; the unrestrained man on the other hand invariably repents his excesses afterwards. Hence the objection that we stated[62] does not hold good; on the contrary, it is the profligate who cannot be cured, whereas the unrestrained man can; for vice resembles diseases like dropsy and consumption, whereas unrestraint is like epilepsy, vice being a chronic, unrestraint an intermittent evil. Indeed unrestraint and vice are entirely different in kind, for vice is unconscious, whereas the unrestrained man is aware of his infirmity.

2 Among the unrestrained themselves, the impulsive[63] sort are better than those who know the right principle but do not keep to it; for these succumb to smaller temptations, and they do not yield without deliberation, as do the impulsive; the unrestrained[64] man is like people who get drunk quickly, and with a small 3 amount of wine, or with less than most men. That unrestraint is not strictly a vice (though it is perhaps vice in a sense) is clear; for unrestraint acts against deliberate choice, vice in accordance with it. But nevertheless in the actions that result from it it resembles vice: just as Demodocus wrote of the people of Miletus –

> Milesians are no fools, 'tis true,
> But yet they act as fools would do.

Similarly the unrestrained are not unjust, but they do unjust things.

4 Again,[65] the unrestrained man is so constituted as to pursue bodily pleasures that are excessive and contrary to right principle without any belief that he ought to do so, whereas the profligate, because he is so constituted as to pursue them, is convinced that he ought to pursue them. Therefore the former can easily be persuaded to change,[66] but the latter cannot. For virtue preserves

the fundamental principle,[67] vice destroys it, and the first principle or starting-point in matters of conduct is the end proposed, which corresponds to the hypotheses[68] of mathematics; hence no more in ethics than in mathematics are the first principles imparted by process of reasoning, but by virtue, whether natural or acquired by training in right opinion as to the first principle. The man of principle therefore is temperate, the 5 man who has lost all principle, profligate. But there is a person who abandons his choice, against right principle, under the influence of passion, who is mastered by passion sufficiently for him not to act in accordance with right principle, but not so completely as to be of such a character as to believe that the reckless pursuit of pleasure is right. This is the unrestrained man: he is better than the profligate, and not absolutely bad, for in him the highest part of man, the fundamental principle, is still preserved. Opposed to the unrestrained man is another, who stands firm by his choice, and does not abandon it under the mere impulse of passion.

It is clear then from these considerations that self-restraint is a good quality and unrestraint a bad one.

ix   Is then a man self-restrained if he stands by a principle or choice of any sort, or must it be the right choice? and is a man unrestrained if he fails to stand by a choice or principle of any sort, or only if he fails to stand by the true principle and the right choice? This difficulty was raised before.[69] Perhaps the answer is, that though accidentally it may be any principle or choice, essentially it is the true principle and the right choice that the one stands by and the other does not; in the sense that if a man chooses or pursues *b* as a means to *a*, *a* is essentially, *b* only accidentally, his object and his choice. And by 'essentially' we mean 'absolutely'; hence while in a sense it is any sort of opinion, speaking absolutely it is the true opinion that the one stands by and the other abandons.

2   But there are some persons who stand by their opinion whom we call 'obstinate', meaning that they are hard to convince, and not easily persuaded to change their convictions. These bear some resemblance to the self-restrained man, as the prodigal does to the liberal, and the reckless to the brave; but they are really different in many respects. The self-restrained man stands firm

against passion and desire: he will be ready on occasion to yield
to persuasion; but the obstinate stand firm against reason: they are

3 not proof against desire, and are often led by pleasure. Types of
obstinacy are the opinionated, the stupid, and the boorish. The
motives of the opinionated are pleasure and pain: the agreeable
sense of victory in not being persuaded to change their minds,
and the annoyance of having the decrees of their sovereign will
and pleasure annulled. Hence they really resemble the unrestrained more than the restrained.

4 And there are some who fail to abide by their resolves from
some other cause than lack of self-restraint, for instance,
Neoptolemus[70] in the *Philoctetes* of Sophocles. It is true that his
motive for changing was pleasure, though a noble pleasure, since
it was pleasant[71] for him to speak the truth, and he had only told
a lie at the instigation of Odysseus. In fact, not everyone whose
conduct is guided by pleasure is either profligate and base, or
unrestrained, but only those who yield to disgraceful pleasures.

5 There is also a character[72] that takes less than the proper
amount of pleasure in the things of the body, and that fails to
stand by principle in that sense. The self-restrained man therefore
is really intermediate between the unrestrained man and the type
described. The unrestrained man departs from principle because
he enjoys bodily pleasures too much, the person described does
so because he enjoys them too little; while the self-restrained
man stands by principle and does not change from either cause.
And inasmuch as self-restraint is good, it follows that both the
dispositions opposed to it are bad, as indeed they appear to be;
but because one of the two is found only in a few people, and is
rarely displayed, unrestraint is thought to be the sole opposite of
self-restraint, just as profligacy is thought to be the sole opposite
of temperance.

6 Many terms are used in an analogical sense, and so we have
come to speak by analogy of the 'self-restraint' of the temperate
man, because the temperate man, as well as the self-restrained, is
so constituted as never to be led by the pleasures of the body to
act against principle. But whereas the self-restrained man has evil
desires,[73] the temperate man has none; he is so constituted as to
take no pleasure in things that are contrary to principle, whereas

7 the self-restrained man does feel pleasure in such things, but does

not yield to it. There is also a resemblance between the unrestrained man and the profligate, though they are really distinct: both pursue bodily pleasures, but the profligate thinks it right to do so, the man who lacks self-restraint does not.

x   Again, the same person cannot be at once unrestrained and prudent, for it has been shown[74] that prudence is inseparable
2 from moral virtue. Also, prudence does not consist only in knowing what is right, but also in doing it; but the unrestrained man does not do the right. (Cleverness[75] on the other hand is not incompatible with unrestraint – which is why it is sometimes thought that some people are prudent and yet unrestrained – because cleverness differs from prudence in the manner explained in our first discourse:[76] as being intellectual faculties[77] they are closely akin, but they differ in that prudence involves deliberate
3 choice.) Nor indeed does the unrestrained man even know the right in the sense of one who consciously exercises his knowledge, but only as a man asleep or drunk can be said to know something. Also, although he errs willingly (for he knows in a sense both what he is doing and what end he is aiming at), yet he is not wicked, for his moral choice is sound, so that he is only half-wicked. And he is not unjust, for he does not deliberately design to do harm,[78] since the one type of unrestrained person does not keep to the resolve he has formed after deliberation, and the other, the excitable type, does not deliberate at all. In fact the unrestrained man resembles a state which passes all the proper enactments, and has good laws, but which never keeps its laws: the condition of things satirised by Anaxandrides –

The state, that recks not of the laws, would fain . . .

4 whereas the bad man is like a state which keeps its laws but whose laws are bad.

Both self-restraint and unrestraint are a matter of extremes as compared with the character of the mass of mankind; the restrained man shows more and the unrestrained man less steadfastness than most men are capable of.

Reformation is more possible with that type of unrestraint which is displayed by persons of an excitable temperament than it is with those who deliberate as to what they ought to do, but do not keep to the resolution they form. And those who have become unrestrained through habit are more easily cured than those who are unrestrained by nature, since habit is easier to change than nature; for even habit is hard to change, precisely because it is a sort of nature, as Evenus says:

> Mark me, my friend, 'tis long-continued training,[79]
> And training in the end becomes men's nature.

5   We have now discussed the nature of self-restraint and unrestraint, and of endurance and softness, and have shown how these dispositions are related to one another.

xi   It is also the business of the political philosopher to examine the nature of pleasure and pain; for he is the master-craftsman, and lays down the end which is the standard whereby we
2 pronounce things good or bad in the absolute sense. Moreover this investigation is fundamental for our study, because we have established[80] that moral virtue and vice are concerned with pleasures and pains, and most people hold that pleasure is a necessary adjunct of happiness, which is why the word denoting 'supreme bliss' is derived from the verb meaning 'to enjoy'.[81]

3   Now (1) some people think that no pleasure is a good thing, whether essentially or accidentally. They argue that good and pleasure are two distinct things.

(2) Others hold that though some pleasures are good, most are bad.

(3) There is also a third view, that even if all pleasures are good, nevertheless pleasure cannot be the supreme good.[82]

4   (1) To prove that pleasure is not a good at all, it is argued that

     (a) Every pleasure is a conscious process towards a natural state; but a process can in no case belong to the same order of things as its end; for example, the process of building cannot be a thing of the same sort as the house built.

     (b) The temperate man avoids pleasures.

     (c) The prudent man pursues freedom from pain, not pleasure.

     (d) Pleasures are a hindrance to prudent deliberation, and the more so the more enjoyable they are; for instance, sexual pleasure: no one could think of anything while indulging in it.

(e) There is no art of pleasure; yet with every good thing there is an art which produces it.

(f) Children and animals pursue pleasures.

5 (2) To prove that not all pleasures are good, it is argued that

(a) Some pleasures are disgraceful, and discredit the man who indulges in them.

(b) Some pleasures are harmful, for certain pleasant things cause disease.

(3) To prove that pleasure is not the supreme good, it is argued that it is not an end but a process.

These then, more or less, are the current views.

xii But the following considerations will show that these arguments are not conclusive to prove (1) that pleasure is not a good at all, nor (3) that it is not the supreme good.

(1) (a) In the first place (i) 'the good' has two meanings: it means both that which is good absolutely, and that which is good for somebody, or relatively. Consequently the term 'good' has the same double meaning when applied to men's natures and dispositions; and therefore also when applied to movements and to processes. Also those processes which are thought to be bad will in some cases, though bad absolutely, be not bad relatively, but in fact desirable for a particular person, or in other cases, though not even desirable generally for the particular person, nevertheless desirable for him in particular circumstances and for a short time although not really desirable. And some such processes[83] are not really pleasures at all, but only seem to be so: I mean the painful processes that are undergone for their curative effects, for instance treatment applied to the sick.

2 Again, (ii) the good is either an *activity* or a *state*. Now the pleasures that restore us to our natural *state* are only accidentally pleasant; while the *activity* of desire is the activity of that part of us which has remained in the natural state:[84] for that matter, there are some pleasures which do not involve pain or desire at all (for instance, the pleasure of contemplation), being experienced without any deficiency from the normal having occurred. That restorative pleasures are only accidentally pleasant is indicated by the fact that we do not enjoy the same things while the natural state is being replenished as we do after it has been restored to the normal; in the normal state we enjoy things that are absolutely

pleasant, but during the process of replenishment we enjoy even their opposites; for instance, sour and bitter things, none of which are naturally or absolutely pleasant, so that the pleasures we get from them are not naturally or absolutely pleasant either, since there is the same distinction between various pleasures as there is between the pleasant things from which they arise.

3   Again, (iii) it does not follow, as some argue, that as the end is better than the process towards it, so there must be something better than pleasure. For pleasures are not really processes, nor are they all incidental to a process: they are activities, and therefore an end; nor do they result from the process of acquiring our faculties, but from their exercise; nor have they all of them some end other than themselves: this is only true of the pleasures of progress towards the perfection of our nature. Hence it is not correct to define pleasure as a 'conscious process'; the term should rather be 'activity of our natural state', and for 'conscious' we must substitute 'unimpeded'. Some thinkers hold that pleasure is a process on the ground that it is good in the fullest sense, because in their view an activity is a process; but really an activity is different from a process.

4   To argue (2) (b) that pleasures are bad because some pleasant things are detrimental to health is the same as to argue that health is bad because some healthy things are bad for the pocket. Both pleasant things and healthy things can be bad in a relative sense, but that does not make them really bad; even contemplation may on occasion be injurious to health.

5   (1) (d) Neither prudence nor any other quality is hampered by its own pleasure, but only by alien pleasures;[85] the pleasures of contemplation and study will enable us to contemplate and study better.

6   (1) (e) That there should be no art devoted to the production of any form of pleasure is only natural; an art never produces an activity, but the capacity for an activity – though in point of fact the arts of perfumery and cookery are generally considered to be arts of pleasure.

7   The arguments (1) (b) that the temperate man avoids pleasure, and (1) (c) that the prudent man pursues freedom from pain, and (1) (f) that animals and children pursue pleasure, are all met by the same reply. It has been explained[86] how some pleasures are

absolutely good, and how not all pleasures are good.[87] Now it is those pleasures which are not absolutely good that both animals and children pursue, and it is freedom from pain arising from the want of those pleasures that the prudent man pursues:[88] that is, the pleasures that involve desire and pain, namely the bodily pleasures (for these are of that nature), or their excessive forms, in regard to which profligacy is displayed. That is why the temperate man avoids excessive bodily pleasures: for even the temperate man has pleasures.

xiii   That pain moreover is an evil and to be avoided is admitted; since all pain is either absolutely evil, or evil as being in some way an impediment to activity. But that which is the opposite of something to be avoided – opposed to it as a thing to be avoided and evil – must be good. It follows therefore that pleasure is a good. Speusippus attempted to refute this argument[89] by saying that, as the greater is opposed to the equal as well as to the less, so pleasure is opposed to a neutral state of feeling as well as to pain. But this refutation does not hold good; for Speusippus would not maintain that pleasure is essentially evil.

2   But granting (2) that some pleasures are bad, it does not therefore follow (3) that a certain pleasure may not nevertheless be the supreme good; just as a certain form of knowledge may be supremely good, although some forms of knowledge are bad. On the contrary (i) since every faculty has its unimpeded activity, the activity of all the faculties, or of one of them (whichever constitutes happiness) when unimpeded, must probably be the most desirable thing there is; but an unimpeded activity is a pleasure; so that on this showing the supreme good will be a particular kind of pleasure, even though most pleasures are bad, and, it may be, bad absolutely. This is why everybody thinks that the happy life must be a pleasant life, and regards pleasure as a necessary ingredient of happiness; and with good reason, since no impeded activity is perfect, whereas happiness is essentially perfect; so that the happy man requires in addition the goods of the body, external goods and the gifts of fortune, in order that his
3   activity may not be impeded through lack of them. (Consequently those who say[90] that, if a man be good, he will be happy even when on the rack, or when fallen into the direst misfortune,
4   are intentionally or unintentionally talking nonsense.) But

because happiness requires the gifts of fortune in addition, some people think that it is the same thing as good fortune; but this is not so, since even good fortune itself when excessive is an impediment to activity, and perhaps indeed no longer deserves to be called good fortune, since good fortune can only be defined in relation to happiness.

5   (ii) Moreover, that all animals and all human beings pursue pleasure is some indication that it is in a sense the supreme good:

> No rumour noised abroad by many peoples
> Comes utterly to naught.[91]

6 But they do not all pursue the same pleasure, since the natural state and the best state neither is nor seems to be the same for them all; yet still they all pursue pleasure. Indeed it is possible that in reality they do not pursue the pleasure which they think and would say they do, but all the same pleasure; for nature has implanted in all things something divine.[92] But as the pleasures of the body are the ones which we most often meet with, and as all men are capable of these, these have usurped the family title; and so men think these are the only pleasures that exist, because they are the only ones which they know.

7   (iii) Moreover, it is clear that if pleasure is not good and activity is not pleasure,[93] the life of the happy man will not necessarily be pleasant. For why should he need pleasure if it is not good? On the contrary, his life may even be painful; for if pleasure is neither good nor evil, no more is pain either, so why should he avoid it? And if the good man's activities are not pleasanter than those of others, his life will not be pleasanter either.

xiv   On the subject of the bodily pleasures, we must examine the view of those who say that though it is true that some pleasures, which they call the noble pleasures, are highly desirable, yet bodily pleasures and those which are the objects of the profligate
2 are not desirable. If so, why are the pains opposed to them evil? since the opposite of evil is good. Perhaps the true view is, that the necessary pleasures are good in the sense that what is not evil is good; or that they are good up to a point: for though you cannot have excessive pleasure from states and movements which cannot themselves be in excess of what is good, you can have excessive pleasure from those which themselves admit of excess.

Now you can have an excess of the bodily goods; and it is pursuing this excess that makes a bad man, not pursuing the necessary pleasures, for everybody enjoys savoury food, wine, and sexual pleasure in some degree, though not everybody to the right degree. With pain it is the other way about:[94] one avoids not merely excessive pain, but all pain; for the opposite of excessive pleasure is not pain at all, except to the man who pursues excessive pleasure.

3   We ought however not only to state the true view, but also to account for the false one, since to do so helps to confirm the true; for when we have found a probable explanation why something appears to be true though it is not true, this increases our belief in the truth.

We have then to explain why it is that bodily pleasures appear to be more desirable than others.

4   (1) Now the first reason is that pleasure drives out pain; and excessive pain leads men to seek excessive pleasure, and bodily pleasure generally, as a restorative. And these restorative pleasures are intense, and therefore sought for, because they are seen in contrast with their opposite. (The view that pleasure is not a good at all is also due to these two facts, as has been said,[95] (a) that some pleasures are actions indicative of an evil nature, whether it be depraved from birth, like the nature of an animal,[96] or corrupted by habit, as is the case with evil men, and (b) that others are restoratives of a defective state,[97] and to be in the natural state is better than to be in process of returning to it. But as a matter of fact the latter sort of pleasures accompany a process towards perfection, so that accidentally they are good.)

5   (2) Another reason is that bodily pleasures are sought for, just because of their intensity, by people who are incapable of enjoying others (for instance, some deliberately take steps to make themselves thirsty): not that there is any objection to this if the pleasures are innocuous, but it is bad if they are productive of harmful results. The fact is that some men have no other sources of enjoyment; and also many are so constituted that a neutral state of feeling is to them positively painful. (This is because a state of strain is the normal condition of an animal organism, as physiology testifies; it tells us that sight and hearing are in fact painful, but we have got used to them in course of time – such is

6 the theory.) Similarly the young are in a condition resembling intoxication, because they are growing, and youth is pleasant in itself; but persons of an excitable nature need a restorative perpetually, because their temperament keeps their bodies in a constant state of irritation, and their appetites are continually active; and any pleasure, if strong, drives out pain, not only the opposite pleasure. This is why excitable men become profligate and vicious.

7   Pleasures unaccompanied by pain, on the other hand – and these are those derived from things naturally and not accidentally pleasant – do not admit of excess. By things accidentally pleasant I mean things taken as restoratives; really their restorative effect is produced by the operation[98] of that part of the system which has remained sound, and hence the remedy itself is thought to be pleasant. Those things on the contrary are naturally pleasant which stimulate the activity of a given nature.[99]

8   Nothing however can continue to give us pleasure always, because our nature is not simple, but contains a second element (which is what makes us perishable beings), and consequently, whenever one of these two elements is active, its activity runs counter to the nature of the other, while when the two are balanced, their action feels neither painful nor pleasant. Since if any man had a simple nature, the same activity would afford him the greatest pleasure always. Hence God enjoys a single simple pleasure perpetually. For there is not only an activity of motion, but also an activity of immobility, and there is essentially a truer pleasure in rest than in motion. But change in all things is sweet, as the poet says,[100] owing to some badness in us; since just as a changeable man is bad, so also is a nature that needs change; for it is not simple nor good.

9   We have now discussed the nature of self-restraint and unrestraint, and of pleasure and pain, and have shown in either case in what sense one of the two is good and the other evil. It remains for us to speak of friendship.

1   Or brutality: the two English words have acquired slightly different shades of meaning, which are combined in the Greek.

2   *Iliad*, xxiv, 258. The preceding words are, 'Hector, who was a god'.

3   literally 'for those who surpass (the rest of) men in vice' (*i.e.*, human, not bestial wickedness).

4   Aristotle holds (I, viii, 7) that the opinions of the mass of mankind, and of philosophers, on matters of conduct are likely to be substantially true; although being stated from different points of view, and sometimes in ambiguous language, they often seem mutually contradictory. The business of ethics is to state them clearly, examine their apparent contradictions, discard such parts of them as really refute each other, and elicit the common residuum of truth: see ii, 12.

5   a quotation from Plato, *Protagoras*, 352 b.

6. that a man may know the right and do the wrong.

7. *cf.* VI, vii, 7 and xii, 10.

8   lines 895–916. See further, ix, 4.

9   because he is foolish.

10 *i.e.*, a profligate. This is another sophistic paradox based on the contradiction between (1) the identification of the unrestrained man with the profligate, and (2) the view (§ 6) that the former acts contrary to his deliberate conviction.

11 A variant gives 'but as it is he is convinced it is wrong but nevertheless does it'.

12 See note 4.

13 This question is not pursued below; indeed the contents of the following chapters are correctly outlined in § 1, and § 2 is superfluous.

14 Not the difference between the two, since of course they are concerned with the same objects, but the difference between both of them and other similar characters; see i, 4.

15 This seems to refer to the dogmatic tone of Heraclitus's teaching in general.

16 The major premise of a practical syllogism is universal, a general

rule; the minor is particular, the application of the rule to the case in hand. The next sentence points out that this application really requires two syllogisms; in the first, the personal term of the major premise is predicated in the minor of the particular person concerned (dry food is good for all men: I am a man: therefore dry food is good for me); in the second, the other universal term is predicated in the minor of a particular thing about which the person is deliberating (dry food is good for me: this stale loaf is dry food: therefore this stale loaf is good for me). It is the minor premise of the second syllogism, *i.e.* the application of the general rule not to himself but to the thing in question, that the unrestrained man seems not to know, or not to think of, at the time.

17 The reference is to persons of weak will uttering sound moral maxims almost at the very moment of yielding to temptation.

18 *i.e.*, asleep or drunk. It may have been some Falstaff of Attic comedy that quoted the moral maxims of Empedocles in his cups.

19 *i.e.*, in this case, psychologically: literally 'with reference to its nature': *cf.* VIII, i, 6; IX, vii, 2 and ix, 7.

20 *i.e.*, determines action (Ross).

21 *cf.* ii, 1.

22 Here τὸ πάθος means ἀκρατεύεσθαι, *cf.* ii, 2; iii, 12 and iv, 6; but in the following line (*cf.* ii, 1) it probably means ἐπιθυμία or θυμός, as iii, 7; v, 5 and vii, 8.

23 See note 31.

24 See III, x.

25 *cf.* i, 7: θυμός, 'spirit', aims at victory, and so is brought into this discussion of 'pleasures and desires' (§ 5); but in chapter vi it is contrasted with desire, and its indulgence in the form of anger is seen to be painful rather than pleasant (vi, 4).

26 This seems to be the meaning of the imperfect tenses. An inscription records that a boxer named Ἄνθρωπος won at Olympia in 456 BC and the Greek commentators say that he is referred to here. His name would appear to have been used in the Peripatetic school as an example of the analogical use of words.

27 *i.e.*, it only requires the addition of three words. Strictly speaking, however, it is impossible to define an individual; moreover, the Olympic victor (a) was a man not merely by analogy but as a member of the species, and (b) was named Man not even by analogy but only homonymously. But a humorous illustration need not be precise.

28 Perhaps Man had some personal peculiarity which somewhat belied his name.

29 Probably this should be amended to 'moderate bodily pains', *cf.* § 4.

30 This parenthesis may be an interpolation.

31 See § 2: a third class is now added, pleasures bad in themselves and not only in excess; and the 'necessary' pleasures are now classed as 'intermediate', neither good nor bad in themselves, though good as a means to life, and bad in excess.

32 This subject is left without its verb, which apparently would be 'are not wicked, nor yet unrestrained in the proper sense'. Though this clause here begins as a parenthesis, it is resumed below at 'well then' as a fresh sentence which really, however, constitutes the apodosis of the protasis that began at the beginning of the section, 'And inasmuch'.

33 Niobe vaunted her children as more beautiful than those of Leto.

34 The Greek commentators tell stories of a certain Satyrus who, when his father died, committed suicide for grief.

35 Perhaps there is a reference to the Lamia of folk-lore.

36 The manuscripts give 'who lend their children to each other for feasting'.

37 See note 39.

38 We must understand 'does not constitute *restraint* or unrestraint'.

39 No such stories about Phalaris are alluded to elsewhere; so Burnet here brackets the name, supposing the subject of κατεῖχεν to be unexpressed, and taking § 2 to refer to Phalaris's well-known practice of burning human victims in a bronze bull. But that was hardly an instance of bestiality.

40 *i.e.*, inhuman vice.

41 Lack of control of the spirit': see note 25.

42 These words are surely an interpolation.

43 the man who is 'unrestrained' in the strict sense, *i.e.*, cannot restrain his desires.

44 This story is developed in Robert Browning's poem 'Halbert and Hob'; it is said also to occur in a German Volkslied.

45 The line seems to have ended Κυπρογένεος πρόπολον (Bergk), 'for the servant of the wile-weaving Cyprus-born', *i.e.*, Peitho, persuasion. It is ascribed by Wilamowitz to Sappho, and the same epithet is applied to Aphrodite in Sappho, i, 2.

46 One of the emblematic figures embroidered on the girdle of Aphrodite, *Iliad*, xiv, 217.

47 ὕβρις means any injury that is insulting to the victim, but here the writer is thinking specially of outrage prompted by lust. The argument is based on the feelings of both agent and victim. Anger, being a painful feeling, does not show wantonness or insolence, for wanton acts are pleasant to the doer. An injury done in anger

therefore arouses less anger in return, less resentment in the victim, than does wanton outrage due to unrestrained desire. Therefore it is less 'unjust', less of an injury: cf. *Rhetoric*, II, iii, 1380 a 34 (anger is not so much resented, because it does not show contempt for its victim).

48 See v, 1, and also i, 3.

49 The writer here seems to regard all animals as unnatural, in the sense of imperfectly developed, because irrational. The order precludes our taking this clause of the exceptional species (asses, wild boars, and pigs according to Greek zoology) just alluded to; moreover, as the excessive appetites of these are analogous to profligacy in men, they are not aberrations from animal nature any more than profligates are from human nature.

50 No two commentators read the same sense into this section, which is 'little more than a series of jottings' (Burnet). The version given largely follows Peters. The insertions in brackets indicate what may possibly have been in the writer's mind.

51 The relevance of this parenthesis is obscure; its meaning, in the light of other passages in Aristotle, may be that injustice is worse in the sense that it is evil *per se* (whereas the unjust man is evil *per accidens*), but the unjust man is worse in the sense that he is productive of evil.

52 III, x.

53 This addition is illogically expressed, but it is a reminder that to take too little of certain 'necessary' pleasures is as wrong as to take too much: see note 31.

54 *i.e.*, necessary things; see the tripartite classification of iv, 5.

55 Incurable, and therefore profligate, ἀκόλαστος, which means literally either 'incorrigible' or 'unchastised': see III, note 88 on p. 82.

56 Not softness strictly, which ranges with unrestraint and is not deliberate.

57 Seneca, *De ira*, ii, 2, says that Xenophantus's martial music made Alexander put out his hand to grasp his weapons (the story is told by Suidas of a Theban flute-player Timotheus, cf. Dryden, *Alexander's Feast*); apparently Alexander's music had a different effect on Xenophantus!

58 Herodotus, i, 105, says that certain Scythians who robbed the temple of Uranian Aphrodite at Askalon were smitten with the 'feminine disease', which affected their descendants ever after, but Hippocrates, Περὶ ἀέρων 22, describes effeminate symptoms prevalent among wealthy and high-born Scythians, due to being too much on horseback.

59 *i.e.*, it is not an excessive proneness to pursue pleasure, and therefore is not profligacy.

60 The variant 'can avoid being tickled by tickling the other person first' seems less likely, but either reading may be doubted. Aristotle elsewhere (*Prob.* 965 a 11) remarks that one is less sensitive to tickling if one is not taken unawares, and that is why one cannot tickle oneself.

61 vii, 2.

62 ii, 10.

63 ἐκστατικός is here used as equivalent to προπετής, 'impetuous', in vii, 8; whereas below, § 5, as in i, 6 and ii, 7, it denotes the quality with which it is here contrasted.

64 *i.e.*, the feeble sort who stop to think and yet succumb; the impulsive man is not the typical unrestrained man.

65 The argument is here resumed from §1.

66 *i.e.*, to change his conduct. The unrestrained man's belief is right already and he needs only to be induced to act up to it; whereas the profligate must be persuaded to change his belief before he will alter his conduct.

67 *cf.* VI, v, 6.

68 The context might indicate that the *definitions* are meant, which, themselves apprehended intuitively, are the starting-points of mathematical deductions. But these are ordinarily distinguished by Aristotle from *hypotheses*, which are assertions of the existence of things, not of their nature. It is therefore suggested that the term here means the *propositions* of mathematics, which are assumed as the starting-point of the analytical process by which a proof of a theorem or solution of a problem may be discovered: *cf.* III, iii, 12.

69 ii, 7.

70 *cf.* ii, 7.

71 The manuscripts, instead of 'pleasant', repeat 'noble' by a slip.

72 *cf.* III, xi, 7.

73 though he conquers them.

74 *cf.* VI, xiii, 6.

75 This parenthesis would come better before the preceding sentence.

76 *cf.* VI, xii, 9.

77 or perhaps 'in definition'.

78 *cf.* vi, 3.

79 *i.e.*, habit is.

80 II, iii, 1.

81 μακάριος from μάλα χαίρειν: *cf.* V, iv, 9.

82   Of these three views, the first is that of Speusippus, Plato's successor as head of the Academy; the second is that of Plato's *Philebus*; the third, which appears at the end of the *Philebus*, is that of Aristotle in Book X below.

83   Certain 'felt processes towards a natural state' (xi, 4), which are obviously not good, are not really pleasant either.

84   *cf.* xiv, 7.

85   *i.e.*, the pleasures arising from the exercise of other qualities.

86   *cf.* iv, 5.

87   *i.e.*, not good absolutely or in themselves, though good (in moderation) as means to life: the 'necessary' and 'neutral' pleasures of iv, 2 and 5.

88   *i.e.*, the prudent man both satisfies his natural desire for the bodily pleasures in moderation, and trains himself not to mind their absence; but does both not for the sake of pleasure, but to avoid the disturbance of pain.

89   See more fully, X, ii, 5.

90   probably the Cynics.

91   Hesiod, *Works and Days*, 763.

92   *cf.* X, ii, 4.

93   The manuscripts give 'if pleasure and activity are not good'.

94   Whereas bodily pleasure is good in moderation and bad only in excess, all pain is bad; but this does not mean that the absence of excessive pleasure is bad, for it is not painful to the good man.

95   The reference is presumably to xii, 1, but the two passages do not correspond very closely.

96   *cf.* note 49.

97   or possibly 'that the restorative pleasures imply a defective state'.

98   It is this which is really pleasant: see xii, 2.

99   *i.e.*, which stimulate the activity of any ἕξις, disposition or faculty, which is in its natural state, in contrast with those pleasures which stimulate the restoration of a faculty to its natural state.

100   Euripides, *Orestes*, 234.

BOOK EIGHT

Friendship

1. Nature and kinds of friendship

i   Introduction: friendship implies virtue; and is valuable as a means to the good life, as natural, as the bond of society, and as morally noble. Three difficulties: (1) Does attraction depend on likeness or unlikeness?
(2) Is friendship only possible between good men? (3) Is it of one kind or several?

ii   Solution of 2nd and 3rd difficulties (chapters ii–iv). Three objects of liking: the good, the pleasant, the useful. (Definition of friendship.)

iii   Three species of friendship corresponding. Friendships of utility and of pleasure. Friendship of virtue, the perfect kind.

iv   The two lower kinds of friendship less permanent; and not confined to good men (2nd difficulty).

v   The genus of friendship: it is a fixed disposition, maintained by active exercise in intercourse.

vi   Friendship and intercourse. The perfect kind of friendship rare. Friendships of pleasure nearer perfect friendship than friendships of utility.

vii   Friendships of unequals.

viii   Inequality redressed by affection. Likeness the basis of true friendship (1st difficulty of i, 6). The attraction of opposites accidental.

2. The social aspect of friendship:
its connection with justice (VIII, ix to X, iii)

ix   Friendship accompanying all social relations.

x   Analogy of private and political relationships. Classification of constitutions. The analogous family relationships.

xi   Corresponding analogy of accompanying affection.

xii   Kinsmen and comrades. Parental and filial affection. Fraternal

i Our next business after this will be to discuss friendship.[1] For friendship is a virtue,[2] or involves virtue; and also it is one of the most indispensable requirements of life. For no one would choose to live without friends, but possessing all other good things. In fact rich men, rulers and potentates are thought especially to require friends, since what would be the good of their prosperity without an outlet for beneficence, which is displayed in its fullest and most praiseworthy form towards friends? and how could such prosperity be safeguarded and preserved without friends? for the greater it is, the greater is its

2 insecurity. And in poverty or any other misfortune men think friends are their only resource. Friends are an aid to the young, to guard them from error; to the elderly, to tend them, and to supplement their failing powers of action; to those in the prime of life, to assist them in noble deeds –

When twain together go –[3]

3 for two are better able both to plan and to execute. And the affection of parent for offspring and of offspring for parent seems to be a natural instinct, not only in man but also in birds and in most animals; as also is friendship between members of the same species; and this is especially strong in the human race; for which reason we praise those who love their fellow men.[4] Even when travelling abroad one can observe that a natural affinity and

4 friendship exist between man and man universally. Moreover, friendship appears to be the bond of the state; and lawgivers seem to set more store by it than they do by justice, for to promote concord, which seems akin to friendship, is their chief aim, while faction, which is enmity, is what they are most anxious to banish. And if men are friends, there is no need of justice between them; whereas merely to be just is not enough – a feeling of friendship also is necessary. Indeed the highest form of justice seems to have an element of friendly feeling in it.[5]

5 And friendship is not only indispensable as a means, it is also

noble in itself. We praise those who love their friends, and it is counted a noble thing to have many friends; and some people think that a true friend must be a good man.

6   But there is much difference of opinion as to the nature of friendship. Some define it as a matter of similarity; they say that we love those who are like ourselves: whence the proverbs 'Like finds his like', 'Birds of a feather flock together',[6] and so on. Others on the contrary say that with men who are alike it is always a case of 'two of a trade'.[7] Some try to find a more profound and scientific explanation of the nature of affection. Euripides[8] writes that 'Earth yearneth for the rain' when dried up, 'And the majestic heaven when filled with rain yearneth to fall to earth.' Heraclitus says, 'Opposition unites', and 'The fairest harmony springs from difference', and ' 'Tis strife that makes the world go on'. Others maintain the opposite view, notably Empedocles, who declares that 'Like seeks after like'.

7   Dismissing then these scientific speculations as not germane to our present enquiry, let us investigate the human aspect of the matter, and examine the questions that relate to man's character and emotions: for instance, whether all men are capable of friendship, or bad men cannot be friends; and whether there is only one sort of friendship or several. Those who hold that all friendship is of the same kind because friendship admits of degree, are relying on an insufficient proof, for things of different kinds also can differ in degree. But this has been discussed before.[9]

ii   Perhaps the answer to these questions will appear if we ascertain what sort of things arouse liking or love. It seems that not everything is loved, but only what is lovable, and that this is either what is good, or pleasant, or useful. But useful may be taken to mean productive of some good or of pleasure, so that the class of things lovable as ends is reduced to the good and the

2   pleasant. Then, do men like what is really good, or what is good for them? for sometimes the two may be at variance; and the same with what is pleasant. Now it appears that each person loves what is good for himself, and that while what is really good is lovable absolutely, what is good for a particular person is lovable for that person. Further, each person loves not what is really good for himself, but what appears to him to be so; however, this

will not affect our argument, for 'lovable' will mean 'what appears lovable'.

3   There being then three motives of love, the term friendship is not applied to love for inanimate objects, since here there is no return of affection, and also no wish for the good of the object – for instance, it would be ridiculous to wish well to a bottle of wine: at the most one wishes that it may keep well in order that one may have it oneself; whereas we are told that we ought to wish our friend well for his own sake. But persons who wish another good for his own sake, if the feeling is not reciprocated, are merely said to feel goodwill for him: only when mutual is

4   such goodwill termed friendship. And perhaps we should also add the qualification that the feeling of goodwill must be known to its object. For a man often feels goodwill towards persons whom he has never seen, but whom he believes to be good or useful, and one of these persons may also entertain the same feeling towards him. Here then we have a case of two people mutually well-disposed, whom nevertheless we cannot speak of as friends, because they are not aware of each other's regard. To be friends therefore, men must (1) feel goodwill for each other, that, is, wish each other's good, and (2) be aware of each other's goodwill, and (3) the cause of their goodwill must be one of the lovable qualities mentioned above.

iii   Now these qualities differ in kind; hence the affection or friendship they occasion may differ in kind also. There are accordingly three kinds of friendship, corresponding in number to the three lovable qualities; since a reciprocal affection, known to either party, can be based on each of the three, and when men love each other, they wish each other well in respect of the quality which is the ground of their friendship.[10] Thus friends whose affection is based on utility do not love each other in themselves, but in so far as some benefit accrues to them from each other. And similarly with those whose friendship is based on pleasure: for instance, we enjoy the society of witty people not because of what they are in themselves, but because they are

2   agreeable to us. Hence in a friendship based on utility or on pleasure men love their friend for their own good or their own pleasure, and not as being the person loved, but as useful or agreeable. And therefore these friendships are based on an

accident, since the friend is not loved for being what he is, but as affording some benefit or pleasure as the case may be.

3 Consequently friendships of this kind are easily broken off, in the event of the parties themselves changing, for if no longer pleasant or useful to each other, they cease to love each other. And utility is not a permanent quality; it differs at different times. Hence when the motive of the friendship has passed away, the friendship itself is dissolved, having existed merely as a means to that end.

4 Friendships of utility seem to occur most frequently between the old, as in old age men do not pursue pleasure but profit; and between those persons in the prime of life and young people whose object in life is gain. Friends of this kind do not indeed frequent each other's company much, for in some cases they are not even pleasing to each other, and therefore have no use for friendly intercourse unless they are mutually profitable; since their pleasure in each other goes no further than their expectations of advantage.

With these friendships are classed family ties of hospitality with foreigners.

5 With the young on the other hand the motive of friendship appears to be pleasure, since the young guide their lives by emotion, and for the most part pursue what is pleasant to themselves, and the object of the moment. And the things that please them change as their age alters; hence they both form friendships and drop them quickly, since their affections alter with what gives them pleasure, and the tastes of youth change quickly. Also the young are prone to fall in love, as love is chiefly guided by emotion, and grounded on pleasure; hence they form attachments quickly and give them up quickly, often changing before the day is out.

The young do desire to pass their time in their friend's company, for that is how they get the enjoyment of their friendship.

6 The perfect form of friendship is that between the good, and those who resemble each other in virtue. For these friends wish each alike the other's good in respect of their goodness,[11] and they are good in themselves; but it is those who wish the good of their friends for their friends' sake who are friends in the fullest

sense, since they love each other for themselves and not accidentally.[12] Hence the friendship of these lasts as long as they continue to be good; and virtue is a permanent quality. And each is good relatively to his friend as well as absolutely, since the good are both good absolutely and profitable to each other. And each is pleasant in both ways also, since good men are pleasant both absolutely and to each other; for everyone is pleased by his own actions, and therefore by actions that resemble his own, and the

7   actions of all good men are the same or similar. Such friendship is naturally permanent, since it combines in itself all the attributes that friends ought to possess. All affection is based on good or on pleasure, either absolute or relative to the person who feels it, and is prompted by similarity[13] of some sort; but this friendship possesses all these attributes in the friends themselves, for they are alike, *et cetera*,[14] in that way.[15] Also the absolutely good is pleasant absolutely as well; but the absolutely good and pleasant are the chief objects of affection; therefore it is between good men that affection and friendship exist in their fullest and best form.

8   Such friendships are of course rare, because such men are few. Moreover they require time and intimacy: as the saying goes, you cannot get to know a man till you have consumed the proverbial amount of salt[16] in his company; and so you cannot admit him to friendship or really be friends, before each has shown the other that he is worthy of friendship and has won his

9   confidence. People who enter into friendly relations quickly have the wish to be friends, but cannot really be friends without being worthy of friendship, and also knowing each other to be so; the wish to be friends is a quick growth, but friendship is not.

iv   This form of friendship is perfect both in point of duration and of the other attributes[17] of friendship; and in all respects either party receives from the other the same or similar benefits, as it is proper that friends should do.

Friendship based on pleasure has a similarity to friendship based on virtue, for good men are pleasant to one another; and the same is true of friendship based on utility, for good men are useful to each other. In these cases also the friendship is most lasting when each friend derives the same benefit, for instance pleasure, from the other, and not only so, but derives it from the same thing, as in a friendship between two witty people, and not

as in one between a lover and his beloved. These do not find
their pleasure in the same things: the lover's pleasure is in gazing
at his beloved, the loved one's pleasure is in receiving the
attentions of the lover; and when the loved one's beauty fades,
the friendship sometimes fades too, as the lover no longer finds
pleasure in the sight of his beloved, and the loved one no longer
receives the attentions of the lover; though on the other hand
many do remain friends if as a result of their intimacy they have
come to love each other's characters, both being alike in
2 character. But when a pair of lovers exchange not pleasure for
pleasure but pleasure for gain, the friendship is less intense and
less lasting.

A friendship based on utility dissolves as soon as its profit
ceases; for the friends did not love each other, but what they got
out of each other.

Friendships therefore based on pleasure and on utility can exist
between two bad men, between one bad man and one good, and
between a man neither good nor bad and another either good,
bad, or neither. But clearly only good men can be friends for
what they are in themselves; since bad men do not take pleasure
in each other, save as they get some advantage from each other.

3 Also friendship between good men alone is proof against
calumny; for a man is slow to believe anybody's word about a
friend whom he has himself tried and tested for many years, and
with them there is the mutual confidence, the incapacity ever to
do each other wrong, and all the other characteristics that are
required in true friendship. Whereas the other forms of friendship are liable to be dissolved by calumny and suspicion.

4 But since people do apply the term 'friends' to persons whose
regard for each other is based on utility, just as states can be
'friends' (since expediency is generally recognised as the motive
of international alliances), or on pleasure, as children make
friends, perhaps we too must call such relationships friendships;
but then we must say that there are several sorts of friendship,
that between good men, as good, being friendship in the primary
and proper meaning of the term, while the other kinds are
friendships in an analogical sense,[18] since such friends are friends
in virtue of a sort of goodness and of likeness[19] in them:
5 insomuch as pleasure is good in the eyes of pleasure-lovers. But

these two secondary forms of friendship are not very likely to coincide: men do not make friends with each other both for utility and for pleasure at the same time, since accidental qualities are rarely found in combination.

6　Friendship then being divided into these species, inferior people will make friends for pleasure or for use, if they are alike in that respect,[20] while good men will be friends for each other's own sake, since they are alike in being good.[21] The latter therefore are friends in an absolute sense, the former accidentally, and through their similarity to the latter.

V　It is with friendship as it is with the virtues; men are called good in two senses, either as having a virtuous disposition or as realising virtue in action, and similarly friends when in each other's company derive pleasure from and confer benefits on each other, whereas friends who are asleep or parted are not actively friendly, yet have the disposition to be so. For separation does not destroy friendship absolutely, though it prevents its active exercise. If however the absence be prolonged, it seems to cause the friendly feeling itself to be forgotten: hence the poet's remark[22]

> Full many a man finds friendship end
> For lack of converse with his friend.

2　The old and the morose do not appear to be much given to friendship, for their capacity to please is small, and nobody can pass his days in the company of one who is distasteful to him, or not pleasing, since it seems to be one of the strongest instincts of nature to shun what is painful and seek what is pleasant. And
3　when persons approve of each other without seeking such other's society, this seems to be goodwill rather than friendship. Nothing is more characteristic of friends than that they seek each other's society: poor men desire their friends' assistance, and even the most prosperous wish for their companionship (indeed they are the last people to adopt the life of a recluse), but it is impossible for men to spend their time together unless they give each other pleasure, or have common tastes. The latter seems to be the bond between the members of a comradeship.[23]
4　Friendship between good men then is the truest friendship, as has been said several times before. For it is agreed that what is

good and pleasant absolutely is lovable and desirable strictly, while what is good and pleasant for a particular person is lovable and desirable relatively to that person; but the friendship of good men for each other rests on both these grounds.[24]

5   Liking[25] seems to be an emotion, friendship a fixed disposition, for liking can be felt even for inanimate things, but reciprocal liking[26] involves deliberate choice, and this springs from a fixed disposition. Also, when men wish the good of those they love for their own sakes, their goodwill does not depend on emotion but on a fixed disposition. And in loving their friend they love their own good, for the good man in becoming dear to another becomes that other's good. Each party therefore both loves his own good and also makes an equivalent return by wishing the other's good, and by affording him pleasure; for there is a saying, 'Amity is equality', and this is most fully realised in the friendships of the good.

vi   Morose and elderly people rarely make friends, as they are inclined to be surly, and do not take much pleasure in society; good temper and sociability appear to be the chief constituents or causes of friendship. Hence the young make friends quickly, but the old do not, since they do not make friends with people if they do not enjoy their company; and the same applies to persons of a morose temper. It is true that the old or morose may feel goodwill for each other, since they may wish each other well and help each other in case of need; but they cannot properly be called friends, as they do not seek each other's society nor enjoy it, and these are thought to be the chief marks of friendship.

2   It is not possible to have many friends in the full meaning of the word friendship, any more than it is to be in love with many people at once (love indeed seems to be an excessive state of emotion, such as is naturally felt towards one person only); and it is not easy for the same person to like a number of people at once, nor indeed perhaps can good men be found in large

3   numbers. Also for perfect friendship you must get to know a man thoroughly, and become intimate with him, which is a very difficult thing to do. But it is possible to like a number of persons for their utility and pleasantness, for useful and pleasant people are plentiful, and the benefits they confer can be enjoyed at once.

4   Of these two inferior kinds of friendship, the one that more

closely resembles true friendship is that based on pleasure, in which the same benefit is conferred by both parties, and they enjoy each other's company, or have common tastes; as is the case with the friendships of young people. For in these there is more generosity of feeling, whereas the friendship of utility is a thing for sordid souls. Also those blessed with great prosperity have no need of useful friends, but do need pleasant ones, since they desire some society; and though they may put up with what is unpleasant for a short time, no one would stand it continually: you could not endure even the absolute good itself for ever, if it bored you; and therefore the rich seek for friends who will be pleasant. No doubt they ought to require them to be good as well as pleasant, and also good for them, since then they would

5 possess all the proper qualifications for friendship. But princes and rulers appear to keep their friends in separate compartments: they have some that are useful, and some that are pleasant, but rarely any that are both at once. For they do not seek for friends who are pleasant because they are good, or are useful for noble purposes, but look for witty people when they desire pleasure, and for the other sort seek men who are clever at executing their commissions; and these two qualities are rarely found in the same

6 person. The good man, as we have said, is both useful and pleasant, but the good man does not become the friend of a superior, unless his superior in rank be also his superior in virtue; otherwise the good man as the inferior party cannot make matters proportionally equal.[27] But potentates of such superior excellence are scarcely common.

7 But to resume: the forms of friendship of which we have spoken are friendships of equality, for both parties render the same benefit and wish the same good to each other, or else exchange[28] two different benefits, for instance pleasure and profit. (These[29] are less truly friendships, and less permanent, as we have said; and opinions differ as to whether they are really friendships at all, owing to their being both like and unlike the same thing. In view of their likeness to friendship based on virtue they do appear to be friendships, for the one contains pleasure and the other utility, and these are attributes of that form of friendship too; but in that friendship based on virtue is proof against calumny, and permanent, while the others quickly

change, besides differing in many other respects, they appear not
to be real friendships, owing to their unlikeness to it.)

vii But there is a different kind of friendship, which involves
superiority of one party over the other, for example, the
friendship between father and son, and generally between an
older person and a younger, and that between husband and wife,
and between any ruler and the persons ruled. These friendships
also vary among themselves. The friendship between parents and
children is not the same as that between ruler and ruled, nor
indeed is the friendship of father for son the same as that of son
for father, nor that of husband for wife as that of wife for
husband; for each of these persons has a different excellence and
function, and also different motives for their regard, and so the
2 affection and friendship they feel are different. Now in these
unequal friendships the benefits that one party receives and is
entitled to claim from the other are not the same[30] on either side;
but the friendship between parents and children will be enduring
and equitable, when the children render to the parents the
services due to the authors of one's being, and the parents to the
children those due to one's offspring. The affection rendered in
these various unequal friendships should also be proportionate:[31]
the better of the two parties, for instance, or the more useful or
otherwise superior as the case may be, should receive more
affection than he bestows; since when the affection rendered is
proportionate to desert, this produces equality in a sense between
the parties, and equality is felt to be an essential element of
friendship.

3 Equality in friendship, however, does not seem to be like
equality in matters of justice. In the sphere of justice, 'equal' (fair)
means primarily proportionate to desert, and 'equal in quantity' is
only a secondary sense; whereas in friendship 'equal in quantity'
4 is the primary meaning, and 'proportionate to desert' only
secondary. This is clearly seen when a wide disparity arises
between two friends in point of virtue or vice, or of wealth, or
anything else; they no longer remain nor indeed expect to
remain friends. This is most manifest in the case of the gods,
whose superiority in every good attribute is pre-eminent; but it is
also seen with princes: in their case also men much below them
in station do not expect to be their friends, nor do persons of no

particular merit expect to be the friends of men of distinguished
5 excellence or wisdom. It is true that we cannot fix a precise limit
in such cases, up to which two men can still be friends; the gap
may go on widening and the friendship still remain;[32] but when
one becomes very remote from the other, as God is remote from
6 man, it can continue no longer. This gives rise to the question, is
it not after all untrue that we wish our friends the greatest of
goods? for instance, can we wish them to become gods? for then
they will lose us as friends, and therefore lose certain goods, for
friends are goods.[33] If then it was rightly said above[34] that a true
friend wishes his friend's good for that friend's own sake, the
friend would have to remain himself, whatever that may be; so
that he will really wish him only the greatest goods compatible
with his remaining a human being. And perhaps not all of these,
for everybody wishes good things for himself most of all.

viii   Most men however, because they love honour, seem to be
more desirous of receiving than of bestowing affection. Hence
most men like flattery, for a flatterer is a friend who is your
inferior,[35] or pretends to be so, and to love you more than you
love him; but to be loved is felt to be nearly the same as to be
2 honoured, which most people covet. They do not however
appear to value honour for its own sake, but for something
incidental to it. Most people like receiving honour from men of
high station, because they hope for something from them: they
think that if they want something, the great man will be able to
give it them; so they enjoy being honoured by him as a token of
benefits to come. Those on the other hand who covet being
honoured by good men, and by persons who know them, do so
from a desire to confirm their own opinion of themselves; so[36]
these like honour because they are assured of their worth by their
confidence in the judgement of those who assert it. Affection on
the other hand men like for its own sake; from which we infer
that it is more valuable than honour, and that friendship is
desirable in itself.
3   But in its essence friendship seems to consist more in giving
than in receiving affection: witness the pleasure that mothers take
in loving their children. Some mothers put their infants out to
nurse, and though knowing and loving them, do not ask to be
loved by them in return, if it be impossible to have this as well,

but are content if they see them prospering; they retain their own love for them even though the children, not knowing them, 4 cannot render them any part of what is due to a mother. As then friendship consists more especially in bestowing affection, and as we praise men for loving their friends, affection seems to be the mark of a good friend. Hence it is friends that love each other as each deserves who continue friends and whose friendship is lasting.

5 Also it is by rendering affection in proportion to desert that friends who are not equals may approach most nearly to true friendship, since this will make them equal. Amity consists in equality and similarity, especially the similarity of those who are alike in virtue; for being true to themselves, these also remain true to one another, and neither request nor render services that are morally degrading. Indeed they may be said actually to restrain each other from evil: since good men neither err themselves nor permit their friends to err. Bad men on the other hand have no constancy in friendship, for they do not even remain true to their own characters; but they can be friends for a short time, while they take pleasure in each other's wickedness.

6 The friendships of useful and pleasant people last longer, in fact as long as they give each other pleasure or benefit. It is friendship based on utility that seems most frequently to spring from opposites, for instance a friendship between a poor man and a rich one, or between an ignorant man and a learned; for a person desiring something which he happens to lack will give something else in return for it. One may bring under this class the friendship between a lover and the object of his affections, or between a plain person and a handsome one. This is why lovers sometimes appear ridiculous when they claim that their love should be equally reciprocated; no doubt if they are equally lovable this is a reasonable demand, but it is ridiculous if they have nothing attractive about them.

7 But perhaps there is no real attraction between opposites as such, but only accidentally, and what they actually desire is the mean between them (since this is the good); the dry for instance striving not to become wet, but to reach an intermediate state, and so with the hot, and everything else. Let us however dismiss this question, as being indeed somewhat foreign to our subject.

ix   The objects and the personal relationships with which friendship is concerned appear, as was said at the outset,[37] to be the
same as those which are the sphere of justice. For in every
partnership we find mutual rights of some sort, and also friendly
feeling: one notes that shipmates and fellow-soldiers speak of
each other as 'my friend', and so in fact do the partners in any
joint undertaking. But their friendship is limited to the extent of
their association in their common business, for so also are their
mutual rights as associates. Again, the proverb says 'Friends'
goods are common property', and this is correct, since
2 community is the essence of friendship. Brothers have all things
in common, and so do members of a comradeship;[38] other
friends hold special possessions in common, more or fewer in
different cases, inasmuch as friendships vary in degree. The claims
of justice also differ in different relationships. The mutual rights
of parents and children are not the same as those between
brothers; the obligations of members of a comradeship not the
same as those of fellow-citizens; and similarly with the other
3 forms of friendship. Injustice therefore also is differently constituted in each of these relationships: wrong is increasingly serious
in proportion as it is done to a nearer friend. For example, it is
more shocking to defraud a comrade of money than a fellow-
citizen; or to refuse aid to a brother than to do so to a stranger; or
to strike one's father than to strike anybody else. Similarly it is
natural that the claims of justice also should increase with the
nearness of the friendship, since friendship and justice exist
between the same persons and are co-extensive in range.
4   But all associations are parts as it were of the association of the
state. Travellers for instance associate together for some advantage, namely to procure some of their necessary supplies. But the
political association too, it is believed, was originally formed, and
continues to be maintained, for the advantage of its members: the
aim of lawgivers is the good of the community, and justice is
sometimes defined as that which is to the common advantage.
5 Thus the other associations aim at some particular advantage; for
example sailors combine to seek the profits of seafaring in the
way of trade or the like, comrades in arms the gains of warfare,
their aim being either plunder, or victory over the enemy or the
capture of a city;[39] and similarly the members of a tribe or parish

[And[40] some associations appear to be formed for the sake of pleasure, for example religious guilds and dining-clubs, which are unions for sacrifice and social intercourse. But all these associations seem to be subordinate to the association of the state, which aims not at a temporary advantage but at one covering the whole of life.] combine to perform sacrifices and hold festivals in connection with them, thereby both paying honour to the gods and providing pleasant holidays for themselves. For it may be noticed that the sacrifices and festivals of ancient origin take place after harvest, being in fact harvest-festivals; this is because that was

6 the season of the year at which people had most leisure. All these associations then appear to be parts of the association of the state; and the limited friendships which we reviewed will correspond to the limited associations from which they spring.

X   Now there are three forms of constitution, and also an equal number of perversions or corruptions of those forms. The constitutions are kingship, aristocracy, and thirdly, a constitution based on a property classification, which it seems appropriate to describe as timocratic, although most people are accustomed to speak of it merely as a constitutional government or republic.

2 The best of these constitutions is kingship, and the worst timocracy. The perversion of kingship is tyranny. Both are monarchies, but there is a very wide difference between them: a tyrant studies his own advantage, a king that of his subjects. For a monarch is not a king[41] if he does not possess independent resources, and is not better supplied with goods of every kind than his subjects; but a ruler so situated lacks nothing, and therefore will not study his own interests but those of his subjects. (A king who is not independent of his subjects will be merely a sort of titular king.[42]) Tyranny is the exact opposite in this respect, for the tyrant pursues his own good. The inferiority of tyranny among the perversions is more evident than that of timocracy among the constitutions, for the opposite of the best must be the worst.

3   When a change of constitution takes place, kingship passes into tyranny, because tyranny is the bad form of monarchy, so that a bad king becomes a tyrant. Aristocracy passes into oligarchy owing to badness in the rulers, who do not distribute what the state has to offer according to desert, but give all or most of its

benefits to themselves, and always assign the offices to the same persons, because they set supreme value upon riches; thus power is in the hands of a few bad men, instead of being in the hands of the best men. Timocracy passes into democracy, there being an affinity between them, inasmuch as the ideal of timocracy also is government by the mass of the citizens, and within the property qualification all are equal. Democracy is the least bad of the perversions, for it is only a very small deviation from the constitutional form of government.[43] These are the commonest ways in which revolutions occur in states, since they involve the smallest change, and come about most easily.

4   One may find likenesses and so to speak models of these various forms of constitution in the household. The relationship of father to sons is regal in type, since a father's first care is for his children's welfare. This is why Homer styles Zeus 'father', for the ideal of kingship is paternal government. Among the Persians paternal rule is tyrannical, for the Persians use their sons as slaves. The relation of master to slaves is also tyrannic, since in it the master's interest is aimed at. The autocracy of a master appears to be right, that of the Persian father wrong; for different subjects
5   should be under different forms of rule. The relation of husband to wife seems to be in the nature of an aristocracy: the husband rules in virtue of fitness, and in matters that belong to a man's sphere; matters suited to a woman he hands over to his wife. When the husband controls everything, he transforms the relationship into an oligarchy, for he governs in violation of fitness, and not in virtue of superiority. And sometimes when the wife is an heiress it is she who rules. In these cases then authority goes not by virtue but by wealth and power, as in an oligarchy.
6   The relation between brothers constitutes a sort of timocracy; they are equals, save in so far as they differ in age; hence, if the divergence in age be great, the friendship between them cannot be of the fraternal type. Democracy appears most fully in households without a master, for in them all the members are equal; but it also prevails where the ruler of the house is weak, and everyone is allowed to do what he likes.

xi   Under each of these forms of government we find friendship existing between ruler and ruled, to the same extent as justice. The friendship of a king for his subjects is one of superiority in beneficence; for a king does good to his subjects, inasmuch as being good he studies to promote their welfare, as a shepherd studies the welfare of his sheep; hence Homer called Agamemnon

2 'shepherd of the people'. The friendship of a father for his child is of the same kind (only here the benefits bestowed are greater, for the father is the source of the child's existence, which seems to be the greatest of all boons, and of its nurture and education; and we also ascribe the same benefits to our forefathers). For it is as natural for a father to rule his children, and forefathers those

3 descended from them, as for a king to rule his subjects. These friendships then involve a superiority of benefits on one side, which is why parents receive honour as well as service.[44] The claims of justice also, therefore, in these relations are not the same on both sides, but proportionate to desert, as is the affection bestowed.

4 The friendship between husband and wife again is the same as that which prevails between rulers and subjects in an aristocracy; for it is in proportion to excellence, and the better party receives the larger share [of good],[45] whilst each party receives what is appropriate to each; and the same is true of the claims of justice on either side.

5 Friendship between brothers is like that between members of a comradeship: the two parties are equal in station and age, and this usually implies identity of feelings and of character. The counterpart of fraternal friendship is that which exists under the timocratic form of constitution; since the ideal of timocracy is that all citizens shall be equal and shall be good, so that they all rule in turn, and all have an equal share of power; and therefore the friendship between them is also one of equality.

6 Under the perverted forms of constitution friendship like justice can have but little scope, and least of all in the worst: there is little or no friendship between ruler and subjects in a tyranny. For where there is nothing in common between ruler and ruled, there can be no friendship between them either, any more than there can be justice. It is like the relation between a craftsman and his tool, or between the soul and the body [or between master and slave][46]: all these instruments it is true are benefited by the persons who use them, but there can be no friendship, nor justice, towards inanimate things; indeed not even towards a

horse or an ox, nor yet towards a slave as slave. For master and slave have nothing in common: a slave is a living tool, just as a
7 tool is an inanimate slave. Therefore there can be no friendship with a slave as slave, though there can be as human being: for there seems to be some room for justice in the relations of every human being with every other that is capable of participating in law and contract, and hence friendship also is possible with
8 everyone so far as he is a human being. Hence even in tyrannies there is but little scope for friendship and justice between ruler and subjects; but there is most room for them in democracies, where the citizens being equal have many things in common.

xii   All friendship, as we have said,[47] involves community; but the friendship between relatives and between members of a comradeship may be set apart as being less in the nature of partnerships than are the friendships between fellow-citizens, fellow-tribesmen, shipmates, and the like; since these seem to be founded as it were on a definite compact. With the latter friendships may be classed family ties of hospitality between foreigners.

2   Friendship between relatives itself seems to include a variety of species, but all appear to derive from the affection of parent for child. For parents love their children as part of themselves, whereas children love their parents as the source of their being. Also parents know their offspring with more certainty than children know their parentage; and progenitor is more attached to progeny than progeny to progenitor, since that which springs from a thing belongs to the thing from which it springs – for instance, a tooth or hair or what not to its owner – whereas the thing it springs from does not belong to it at all, or only in a less degree. The affection of the parent exceeds that of the child in duration also; parents love their children as soon as they are born, children their parents only when time has elapsed and they have
3 acquired understanding,[48] or at least perception. These considerations[49] also explain why parental affection is stronger in the mother. Parents then love their children as themselves (one's offspring being as it were another self – other because separate);[50] children love their parents as the source of their being; brothers love each other as being from the same source, since the identity of their relations to that source identifies them with one another,

which is why we speak of 'being of the same blood' or 'of the same stock' or the like; brothers are therefore in a manner the 4 same being, though embodied in separate persons. But friendship between brothers is also greatly fostered by their common upbringing and similarity of age; 'two of an age agree',[51] and 'familiarity breeds fellowship', which is why the friendship between brothers resembles that between members of a comradeship. Cousins and other relatives derive their attachment from the fraternal relationship, since it is due to their descent from the same ancestor; and their sense of attachment is greater or less, according as the common ancestor is nearer or more remote.

5   The affection of children for their parents, like that of men for the gods, is the affection for what is good, and superior to oneself; for their parents have bestowed on them the greatest benefits in being the cause of their existence and rearing, and later of their 6 education. Also the friendship between parents and children affords a greater degree both of pleasure and of utility than that between persons unrelated to each other, inasmuch as they have more in common in their lives.

Friendship between brothers has the same characteristics as that between members of a comradeship, and has them in a greater degree, provided they are virtuous, or resemble one another in any way;[52] inasmuch as brothers belong more closely to each other, and have loved each other from birth, and inasmuch as children of the same parents, who have been brought up together and educated alike, are more alike in character; also with brothers 7 the test of time has been longest and most reliable. The degrees of friendship between other relatives vary correspondingly.[53]

The friendship between husband and wife appears to be a natural instinct; since man is by nature a pairing creature even more than he is a political creature,[54] inasmuch as the family is an earlier and more fundamental institution than the state, and the procreation of offspring a more general[55] characteristic of the animal creation. So whereas with the other animals the association of the sexes aims only at continuing the species, human beings cohabit not only for the sake of begetting children but also to provide the needs of life; for with the human race division of labour begins at the outset, and man and woman have different functions; thus they supply each other's wants, putting their special capacities into the common stock. Hence the friendship of man and wife seems to be one of utility and pleasure combined. But it may also be based on virtue, if the partners be of high moral character; for either sex has its special virtue, and this may be the ground of attraction. Children, too, seem to be a bond of union, and therefore childless marriages are more easily dissolved; for children are a good possessed by both parents in common, and common property holds people together.

8 The question what rules of conduct should govern the relations between husband and wife, and generally between friend and friend, seems to be ultimately a question of justice. There are different claims of justice between friends and strangers, between members of a comradeship and schoolfellows.

xiii There are then, as we said at the outset, three kinds of friendship, and in each kind there are both friends who are on an equal footing and friends on a footing of disparity; for two equally good men may be friends, or one better man and one worse; and similarly with pleasant friends and with those who are friends for the sake of utility, who may be equal or may differ in the amount of the benefits[56] which they confer. Those who are equals must make matters equal by loving each other, etc.,[57] equally; those who are unequal by making a return[58] proportionate to the superiority of whatever kind on the one side.

2 Complaints and recriminations occur solely or chiefly in friendships of utility, as is to be expected. In a friendship based on virtue each party is eager to benefit the other, for this is characteristic of virtue and of friendship; and as they vie with each other in giving and not in getting benefit, no complaints nor quarrels can arise, since nobody is angry with one who loves him and benefits him, but on the contrary, if a person of good feeling, requites him with service in return; and the one who outdoes the other in beneficence will not have any complaint against his friend, since he gets what he desires, and what each 3 man desires is the good.[59] Nor again are complaints likely to occur between friends whose motive is pleasure either; for if they enjoy each other's company, both alike get what they wish for; and indeed it would seem ridiculous to find fault with somebody for not being agreeable to you, when you need not associate with 4 him if you do not want to do so. But a friendship whose motive

is utility is liable to give rise to complaints. For here the friends associate with each other for profit, and so each always wants more, and thinks he is getting less than his due; and they make it a grievance that they do not get as much as they want and deserve; and the one who is doing a service can never supply all that the one receiving it wants.

5   It appears that, as justice is of two kinds, one unwritten and the other defined by law, so the friendship based on utility may be either moral[60] or legal. Hence occasions for complaint chiefly occur when the type of friendship in view at the conclusion of the transaction is not the same as when the relationship was

6 formed. Such a connection when on stated terms is one of the legal type, whether it be a purely business matter of exchange on the spot, or a more liberal accommodation for future repayment,[61] though still with an agreement as to the *quid pro quo;* and in the latter case the obligation is clear and cannot cause dispute, though there is an element of friendliness in the delay allowed, for which reason in some states there is no action at law in these cases, it being held that the party to a contract involving credit must abide

7 by the consequences. The moral type on the other hand is not based on stated terms, but the gift or other service is given as to a friend, although the giver expects to receive an equivalent or greater return, as though it had not been a free gift but a loan; and as he ends the relationship in a different spirit from that in

8 which he began it, he will complain.[62] The reason of this is that all men, or most men, wish what is noble but choose what is profitable; and while it is noble to render a service not with an eye to receiving one in return, it is profitable to receive one. One

9 ought therefore, if one can, to return the equivalent of services received, and to do so willingly; for one ought not to make a man one's friend if one is unwilling to return his favours. Recognising therefore that one has made a mistake at the beginning and accepted a service from a wrong person – that is, a person who was not a friend, and was not acting disinterestedly[63] – one should accordingly end the transaction as if one had accepted the service on stated terms. Also, one would agree[64] to repay a service if able to do so (and if one were not able, the giver on his side too would not have expected repayment); hence, if possible, one ought to make a return. But one ought to consider at the

beginning from whom one is receiving the service, and on what terms, so that one may accept it on those terms or else decline it.

10   Dispute may arise however as to the value of the service rendered. Is it to be measured by the benefit to the recipient, and the return made on that basis, or by the cost to the doer? The recipient will say that what he received was only a trifle to his benefactor, or that he could have got it from someone else: he beats down the value. The other on the contrary will protest that it was the most valuable thing he had to give, or that it could not have been obtained from anybody else, or that it was bestowed at
11   a time of danger or in some similar emergency. Perhaps then we may say that, when the friendship is one of utility, the measure of the service should be its value to the recipient, since it is he who wants it, and the other comes to his aid in the expectation of an equivalent return; therefore the degree of assistance rendered has been the amount to which the recipient has benefited, and so he ought to pay back as much as he has got out of it; or even more, for that will be more noble.

In friendships based on virtue, complaints do not arise, but the measure of the benefit seems to be the intention[65] of the giver; for intention is the predominant factor in virtue and in character.

xiv   Differences also arise in friendships where there is disparity between the parties. Each claims to get more than the other, and this inevitably leads to a rupture. If one is a better man than the other, he thinks he has a right to more, for goodness deserves the larger share. And similarly when one is more useful than the other: if a man is of no use, they say, he ought not to have an equal share, for it becomes a charity and not a friendship at all, if what one gets out of it is not enough to repay one's trouble. For men think that it ought to be in a friendship as it is in a business partnership, where those who contribute more capital take more of the profits. On the other hand the needy or inferior person takes the opposite view: he maintains that it is the part of a good friend to assist those in need; what is the use (he argues) of being friends with the good and great if one is to get nothing out of it?

2   Now it appears that each of these rival claims is right. Both parties should receive a larger share from the friendship, but not a larger share of the same thing: the superior should receive the

larger share of honour, the needy one the larger share of profit; for honour is the due reward of virtue and beneficence, while need obtains the aid it requires in pecuniary gain.

3   The same principle is seen to obtain in public life.[66] A citizen who contributes nothing of value to the common stock is not held in honour, for the common property is given to those who benefit the community, and honour is a part of the common property. For a man cannot expect to make money out of the community and to receive honour as well. For[67] nobody is content to have the smaller share all round, and so we pay honour to the man who suffers money loss by holding office, and give money to the one who takes bribes; since requital in accordance with desert restores equality, and is the preservative of friendship,[68] as has been said above.

       This principle therefore should also regulate the intercourse of friends who are unequal: the one who is benefited in purse or
4   character must repay what he can, namely honour. For friendship exacts what is possible, not what is due; requital in accordance with desert is in fact sometimes impossible, for instance in honouring the gods, or one's parents: no one could ever render them the honour they deserve, and a man is deemed virtuous if he pays them all the regard that he can. Hence it would appear that a son never ought to disown his father, although a father may disown his son; for a debtor ought to pay what he owes, but nothing that a son can do comes up to the benefits he has received, so that a son is always in his father's debt. But a creditor may discharge his debtor, and therefore a father may disown his son. At the same time, no doubt it is unlikely that a father ever would abandon a son unless the son were excessively vicious; for natural affection apart, it is not in human nature to reject the assistance that a son will be able to render. Whereas a bad son will look on the duty of supporting his father as one to be avoided, or at all events not eagerly undertaken; for most people wish to receive benefits, but avoid bestowing them as unprofitable. So much then for a discussion of these subjects.

1 φιλία, 'friendship', sometimes rises to the meaning of affection or love, but also includes any sort of kindly feeling, even that existing between business associates, or fellow-citizens. The corresponding verb means both 'to like' and 'to love'; the adjective is generally passive, 'loved', 'liked', 'dear', but sometimes active: 'loving', 'liking', and so on, as a noun 'a friend'.

2 That is, the social grace of friendliness describe in IV, vi; it is there said to be nameless, but it is called φιλία at II, vii, 13.

3 Homer, *Iliad*, X, 224.

4 φιλάνθρωπος means 'humane', 'kindly'.

5 or possibly, 'And the just are thought to possess friendliness in its highest form'.

6 literally 'jackdaw to jackdaw'.

7 Literally, 'all such men are potters to each other', an allusion to Hesiod, *Works and Days*, 25, 'Potter with potter contends, and joiner quarrels with joiner'.

8 Fr. 890 Dindorf, from an unknown play.

9 No passage in the *Ethics* answers exactly to this reference.

10 *i.e.*, they wish each other to become more virtuous, pleasant, or useful as the case may be; so that there is a different species of well-wishing in each case.

11 see § 1 above, and note 10.

12 *i.e.*, for some accidental (temporary or not essential) quality: *cf.* §§ 2, 3.

13 There is some uncertainty here and elsewhere in these chapters whether 'similarity' refers to resemblance between the friends (as § 6, and *cf.* 1139 a 10, καθ' ὁμοιότητά τινα), or between the different forms of friendship (καθ' ὁμοιότητα, 1157 a 32, 1158 b 6), friendships based on pleasure or profit being only so called 'by way of resemblance', *i.e.* in an analogical and secondary sense. But the latter consideration seems irrelevant here, and is first developed in the next chapter (§§ 1, 4). It is true that whether similarity between the parties is an element in all friendship (although this is implied by the words 'who resemble each other in virtue' in § 6) is nowhere clearly decided, and it can hardly be predicated of some friendships considered below.

14 *i.e.*, absolutely and relatively good and pleasant: *cf.* iv, 1.

15 in themselves, and not accidentally.

16 *cf. Eudemian Ethics*, 1238 a 2, διὸ εἰς παροιμίαν ἐλήλυθεν ὁ μέδιμνος τῶν ἁλῶν, 'hence "the peck of salt" has passed into a proverb.'

17 *cf.* note 13.

18 literally, 'by way of resemblance to true friendship': see iii, 7, note.

19 Perhaps the words 'and of likeness' are interpolated; the following clause explains 'goodness' only. That utility is 'a sort of goodness' is assumed.

20 *i.e.*, in being pleasant or useful to each other; or possibly 'since they are alike in loving pleasure or profit'.

21 or possibly 'since they like each other as being good'.

22 The source of this is unknown.

23 The ἑταιρεῖαι, or comradeships, at Athens were associations of men of the same age and social standing. In the fifth century they had a political character, and were oligarchical in tendency, but in Aristotle's day they seem to have been no more than social clubs, whose members were united by personal regard, and were felt to have claims on each other's resources. See ix, 2; xi, 5; xii, 4 and 6; IX, ii, 1, 3 and 9; x, 6.

24 *i.e.*, good men love each other because they are both good and pleasant absolutely and good and pleasant for each other.

25 This sentence would come better after the following one.

26 *cf.* ii, 3.

27 For this 'proportional equalisation' of the parties to an unequal friendship see vii, 2; xiii, 1. It would appear that the meaning here is, that unless the great man is also better than the good man, the good man cannot give more love or respect to the great man than the great man gives to him, which is the only way in which the good man can compensate the great man for giving more benefits than he gets, and so be put on an equality; see further on IX, i, 1.

28 *i.e.*, equivalent amounts of two different things.

29 *i.e.*, friendships based on pleasure or utility or both in contrast to those based on virtue; although the latter also are, of course, 'friendships of equality'. The parenthesis breaks the flow of the argument.

30 They are not only different in kind but unequal in value.

31 *i.e.*, unequal, and proportionate to the benefits received.

32 Literally 'though many things are taken away, (friendship) still remains'; apparently an allusion to the Sorites fallacy (*ratio ruentis acervi*, Horace, *Epistles* II, i, 47), How many grains can be taken

from a heap of corn for it still to be a heap?

33 It is a contradiction in terms to wish a friend a good that involves a loss of good.

34 ii, 3.

35 *i.e.*, the party to the friendship who gets more than he gives, and redresses the balance by repaying more affection or esteem than he receives.

36 or possibly 'so what they really enjoy is being assured', etc.

37 i, 4.

38 See note 23.

39 literally 'plunder or victory or a city'; the last words may refer either to colonists or exiles who obtain a new abode by conquest, or to civil war; but the expression is improbable, and perhaps should be emended to 'or to defend the city'.

40 The bracketed sentences, as Cook Wilson points out, look like an interpolated fragment of a parallel version.

41 Probably the text should read 'a king is not a king at all unless – '

42 Literally 'a king elected by lot', like the annual archon at Athens, who had the title of king, but retained only certain religious functions from the primitive monarchy.

43 *i.e.*, timocracy: see § 1.

44 because their children cannot fully repay their services in kind.

45 The word 'good' looks like an interpolation. The sense seems to require 'a larger share of affection'; it is clear throughout that in an unequal friendship the superior party receives not more but less benefit (though more affection) than the inferior. In x, 5 the conjugal association is compared to the aristocratic polity in virtue of the fact that the superior party has more power, not more benefit; and from x, 3 it appears that when the ruling class takes all or most of the benefits for itself, the government is no longer an aristocracy but an oligarchy.

46 These words are better omitted, as they anticipate what comes below.

47 ix, 1.

48 *cf.* VI, xi, 2 and note 70 on p. 166.

49 *i.e.*, greater certainty of parentage, closer affinity and earlier commencement of affection.

50 or 'a second self produced by separation from oneself'.

51 ἧλιξ ἥλικα *sc.* τέρπει, *Rhetoric*, I, xi, 1371 b 15. 'Crabbed age and youth cannot live together.' In its fuller form the proverb continues, 'the old get on with the old', ἧλιξ ἥλικα τέρπε, γέρων δέ τε τέρπε γέροντα: scholiast on Plato, *Phaedrus* 240 c. The next

phrase appears to be a proverb as well.

52 *sc.* not only when they are alike in virtue.

53 *i.e.*, in proportion to the closeness of the relationship: *cf.* § 4.

54 See I, note 34 on p. 27.

55 more universal than the gregarious instinct, which finds its highest expression in the state.

56 *i.e.*, the pleasure or utility as the case may be.

57 *i.e.*, 'and by being good or pleasant or useful'.

58 The one who is less good or pleasant or useful must give more affection: see note 27.

59 The last clause is suspected as an interpolation.

60 *i.e.*, either a 'moral obligation' or a contract enforceable at law. It is noteworthy that the term 'friendship' is stretched to include the latter.

61 or 'more liberal in point of time'.

62 if disappointed of the return he expects.

63 Literally 'was not doing the service for its own sake', or perhaps 'for the sake of friendship'. But probably the text should be corrected to read 'was not doing the service for one's own sake': *cf.* IX, i, 7 and x, 6.

64 *i.e.*, in any case of the sort, if at the outset the question of repayment were raised.

65 literally 'choice' in Aristotle's technical sense.

66 *cf.* V, ii, 12 and iv, 2.

67 This explains why a benefactor of the commonwealth must receive a reward in the shape of honour.

68 *i.e.*, the friendly feeling between the citizens as such, see xi, 1. But that this is maintained by τὸ κατ' ἀξίαν has not been said before: indeed the phrase is an odd description of what precedes, and its applicability to private friendship is denied just below. Perhaps 'since requital . . . above' is an interpolation.

BOOK NINE

Friendship (*continued*)

The claims of friendship (*continued*): three difficulties solved

i   First difficulty: how and by which party is the due return for a service to be measured? Answer: its measure should be the value of the service to the recipient.

ii Second difficulty: conflict of claims of different friends. Two general rules:
    (i) No one has an absolute claim to preference
    (ii) Different relations have different claims.

iii Third difficulty: what justifies a dissolution of friendship? Answer:
    (i) In the inferior kinds of friendship, the cessation of the pleasure or utility derived from them.
    Hypocritical friendships.
    (ii) In friendships based on virtue, an extreme moral decline, or improvement, in one of the parties.

3. (Appendix to 1) Friendship distinguished from kindred qualities

iv (1) Self-love, the type and basis of love for others. True self-esteem impossible for the base.

v   (2) Goodwill, the germ of true friendship.

vi (3) Concord.

4. Five further difficulties solved

vii (1) Why does the benefactor love the beneficiary more than the latter loves the former? Not solely on selfish grounds.
    (a) We love what we have created;
    (b) Beneficence is noble;
    (c) Affection an active principle. What has cost us trouble.

viii (2) Is self-love right or wrong? Two meanings of self-love.

Noble self-love a duty.

ix   (3) Is friendship necessary for happiness? Yes,

    (a)   as an external good;

    (b)   as an opportunity for beneficence;

    (c)   Man a social being.

    (d) The society of the good: (α) affords the spectacle of others' noble actions, (β) assists our own, (γ) makes us more virtuous.

    (e) Psychological argument: sympathy enlarges our consciousness and therefore our happiness.

x   (4) Should the number of our friends be limited? Yes, in all three kinds of friendship.

xi   (5) Are friends more needed in prosperity or adversity? Answer, they are needed in both.

5. Conclusion: the value of the society of friends

xii   The influence of their character on ours.

i In all dissimilar[1] friendships, it is proportion, as has been said, that establishes equality and preserves the friendship; just as, in the relations between fellow-citizens, the shoemaker receives payment for his shoes, and the weaver and the other craftsmen for their
2 products, according to value rendered. In these business relationships then a common measure has been devised, namely money, and this is a standard to which all things are referred and by which they are measured. But in sentimental friendships, the lover sometimes complains that his warmest affection meets with no affection in return, it may be because there is nothing in him to arouse affection; while the person loved frequently complains that the lover who formerly promised everything now fulfils none of his
3 promises. Such disputes occur when pleasure is the motive of the friendship on the lover's side and profit on the side of the beloved, and when they no longer each possess the desired attribute. For in a friendship based on these motives, a rupture occurs as soon as the parties cease to obtain the things for the sake of which they were friends; seeing that neither loved the other in himself, but some attribute he possessed that was not permanent; so that these friendships are not permanent either. But friendship based on character is disinterested, and therefore lasting, as has been said.[2]

4 Differences arise when the friends do not obtain what they desire, but something else; for not to get what you want is almost the same as not to get anything at all. For instance, there is the story of the man who hired a harper, and promised that the better he played the more he would pay him; but next morning, when the harper asked him to fulfil his promise, he said that he had already paid for the pleasure he had received by the pleasure he had given.[3] This would have been all right if both had wanted pleasure; but when one wants amusement and the other gain, and one gets what he wants and the other does not, it would not be a fair bargain; for it is the thing that a man happens to need that he sets his heart on, and only to get that is he ready to give what he does.

5   Which party's business is it to decide the amount of the return due? Should it be assessed by the one who proffers the initial service? Or rather by the one who receives[4] it, since the other by proffering it seems to leave the matter to him? This we are told was the practice of Protagoras;[5] when he gave lessons in any subject, he used to tell his pupil to estimate the value he set upon

6   his knowledge, and accepted a fee of that amount. In such matters however some people prefer the principle of 'the wage stated'.[6] But people who take the money in advance, and then, having made extravagant professions, fail to perform what they undertook, naturally meet with complaints because they have

7   not fulfilled their bargain. Perhaps however the sophists are bound to demand their fees in advance, since nobody would pay money for the knowledge which they possess.[7] Persons paid in advance then naturally meet with complaints if they do not perform the service for which they have taken the pay.

But in cases where no agreement is come to as to the value of the service, if it is proffered for the recipient's own sake, as has been said above,[8] no complaint arises, for a friendship based on virtue does not give rise to quarrels; and the return made should be in proportion to the intention of the benefactor, since intention is the measure of a friend, and of virtue. This is the principle on which it would seem that payment ought to be made to those who have imparted instruction in philosophy; for the value of their service is not measurable in money, and no honour paid them could be an equivalent, but no doubt all that can be expected is that to them, as to the gods and to our parents, we should make such return as is in our power.

8   When on the other hand the gift is not disinterested but made with a view to a recompense, it is no doubt the best thing that a return should be made such as both parties concur in thinking to be what is due. But failing such concurrence, it would seem to be not only inevitable but just that the amount of the return should be fixed by the party that received the initial service, since the donor will have recovered what the recipient really owes when he has been paid the value of the service to him, or the sum that he would have been willing to pay as the price of the pleasure.

9   For in buying and selling also this seems to be the practice;[9] and in some countries the law does not allow actions for the

enforcement of voluntary covenants,[10] on the ground that when you have trusted a man you ought to conclude the transaction as you began it. For it is thought fairer for the price to be fixed by the person who received credit than by the one who gave credit.[11] For as a rule those who have a thing value it differently from those who want to get it. For one's own possessions and gifts always seem to one worth a great deal; but nevertheless the repayment is actually determined by the valuation of the recipient. But he ought no doubt to estimate the gift not at what it seems to him to be worth now that he has received it, but at the value he put on it before he received it.

ii   Other questions that may be raised are such as these: Does a man owe his father unlimited respect and obedience, or ought he when ill to take the advice of a physician, and when electing a general to vote for the best soldier? and similarly, ought he to do a service to a friend rather than to a virtuous man, and ought he to repay his obligation to a benefactor rather than make a present to a comrade, when he is not in a position to do both?

2   Now perhaps with all these matters it is not easy to lay down an exact rule, because the cases vary indefinitely in importance or
3 unimportance, and in nobility or urgency. But it is quite clear that no one person is entitled to unlimited consideration. As a general rule one ought to return services rendered rather than do favours to one's comrades, just as one ought to pay back a loan to a
4 creditor rather than give the money to a friend. Yet perhaps even this rule is not without exceptions. For example, (a) suppose one has been ransomed from brigands; ought one to ransom one's ransomer in turn, whoever he may be – or even if he has not been captured himself but asks for his money back, ought one to repay him – or ought one to ransom one's own father? for it might be thought to be a man's duty to ransom his father even
5 before himself. As a general rule then, as has been said, one ought to pay back a debt, but if the balance of nobility or urgency is on the side of employing the money for a gift, then one ought to decide in favour of the gift. For (b) there are occasions when it would be actually unfair to return the original service; as for instance when A has done B a service knowing him to be a good man, and B is called upon to return the service to A whom he believes to be a bad man. For even when A has lent B a loan, B is

not always bound to lend A a loan in turn: A may have lent money to B, who is an honest man, expecting to get his money back, while B would have no hope of recovering from A, who is a rascal. If A is really a rascal, the return he asks for is not a fair one; and even if A is not a rascal, but people think[12] he is, it would not be deemed unreasonable for B to refuse.

6   Hence, as has been frequently remarked already,[13] discussions about our emotions and actions only admit of such degree of definiteness as belongs to the matters with which they deal.

7   It is quite clear therefore that all people have not the same claim upon us, and that even a father's claim is not unlimited, just as Zeus does not have all the sacrifices. Since the claims of parents and brothers, comrades and benefactors, are different, we ought to render to each that which is proper and suitable to each. This is in fact the principle on which men are observed to act. They invite their relatives to a wedding, because they are members of the family, and therefore concerned in the family's affairs; also it is thought to be specially incumbent on relations to attend funerals,

8   for the same reason. It would be felt that our parents have the first claim on us for maintenance, since we owe it to them as a debt, and to support the authors of our being stands before self-preservation in moral nobility. Honour also is due to parents, as it is to the gods, though not indiscriminate honour: one does not owe to one's father the same honour as to one's mother, nor yet the honour due to a great philosopher or general, but one owes to one's father the honour appropriate to a father, and to one's

9   mother that appropriate to her. Again, we should pay to all our seniors the honour due to their age, by rising when they enter, offering them a seat, and so on. Towards comrades and brothers on the other hand we should use frankness of speech, and share all our possessions with them. Kinsmen also, fellow-tribesmen, fellow-citizens, and the rest – to all we must always endeavour to render their due, comparing their several claims in respect of

10   relationship and of virtue or utility. Between persons of the same kind discrimination is comparatively easy; but it is a harder matter when they are differently related to us. Nevertheless we must not shirk the task on that account, but must decide their claims as well as we are able.

iii   Another question is, whether a friendship should or should not be broken off when the friends do not remain the same.

It may be said that where the motive of the friendship is utility or pleasure, it is not unnatural that it should be broken off when our friends no longer possess the attribute of being useful or agreeable. It was those attributes that we loved, and when they have failed it is reasonable that love should cease. But a man might well complain, if, though we really liked him for the profit or pleasure he afforded, we had pretended to love him for his character. As was said at the outset,[14] differences between friends most frequently arise when the nature of their friendship is not
2 what they think it is. When therefore a man has made a mistake, and has fancied that he was loved for his character, without there having been anything in his friend's behaviour to warrant the assumption, he has only himself to blame. But when he has been deceived by his friend's pretence, there is ground for complaint against the deceiver: in fact he is a worse malefactor than those who counterfeit the coinage,[15] inasmuch as his offence touches something more precious than money.

3 Again, supposing we have admitted a person to our friendship as a good man, and he becomes, or we think he has become, a bad man: are we still bound to love him? Perhaps it is impossible to do so, since only what is good is lovable; and also wrong, for we ought not to be lovers of evil, nor let ourselves become like what is worthless; and, as has been said above,[16] like is the friend of like. Should we therefore break off the friendship at once? Perhaps not in every case, but only when our friends have become incurably bad; for so long as they are capable of reform we are even more bound to help them morally than we should be to assist them financially, since character is a more valuable thing than wealth and has more to do with friendship. However, one could not be held to be doing anything unnatural if one broke off the friendship; for it was not a man of that sort that one loved: he has altered, and if one cannot restore him, one gives him up.

4 On the other hand, suppose one friend to have remained the same while the other has improved, and become greatly the superior in virtue: ought the latter to keep up the friendship? Perhaps it is out of the question; and this becomes especially clear when the gap between them is a wide one, as may happen with

two people who were friends in boyhood. One may have
remained a boy in mind, while the other is a man of the highest
ability; how can they be friends, when they have different tastes
and different likes and dislikes? They will no longer even enjoy
each other's society; but without this, intercourse and therefore
friendship are, as we saw,[17] impossible. But this has been
discussed already.

5   Are we then to behave towards a former friend in exactly the
same way as if he had never been our friend at all? Perhaps we
ought to remember our past intimacy, and just as we think it
right to show more kindness to friends than to strangers, so
likewise some attention should be paid, for the sake of old times,
to those who were our friends in the past, that is, if the rupture
was not caused by extreme wickedness on their part.

iv   The forms which friendly feeling for our neighbours takes, and
the marks by which the different forms of friendship are defined,
seem to be derived from the feelings of regard which we
entertain for ourselves. A friend is defined as (a) one who wishes,
and promotes by action, the real or apparent good of another for
that other's sake; or (b) one who wishes the existence and
preservation of his friend for the friend's sake. (This is the feeling
of mothers towards their children, and of former friends who
have quarrelled.[18]) Others say that a friend is (c) one who
frequents another's society, and (d) who desires the same things as
he does, or (e) one who shares his friend's joys and sorrows. (This
2   too is very characteristic of mothers.) Friendship also is defined
by one or other of these marks.[19] But each of them is also found
in a good man's feelings towards himself (and in those of all other
men as well, in so far as they believe themselves to be good; but,
as has been said, virtue and the virtuous man seem to be the
3   standard in everything). For (d) the good man is of one mind
with himself, and desires the same things with every part of his
nature. Also (a) he wishes his own good, real as well as apparent,
and seeks it by action (for it is a mark of a good man to exert
himself actively for the good); and he does so for his own sake
(for he does it on account of the intellectual part of himself, and
this appears to be a man's real self). Also (b) he desires his own
4   life and security, and especially that of his rational part. For
existence is good for the virtuous man; and everyone wishes his

own good: no one would choose to possess every good in the world on condition of becoming somebody else (for God possesses the good even as it is),[20] but only while remaining himself, whatever he may be; and it would appear that the
5 thinking part is the real self, or is so more than anything else. And (c) the good man desires his own company; for he enjoys being by himself, since he has agreeable memories of the past, and good hopes for the future, which are pleasant too; also his mind is stored with subjects for contemplation. And (e) he is keenly conscious of his own joys and sorrows; for the same things give him pleasure or pain at all times, and not different things at different times, since he is not apt to change his mind.

It is therefore because the good man has these various feelings towards himself, and because he feels towards his friend in the same way as towards himself (for a friend is another self), that friendship also is thought to consist in one or other of these feelings, and the possession of them is thought to be the test of a friend.

6 Whether a man can be said actually to feel friendship for himself is a question that may be dismissed for the present; though it may be held that he can do so in so far[21] as he is a dual or composite being, and because very intense friendship resembles self-regard.

7 As a matter of fact, the feelings of self-regard described appear to be found in most people, even though they are of inferior moral worth. Perhaps men share them in so far as they have their own approval and believe in their own virtue; since the utterly worthless and criminal never possess them, or even have the
8 appearance of doing so. Indeed it may almost be said that no morally inferior persons possess them. For (d) such persons are at variance with themselves, desiring one thing and wishing another: this is the mark of the unrestrained, who choose what is pleasant but harmful instead of what they themselves think to be good. (a) Others again, out of cowardice and idleness, neglect to do what they think best for their own interests. And (b) men who have committed a number of crimes, and are hated for their wickedness, actually flee from life and make away with them-
9 selves. Also (c) bad men constantly seek the society of others and shun their own company, because when they are by themselves

they recall much that was unpleasant in the past and anticipate the same in the future, whereas with other people they can forget. Moreover they feel no affection for themselves, because they have no lovable qualities. Hence (e) such men do not enter into their own joys and sorrows, as there is civil war in their souls; one part of their nature, owing to depravity, is pained by abstinence from certain indulgences while another part is pleased by it; one part pulls them one way and another the other, as if
10 dragging them asunder. Or if it be impossible to feel pain and pleasure at the same time, at all events after indulging in pleasure they regret it a little later, and wish they had never acquired a taste for such indulgences; since the bad are always changing their minds.

Thus a bad man appears to be devoid even of affection for himself, because he has nothing lovable in his nature. If then such a state of mind is utterly miserable, we should do our utmost to shun wickedness and try to be virtuous. That is the way both to be friends with ourselves and to win the friendship of others.

v   Goodwill appears to be an element of friendly feeling, but it is not the same thing as friendship; for it can be felt towards strangers, and it can be unknown to its object, whereas friendship cannot. But that has been discussed already.[22]

Neither is goodwill the same as affection. For it has no intensity, nor does it include desire, but these things are
2 necessarily involved in affection. Also affection requires intimate acquaintance, whereas goodwill may spring up all of a sudden, as happens for instance in regard to the competitors in a contest; the spectators conceive goodwill and sympathy for them, though they would not actively assist them, for as we said, their goodwill is a sudden growth, and the kindly feeling is only superficial.

3   Goodwill seems therefore to be the beginning of friendship, just as the pleasure of the eye is the beginning of love. No one falls in love without first being charmed by beauty, but one may delight in another's beauty without necessarily being in love: one is in love only if one longs for the beloved when absent, and eagerly desires his presence. Similarly men cannot be friends without having conceived mutual goodwill, though well-wishers are not necessarily friends: they merely desire the good of those whose well-wishers they are, and would not actively assist them

to attain it, nor be put to any trouble on their behalf. Hence extending the meaning of the term friendship we may say that goodwill is inoperative friendship, which when it continues and reaches the point of intimacy may become friendship proper – not the sort of friendship whose motive is utility or pleasure, for these do not arouse goodwill. Goodwill is indeed rendered in return for favours received, but this is merely the payment of a due; and that desire for another's welfare which springs from the anticipation of favours to come does not seem really to show goodwill for one's benefactor, but rather for oneself; just as to court a man for some interested motive is not friendship.

4 Speaking generally, true goodwill is aroused by some kind of excellence or moral goodness: it springs up when one person thinks another beautiful or brave or the like, as in the case we mentioned of competitors in a contest.

vi   Concord also seems to be a friendly feeling. Hence it is not merely agreement of opinion, for this might exist even between strangers. Nor yet is agreement in reasoned judgements about any subject whatever, for instance astronomy, termed concord; to agree about the facts of astronomy is not a bond of friendship. Concord is said to prevail in a state, when the citizens agree as to their interests, adopt the same policy, and carry their common

2 resolves into execution. Concord then refers to practical ends, and practical ends of importance, and able to be realised by both or all the parties: for instance, there is concord in the state when the citizens unanimously decree that the offices of state shall be elective, or that an alliance shall be made with Sparta, or that Pittacus shall be dictator (when Pittacus was himself willing to be dictator).[23] When each of two persons wishes himself to rule, like the rivals[24] in the *Phoenissae*,[25] there is discord; since men are not of one mind merely when each thinks the same thing (whatever this may be), but when each thinks the same thing in relation to the same person: for instance, when both the common people and the upper classes wish that the best people shall rule; for only so can all parties get what they desire.

Concord appears therefore to mean friendship between citizens, which indeed is the ordinary use of the term; for it refers to the interests and concerns of life.

3   Now concord in this sense exists between good men, since

these are of one mind both with themselves and with one another, as they always stand more or less on the same ground; for good men's wishes are steadfast, and do not ebb and flow like the tide, and they wish for just and expedient ends, which they
4 strive to attain in common. The base on the other hand are incapable of concord, except in some small degree, as they are of friendship, since they try to get more than their share of advantages, and take less than their share of labours and public burdens. And while each desires this for himself, he spies on his neighbour to prevent him from doing likewise; for unless they keep watch over one another, the common interests go to ruin. The result is discord, everybody trying to make others do their duty but refusing to do it themselves.

vii   Benefactors seem to love those whom they benefit more than those who have received benefits love those who have conferred them; and it is asked why this is so, as it seems to be unreasonable. The view most generally taken is that it is because the one party is in the position of a debtor and the other of a creditor; just as therefore in the case of a loan, whereas the borrower would be glad to have his creditor out of the way, the lender actually watches over his debtor's safety, so it is thought that the conferrer of a benefit wishes the recipient to live in order that he may receive a return, but the recipient is not particularly anxious to make a return. Epicharmus no doubt would say that people who give this explanation are 'looking at the seamy side'[26] of life; but all the same it appears to be not untrue to human nature, for most men have short memories, and are more desirous of receiving benefits than of bestowing them.

2   But it might be held that the real reason lies deeper,[27] and that the case of the creditor is not really a parallel. With him it is not a matter of affection, but only of wishing his debtor's preservation for the sake of recovering his money; whereas a benefactor feels friendship and affection for the recipient of his bounty even though he is not getting anything out of him and is never likely to do so.

3   The same thing happens with the artist: every artist loves his own handiwork more than that handiwork if it were to come to life would love him. This is perhaps especially true of poets, who have an exaggerated affection for their own poems and love

4 them as parents love their children. The position of the benefactor then resembles that of the artist; the recipient of his bounty is his handiwork, and he therefore loves him more than his handiwork loves its maker. The reason of this is that all things desire and love existence; but we exist in activity, since we exist by living and doing; and in a sense[28] one who has made something exists actively, and so he loves his handiwork because he loves existence. This is in fact a fundamental principle of nature: what a thing is potentially, that its work reveals in actuality.

5 Moreover for the benefactor there is an element of nobility in the act, and so he feels pleased with the person who is its object; but there is nothing noble for the recipient of the benefit in his relation to his benefactor: at most, it is profitable; and what is profitable is not so pleasant or lovable as what is noble. The

6 doer's achievement therefore remains, for nobility or beauty is long-lived, but its utility to the recipient passes away.[29] But while the actuality of the present, the hope of the future, and the memory of the past are all pleasant, actuality is the most pleasant of the three, and the most loved. Also whereas the memory of noble things is pleasant, that of useful ones is hardly at all so, or at least less so; although with anticipation the reverse seems to be the case.

7 Again, loving seems to be an active experience, being loved a passive one; hence affection and the various forms of friendly feeling are naturally found in the more active party to the relationship.

Again, everybody loves a thing more if it has cost him trouble: for instance those who have made money love money more than those who have inherited it. Now to receive a benefit seems to involve no labour, but to confer one is an effort. (This is why mothers love their children more than fathers, because parent-hood costs the mother more trouble [and the mother is more certain that the child is her own][30].) This also then would seem to be a characteristic of benefactors.

viii The question is also raised whether one ought to love oneself or someone else most. We censure those who put themselves first, and 'lover of self' is used as a term of reproach. And it is thought that a bad man considers himself in all he does, and the more so the worse he is – so it is a complaint against him for instance that 'he never does a thing unless you make him' – whereas a good man acts from a sense of what is noble, and the better he is the more he so acts, and he considers his friend's interest, disregarding his own.

2   But the facts do not accord with these theories; nor is this surprising. For we admit that one should love one's best friend most; but the best friend is he that, when he wishes a person's good, wishes it for that person's own sake, even though nobody will ever know of it. Now this condition is most fully realised in a man's regard for himself, as indeed are all the other attributes that make up the definition of a friend; for it has been said already[31] that all the feelings that constitute friendship for others are an extension of regard for self. Moreover, all the proverbs agree with this; for example, 'Friends have one soul between them',[32] 'friends' goods are common property', 'Amity is equality', 'The knee is nearer than the shin.'[33] All of these sayings will apply most fully to oneself; for a man is his own best friend. Therefore he ought to love himself most.

So it is naturally debated which of these two views we ought to adopt, since each of them has some plausibility.

3   Now where there is a conflict of opinion the proper course is doubtless to get the two views clearly distinguished, and to define how far and in what way each of them is true. So probably the matter may become clear if we ascertain what meaning each side attaches to the term 'self-love'.

4   Those then who make it a term of reproach call men lovers of self when they assign to themselves the larger share of money, honours, or bodily pleasures; since these are the things which most men desire and set their hearts on as being the greatest goods, and which accordingly they compete with each other to obtain. Now those who take more than their share of these things are men who indulge their appetites, and generally their passions and the irrational part of their souls. But most men are of this kind. Accordingly the use of the term 'lover of self' as a reproach has arisen from the fact that self-love of the ordinary kind is bad. Hence self-love is rightly censured in those who are
5 lovers of self in this sense. And that it is those who take too large a share of things of this sort whom most people usually mean

when they speak of lovers of self, is clear enough. For if a man were always bent on outdoing everybody else in acting justly or temperately or in displaying any other of the virtues, and in general were always trying to secure for himself moral nobility, no one will charge him with love of self nor find any fault with

6 him. Yet as a matter of fact such a man might be held to be a lover of self in an exceptional degree. At all events he takes for himself the things that are noblest and most truly good. Also it is the most dominant part of himself that he indulges and obeys in everything. But (a) as in the state it is the sovereign that is held in the fullest sense to *be* the state, and in any other composite whole it is the dominant part that is deemed especially to be that whole, so it is with man. He therefore who loves and indulges the dominant part of himself is a lover of self in the fullest degree. Again (b), the terms 'self-restrained' and 'unrestrained' denote being restrained or not by one's intellect, and thus imply that the intellect is the man himself. Also (c) it is our reasoned acts that are felt to be in the fullest sense *our own* acts, *voluntary* acts. It is therefore clear that a man is or is chiefly the dominant part of himself, and that a good man values this part of himself most. Hence the good man will be a lover of self in the fullest degree, though in another sense than the lover of self so-called by way of reproach, from whom he differs as much as living by principle differs from living by passion, and aiming at what is noble from

7 aiming at what seems expedient. Persons therefore who are exceptionally zealous in noble actions are universally approved and commended; and if all men vied with each other in moral nobility and strove to perform the noblest deeds, the common welfare would be fully realised, while individuals also could enjoy the greatest good.

Therefore the good man ought to be a lover of self, since he will then both benefit himself by acting nobly and aid his fellows; but the bad man ought not to be a lover of self, since he will follow his base passions, and so injure both himself and his

8 neighbours. With the bad man therefore, what he does is not in accord with what he ought to do, but the good man does what he ought, since intelligence always chooses for itself that which is best, and the good man obeys his intelligence.

9 But it is also true that the virtuous man's conduct is often guided

by the interests of his friends and of his country, and that he will if necessary lay down his life in their behalf. For he will surrender wealth and power and all the goods that men struggle to win, if he can secure nobility for himself; since he would prefer an hour of rapture to a long period of mild enjoyment, a year of noble life to many years of ordinary existence, one great and glorious exploit to many small successes. And this is doubtless the case with those who give their lives for others; thus they choose great nobility for themselves. Also the virtuous man is ready to forgo money if by that means his friends may gain more money; for thus, though his friend gets money, he himself achieves nobility, and so he assigns
10 the greater good to his own share. And he behaves in the same manner as regards honours and offices also: all these things he will relinquish to his friend, for this is noble and praiseworthy for himself. He is naturally therefore thought to be virtuous, as he chooses moral nobility in preference to all other things. It may even happen that he will surrender to his friend the performance of some achievement, and that it may be nobler for him to be the cause of his friend's performing it than to perform it himself.

11 Therefore in all spheres of praiseworthy conduct it is manifest that the good man takes the larger share of moral nobility for himself. In this sense then, as we said above, it is right to be a lover of self, though self-love of the ordinary sort is wrong.

ix Another debated question is whether friends are necessary or not for happiness. People say that the supremely happy are self-sufficing, and so have no need of friends: for they have the good things of life already, and therefore, being complete in themselves, require nothing further; whereas the function of a friend, who is a second self, is to supply things we cannot procure for ourselves. Hence the saying[34]

When fortune favours us, what need of friends?

2 But it seems strange that if we attribute all good things to the happy man we should not assign him friends, which we consider the greatest of external goods. Also if it be more the mark of a friend to give than to receive benefits, and if beneficence is a function of the good man and of virtue, and it is nobler to benefit friends than strangers, the good man will need friends as the objects of his beneficence.

Hence the further question is asked: Are friends more needed in prosperity or in adversity? It is argued that the unfortunate need people to be kind to them, but also that the prosperous need people to whom they may be kind.

3   Also perhaps it would be strange to represent the supremely happy man as a recluse. Nobody would choose to have all possible good things on the condition that he must enjoy them alone; for man is a social being,[35] and designed by nature to live with others; accordingly the happy man must have society, for he has everything that is naturally good. And it is obviously preferable to associate with friends and with good men than with strangers and chance companions. Therefore the happy man requires friends.

4   What then do the upholders of the former view mean, and in what sense is it true? Perhaps the explanation of it is that most men think of friends as being people who are useful to us. Now it is true that the supremely happy man will have no need of friends of that kind, inasmuch as he is supplied with good things already. Nor yet will he want friends of the pleasant sort, or only to a very small extent, for his life is intrinsically pleasant and has no need of adventitious pleasure. And as he does not need useful or pleasant friends, it is assumed that he does not require friends at all.

5   But perhaps this inference is really untrue. For as we said at the beginning,[36] happiness is a form of activity, and an activity clearly is something that comes into being, not a thing that we possess all the time, like a piece of property. But if happiness consists in life and activity, and the activity of a good man, as was said at the beginning,[37] is good and so pleasant in itself, and if the sense that a thing is our own is also pleasant, yet we are better able to contemplate our neighbours than ourselves, and their actions than our own, and thus good men find pleasure in the actions of other good men who are their friends, since those actions possess both these essentially pleasant qualities,[38] it therefore follows that the supremely happy man will require good friends, insomuch as he desires to contemplate actions that are good and that are his own, and the actions of a good man that is his friend are such. Also men think that the life of the happy man ought to be pleasant. Now a solitary man has a hard life, for it is not easy to

keep up continuous activity by oneself; it is easier to do so with
6 the aid of and in relation to other people. The good man's
activity therefore, which is pleasant in itself, will be more
continuous if practised with friends;[39] and the life of the
supremely happy should be continuously pleasant (for[40] a good
man, in virtue of his goodness, enjoys actions that conform with
virtue and dislikes those that spring from wickedness, just as a
skilled musician is pleased by good music and pained by bad).
7 Moreover the society of the good may supply a sort of training in
goodness, as Theognis[41] remarks.

Again, if we examine the matter more fundamentally, it
appears that a virtuous friend is essentially desirable for a virtuous
man. For as has been said above, that which is essentially good is
good and pleasing in itself to the virtuous man. And life is
defined, in the case of animals, by the capacity for sensation; in
the case of man, by the capacity for sensation and thought. But a
capacity is referred to its activity, and in this its full reality consists.
It appears therefore that life in the full sense is sensation or
thought. But life is a thing good and pleasant in itself, for it is
definite, and definiteness is a part of the essence of goodness, and
what is essentially good is good for the good man, and hence
8 appears to be pleasant to all men. We must not argue from a
vicious and corrupt life, or one that is painful, for such a life is
indefinite, like its attributes.[42] (The point as to pain will be clearer
9 in the sequel.)[43] But if life itself is good and pleasant (as it appears
to be, because all men desire it, and virtuous and supremely
happy men most of all, since their way of life is most desirable
and their existence the most blissful); and if one who sees is
conscious[44] that he sees, one who hears that he hears, one who
walks that he walks, and similarly for all the other human
activities there is a faculty that is conscious of their exercise, so
that whenever we perceive, we are conscious that we perceive,
and whenever we think, we are conscious that we think, and to
be conscious that we are perceiving or thinking is to be conscious
that we exist (for existence, as we saw, is sense-perception or
thought); and if to be conscious one is alive is a pleasant thing in
itself (for life is a thing essentially good, and to be conscious that
one possesses a good thing is pleasant); and if life is desirable, and
especially so for good men, because existence is good for them,

and so pleasant (because they are pleased by the perception of
10 what is intrinsically good); and if the virtuous man feels towards
his friend in the same way as he feels towards himself (for his
friend is a second self) – then, just as a man's own existence is
desirable for him, so, or nearly so, is his friend's existence also
desirable. But, as we saw, it is the consciousness of oneself as
good[45] that makes existence desirable, and such consciousness is
pleasant in itself. Therefore a man ought also to share his friend's
consciousness of his existence, and this is attained by their living
together and by conversing and communicating their thoughts to
each other; for this is the meaning of living together as applied to
human beings, it does not mean merely feeding in the same
place, as it does when applied to cattle.

If then to the supremely happy man existence is desirable in
itself, being good and pleasant essentially, and if his friend's
existence is almost equally desirable to him, it follows that a
friend is one of the things to be desired. But that which is
desirable for him he is bound to have, or else his condition will
be incomplete in that particular. Therefore to be happy a man
needs virtuous friends.

X   Ought we then to make as many friends as possible? or, just as
it seems a wise saying about hospitality –

Neither with troops of guests nor yet with none – [46]

so also with friendship perhaps it will be fitting neither to be
2 without friends nor yet to make friends in excessive numbers.
This rule would certainly seem applicable to those friends whom
we choose for their utility;[47] for it is troublesome to have to
repay the services of a large number of people, and life is not long
enough for one to do it. Any more therefore than are sufficient
for the requirements of one's own life will be superfluous, and a
hindrance to noble living, so one is better without them. Of
friends for pleasure also a few are enough, just as a small amount
3 of sweets is enough in one's diet. But should one have as many
good friends as possible? or is there a limit of size for a circle of
friends, as there is for the population of a state? Ten people
would not make a city, and with a hundred thousand it is a city
no longer; though perhaps the proper size is not one particular
number, but any number between certain limits. So also the

number of one friends must be limited, and should perhaps be the largest number with whom one can constantly associate; since, as we saw,[48] to live together is the chief mark of friendship,

4 but it is quite clear that it is not possible to live with and to share oneself among a large number of people. Another essential is that one's friends must also be the friends of one another, if they are all to pass the time in each other's company; but for a large

5 number of people all to be friends is a difficult matter. Again, it is difficult to share intimately in the joys and sorrows of many people; for one may very likely be called upon to rejoice with one and to mourn with another at the same time.

Perhaps therefore it is a good rule not to seek to have as many friends as possible, but only as many as are enough to form a circle of associates. Indeed it would appear to be impossible to be very friendly with many people, for the same reason as it is impossible to be in love with several people. Love means friendship in the superlative degree, and that must be with one person only; so also warm friendship is only possible with a few.

6 This conclusion seems to be supported by experience. Friendships between comrades[49] only include a few people, and the famous examples of poetry[50] are pairs of friends. Persons of many friendships, who are hail-fellow-well-met with everybody, are thought to be real friends of nobody (otherwise than as fellow-citizens are friends): I mean the sort of people we call obsequious. It is true that one may be friendly with many fellow-citizens and not be obsequious, but a model of excellence; but it is not possible to have many friends whom we love for their virtue and for themselves. We may be glad to find even a few friends of this sort.

xi But do we need friends more in prosperity or in adversity? As a matter of fact men seek friends in both. The unfortunate require assistance; the prosperous want companions, and recipients of their bounty, since they wish to practise beneficence. Hence friendship is more necessary in adversity, so then it is useful friends that are wanted; but it is nobler in prosperity, so the prosperous seek also for good men as friends, since these are preferable both as objects of beneficence and as associates.

2 Also[51] the mere presence of friends is pleasant both in prosperity and adversity. Sorrow is lightened by the sympathy of friends. Hence the question may be raised whether friends actually share

the burden of grief, or whether, without this being the case, the pain is nevertheless diminished by the pleasure of their company and by the consciousness of their sympathy. Whether one of these reasons or some other gives the true explanation of the consoling power of friendship need not now be considered, but in any case it appears to have the effect described.

3   Yet the pleasure that the company of friends affords seems to be of a mixed nature. It is true that the very sight of them is pleasant, especially in time of misfortune, and is a considerable help in assuaging sorrow; for a friend, if tactful, can comfort us with look and word, as he knows our characters and what things

4 give us pleasure and pain. But on the other hand to see another pained by our own misfortunes is painful, as everyone is reluctant to be a cause of pain to his friends. Hence manly natures shrink from making their friends share their pain, and unless a man is excessively insensitive, he cannot bear the pain that his pain gives to them; and he will not suffer others to lament with him, because he is not given to lamentation himself. But weak women and womanish men like those who mourn with them, and love them as true friends and sympathisers. However, it is clear that in everything we ought to copy the example of the man of nobler nature.

5   In prosperity again the company of friends sweetens our hours of leisure, and also affords the pleasure of being conscious of their pleasure in our welfare.

Hence it may be thought that we ought to be eager to invite our friends to share our good fortune (since it is noble to wish to bestow benefits), but reluctant to ask them to come to us in misfortune (since we should impart to others as little as possible of what is evil: whence the proverb 'My own misfortune is enough'). We should summon our friends to our aid chiefly when they will be of great service to us at the cost of little trouble to themselves.

6   So, conversely, it is perhaps fitting that we should go uninvited and readily to those in misfortune (for it is the part of a friend to render service, and especially to those in need, and without being asked, since assistance so rendered is more noble and more pleasant for both parties); but to the prosperous, though we should go readily to help them (for even prosperity needs the

co-operation of friends),[52] we should be slow in going when it is a question of enjoying their good things (for it is not noble to be eager to receive benefits). But doubtless we should be careful to avoid seeming churlish in repulsing their advances, a thing that does sometimes occur.

It appears therefore that the company of friends is desirable in all circumstances.

xii   As then lovers find their greatest delight in seeing those they love, and prefer the gratification of the sense of sight to that of all the other senses, that sense being the chief seat and source of love, so likewise for friends (may we not say?) the society of each other is the most desirable thing there is. For (i) friendship is essentially a partnership. And (ii) a man stands in the same relation to a friend as to himself;[53] but the consciousness of his own existence is a good; so also therefore is the consciousness of his friend's existence; but this[54] consciousness is actualised in intercourse; hence friends naturally desire each other's society.

2   And (iii) whatever pursuit it is that constitutes existence for a man or that makes his life worth living, he desires to share that pursuit with his friends. Hence some friends drink or dice together, others practise athletic sports and hunt, or study philosophy, in each other's company; each sort spending their time together in the occupation that they love best of everything in life; for wishing to live in their friends' society, they pursue and take part with them in these occupations as best they can.[55]

3   Thus the friendship of inferior people is evil, for they take part together in inferior pursuits [being unstable,][56] and by becoming like each other are made positively evil. But the friendship of the good is good, and grows with their intercourse. And they seem actually to become better by putting their friendship into practice, and because they correct each other's faults, for each takes the impress from the other of those traits in him that give him pleasure – whence the saying:

Noble deeds from noble men.[57]

So much for our treatment of friendship. Our next business will be to discuss pleasure.

1   Or 'heterogeneous', *i.e.* friendships between dissimilar people, e.g.
    one pleasant and the other useful, so that the benefits they confer
    on each other are different in kind. This class of friendship has not
    been named before, though it has been recognised, e.g. VIII, iv, 1,
    2. It is however incorrectly stated here that the notion of
    proportion has been applied to it; for the benefits exchanged in
    such friendships, though different in kind, are not 'proportional',
    but actually equal in amount or value, just as much as in the
    friendships where they are the same in kind; see VIII, vi, 7. The
    term 'proportion' has hitherto been used of 'unequal' friendships,
    where the superior party bestows more benefit (of whatever kind)
    than he receives, and equality is only restored by his receiving more
    affection than he bestows: see VIII, vii, 2, xiii, 1 (and also xiv, 3, to
    which at first sight this passage might be taken to refer). No doubt a
    friendship might be both 'dissimilar' and 'unequal'. That between a
    good man and a superior in rank who also surpasses him in
    goodness, which seems to be contemplated at VIII, vi, 6, is a
    complex example of this nature; the great man confers both
    material benefit and moral edification, the good man returns moral
    edification only, but makes up the deficit by the greater regard
    which the great man's superior goodness enables him to feel.

2   VIII, iii, 7.

3   Plutarch, *De Alexandri fortuna*, ii, 1, tells the story of the tyrant
    Dionysius, who promised the musician a talent (there seems no
    particular point in the sliding scale of payment which Aristotle's
    version introduces), but next day told him that he had already been
    sufficiently paid by the pleasure of anticipation.

4   literally 'the one who receives first', and now has to give a service
    in return.

5   *cf.* Plato, *Protagoras*, 328 b.

6   Hesiod, *Works and Days*, 370, μισθὸς δ' ἀνδρὶ φίλῳ εἰρημένος
    ἄρκιος ἔστω, 'let the wage stated to a friend stand good'.

7   *i.e.*, after he has found out in the course of the lessons what that
    knowledge amounts to.

8   *cf.* VIII, xiii, 2.

9   The price is fixed by what the buyer is willing to pay.

10 *cf.* VIII, xiii, 6. The phrase occurs in Plato, *Republic*, 556 a: *cf.* the 'voluntary private transactions' of V, ii, 13.

11 This sentence seems to come in better at the end of the chapter. The sentences immediately preceding and following have been plausibly rejected as interpolations.

12 Perhaps the text should be emended to 'but B thinks he is'.

13 See I, iii, 4 and II, ii, 3.

14 *cf.* VIII, xiii, 5

15 At Athens the penalty for coining was death.

16 *cf.* VIII, i, 6.

17 *cf.* VIII, v, 3.

18 *i.e.*, have had a difference which keeps them from meeting, but still leaves them well disposed to each other.

19 These five notes of friendship are taken seriatim in §§ 2–5, and again in §§ 8, 9, but in both cases the fourth is dealt with first.

20 The parenthesis seems to mean that as no one gains by God's now having the good, he would not gain if a new person which was no longer himself were to possess it (Ross). But 'and every one . . . whatever he may be' should perhaps be rejected as interpolated.

21 The manuscripts give 'in so far as two or more of the characteristics specifed are present', which hardly gives a sense. The words 'though it may be held . . . self-regard', have been suspected as an interpolation.

22 See VIII, ii, 3.

23 Pittacus was elected dictator of Mitylene early in the sixth century BC; he ruled for fourteen years, and then laid down his office. All the citizens wished him to continue, but this was not strictly unanimity or concord, since there was one dissentient, Pittacus himself.

24 Eteocles and Polyneices.

25 Euripides, *Phoen.* 588 ff.

26 This half-line of verse (Epicharmus doubtless wrote θαμένους) is otherwise unknown.

27 *cf.* VII, iii, 9.

28 In a sense he exists 'actually' as long as his work lasts, though strictly speaking he exists as an actual maker only while the act of making is going on. A possible variant rendering is 'and in a sense the work is its maker actualised'.

29 This sentence in the manuscripts follows the next.

30 This seems an irrelevant insertion from VIII, xii, 2 f.

31 See iv.

32 Euripides, *Orestes,* 1046.

33 'Charity begins at home' (Ross).

34 Euripides, *Orestes*, 665.

35 See I, note 34 on p. 27.

36 I, vii, 15. The argument for friendship from the definition of happiness as virtuous and therefore pleasant activity is threefold: (α) the virtuous actions of our friends give us (by sympathy) the same pleasure as our own; (β) good activities (e.g. study) can be carried on longer (because less liable to fatigue); (γ) virtuous friends increase our own virtue (as we unconsciously imitate their acts). Hence friends useful and pleasant because virtuous (though not useful or pleasant friends in the ordinary sense) are necessary adjuncts of happiness.

37 I, viii, 13.

38 *i.e.,* they are good, and they are their own, *i.e.* like their own.

39 The last four words are implied by the context.

40 This parenthesis comes better in § 5 above, after the words, 'the activity of a good man . . . is good and pleasant in itself'.

41 Theognis 35, ἐσθλῶν μὲν γὰρ ἄπ᾽ ἐσθλὰ μαθήσεαι.

42 *i.e.,* vice and pain.

43 X, i–v.

44 αἰσθάνεσθαι is used throughout to denote 'consciousness' (as well as, where needed, 'sensation'). At 1170 b 11 συναισθάνεσθαι expresses sympathetic consciousness of another's thoughts and feelings; it is probable therefore that in line 4 the compound verb is a copyist's mistake.

45 Perhaps to be emended 'of its goodness'. It is consciousness of life as good that makes it pleasant and desirable.

46 μηδὲ πολύξεινον μηδ᾽ ἄξεινον καλέεσθαι (Hesiod, *Works and Days*, 715).

47 but *cf.* VIII, vi, 3.

48 *cf.* VIII, v, 1.

49 See VIII, note 23 on p. 228.

50 Such as Achilles and Patroclus, Orestes and Pylades, Theseus and Pirithous. It is not quite clear whether they are quoted as examples of comradeship or of friendship in general.

51 This gives a further reason for the second sentence of the chapter, and adds the motive of pleasure to those of utility and virtue.

52 *cf.* VIII, i, 1 *fin.*, 2 *fin.*

53 See chapter iv, and ix, 5.

54 Or possibly, 'and friendship is realised in intercourse', a separate reason for the thesis of the first sentence.

55 The text is doubtful; most manuscripts give, 'by which they think that they live in their society'.

56 It seems best to excise these words as an inapposite reminiscence of iv, 10.

57 *cf.* ix, 7.

    (v) the senses themselves differ in purity (*i.e.* capacity for apprehending form without matter).

   (vi) different species have different pleasures; and so do different individuals of the human species. Ethical inference: the pleasures of the good man, whose activities constitute happiness, are good or real pleasures, and distinctively human.

Conclusion

vi Content of happiness (as defined I, vii, 15). Recapitulation: happiness is activity chosen for its own sake; but it must be activity manifesting virtue or excellence, not merely pursued for amusement.

vii Therefore perfect happiness is that activity which exercises the highest virtue (speculative wisdom), namely contemplation: since this activity is

    (i)   that of our highest part,

   (ii)   most continuous,

  (iii)   pleasantest,

  (iv)   most self-sufficient,

   (v)   an end in itself,

  (vi)   most leisured;

 (vii)   and it is the activity of the divine in man,

(viii)   which is the true self.

Therefore the life of the intellect is the happiest.

viii Further arguments for the pre-eminence of the life of contemplation:

    (i)   the life of virtuous action affords only a secondary happiness, being merely human. (Connection of prudence and moral goodness.)

   (ii)   contemplation needs few external goods.

  (iii)   it is the sole activity conceivable in God.

  (iv) it distinguishes man from animals.

Happiness therefore needs but moderate wealth, even in its secondary form. Our view thus agrees with those of philosophers, but must also be tested by the facts of life. (The man who lives for the intellect must be dearest to the gods, and therefore happiest.)

ix Transition from ethics to politics. Ethical theory only influences exceptionally gifted natures. Teaching is powerless without a foundation of good habits. The necessary discipline is best supplied by the state; since public authority is stronger and less invidious than private. But in default of a public system of education, paternal discipline has the support of affection, and can be adapted to the particular pupil. But the educator must know the principles of government. These at present are only taught by the sophists, who confuse politics with rhetoric, and rely on compilations of existing codes of law; but those are of no value to the student without practical experience. Our science of man must therefore include law and politics. Outline of the sequel, a treatise on politics.

i Our next business after this is doubtless to discuss pleasure. For pleasure is thought to be especially congenial to mankind; and this is why pleasure and pain are employed in the education of the young, as means whereby to steer their course. Moreover, to like and to dislike the right things is thought to be a most important element in the formation of a virtuous character. For pleasure and pain extend throughout the whole of life, and are of great moment and influence for virtue and happiness; since men choose what is pleasant and avoid what is painful.

2 It would therefore seem by no means proper to omit so important a subject, especially as there is much difference of opinion about it. Some people maintain that pleasure is the good. Others on the contrary say that it is altogether bad: some of them perhaps from a conviction that it is really so, but others because they think it to be in the interests of morality to make out that pleasure is bad, even if it is not, since most men (they argue) have a bias towards it, and are the slaves of their pleasures, so that they have to be driven in the opposite direction in order to arrive at the due mean.

3 Possibly however this view is mistaken. In matters of emotion and of action, words are less convincing than deeds; when therefore our theories are at variance with palpable facts, they provoke contempt, and involve the truth in their own discredit. If one who censures pleasure is seen sometimes to desire it himself, his swerving towards it is thought to show that he really believes that all pleasure is desirable; for the mass of mankind cannot
4 discriminate. Hence it appears that true theories are the most valuable for conduct as well as for science; harmonising with the facts, they carry conviction, and so encourage those who understand them to guide their lives by them.

With so much by way of introduction, let us now review the theories about pleasure that have been advanced.

ii That pleasure is the good was held by Eudoxus, on the following grounds. He saw that all creatures, rational and irrational alike, seek to obtain it; but in every case (he argued) that which is desirable is good, and that which is most desirable is the best; therefore the fact that all creatures 'move in the direction of '[1] the same thing indicates that this thing is the supreme good for all (since everything finds its own particular good, just as it finds its own proper food); but that which is good for all, and which all seek to obtain, is the good.

His arguments owed their acceptance however more to the excellence of his character than to their own merit. He had the reputation of being a man of exceptional temperance, and hence he was not suspected of upholding this view because he was a lover of pleasure, but people thought it must really be true.

2   He also held that the goodness of pleasure was equally manifest from the converse: pain is intrinsically an object of avoidance to all, therefore its opposite must be intrinsically an object of desire to all.

Again, he argued that that thing is most desirable which we choose not as a means to or for the sake of something else; but such admittedly is pleasure: we never ask a man for what purpose he indulges in pleasure – we assume it to be desirable in itself.

He also said that the addition of pleasure to any good – for instance, just or temperate conduct – makes that good more desirable; but only the good can enhance the good.

3   Now as for the last argument, it seems only to prove that pleasure is a good, and not that it is in any way better than any other good; for every good is more desirable when combined with some other good than in isolation. In fact, a similar argument is employed by Plato[2] to refute the view that pleasure is the good: the life of pleasure, he urges, is more desirable in combination with intelligence than without it; but if pleasure combined with something else is better than pleasure alone, it is not the good, for the good is not rendered more desirable by the addition of anything to it. And it is clear that nothing else either will be the good if it becomes more desirable when combined

4   with something good in itself. What thing is there then of this nature,[3] which is attainable by us? for it is something of this nature that we are in search of.

Those[4] on the other hand who deny that that which all creatures seek to obtain is good, are surely talking nonsense. For what all think to be good, that, we assert, is good; and he that subverts our belief in the opinion of all mankind, will hardly persuade us to believe his own either. If only the irrational creatures strove to obtain what is pleasant, there would have been some sense in this contention; but inasmuch as beings endowed with intelligence do so too, how can it be right? And perhaps even the lower animals possess an instinct superior to their own natures, which seeks to obtain the good appropriate to their kind.

5 Again, these thinkers' refutation of the argument from the converse appears equally unsound. They say, if pain is bad, it does not follow therefore that pleasure is good: for an evil can also be opposed to an evil and to a thing that is neither good nor evil: a statement which is indeed sound enough, but which does not apply to the things in question. If both pleasure and pain were in the class of evils, both would be also of necessity things to be avoided, and if in the class of things neutral, neither ought to be avoided, or they ought to be avoided alike; but as it is we see men avoid pain as evil and choose pleasure as good; it is therefore as good and evil that they are opposed.

iii Nor yet does it follow that if pleasure is not a quality, therefore it is not a good. Virtuous activities are not qualities either, nor is happiness.

2 Again they argue[5] that good is definite, but that pleasure is indefinite, because it admits of degrees. Now (a) if they base this judgement on the fact that one can be more or less pleased, the same argument will apply to justice and the other virtues, the possessors of which are clearly spoken of as being more or less virtuous; for example, A may be more just or brave, and may act more, or less, justly or temperately, than B. If on the other hand (b) they judge by the nature of the pleasures themselves, I am afraid they do not state the right ground for their conclusion, if it be true that there are two kinds of pleasures, unmixed as well as mixed.[6]

3 Again, (c) why should not pleasure be like health, which is definite although it admits of degrees? For health is not consti-tuted by the same proportion of elements in all persons; nor yet by one particular proportion in the same person always, but when it is in process of dissolution it still lasts for a certain time, and therefore it varies in degree. It is possible therefore that the

same may be the case with pleasure.

4   Again, they postulate[7] that the good is perfect, whereas a motion or process of generation is imperfect, and then they attempt to prove that pleasure is a motion or process. This appears to be a mistake. (a) It would seem that pleasure is not a motion; for we hold it to be a property of all motion to be quick or slow – if (as with the motion[8] of the firmament) not absolutely, then relatively to some other moving body. But pleasure possesses neither absolute nor relative velocity. You can *become* pleased quickly, just as you can get angry quickly: but you cannot *be* pleased quickly, nor yet more quickly than somebody else, as you can walk, grow, etc., more quickly than somebody else. It is possible to pass *into* a pleasurable state quickly or slowly, but not to function *in* that state – *i.e.* to feel pleasure – quickly.

5   And (b) in what sense can pleasure be a process of generation? We do not think that any chance thing can be generated from any other chance thing, but that a thing at its dissolution is resolved into that from which it is generated; and if pleasure is the generation of something, pain is the destruction of that thing.

6   Also (c) they say[9] that pain is a deficiency of the natural state and pleasure is its replenishment. But these are bodily experiences. Now if pleasure is a replenishment of the natural state, the pleasure will be felt by the thing in which the replenishment takes place. Therefore it is the body that feels pleasure. But this does not seem to be the case. Therefore pleasure is not a process of replenishment, though while replenishment takes place, a feeling of pleasure may accompany it, just as a feeling of pain may accompany a surgical operation.[10] The belief that pleasure is a replenishment seems to have arisen from the pains and pleasures connected with food: here the pleasure does arise from a

7 replenishment, and is preceded by the pain of a want. But this is not the case with all pleasures: the pleasures of knowledge, for example, have no antecedent pain; nor have certain of the pleasures of sense, namely those whose medium is the sense of smell, as well as many sounds and sights; and also memories and hopes. If these are processes of generation, generation of what? No lack of anything has occurred that may be replenished.

8   In reply to those who bring forward the disreputable pleasures, one may (a) deny that these are really pleasant: for granted they

are pleasant to ill-conditioned people, it cannot therefore be assumed that they are actually pleasant, except to them, any more than things healthy or sweet or bitter to invalids are really so, or any more than things that seem white to people with a disease of
9 the eyes are really white. Or (b) one may take the line that, though the pleasures themselves are desirable, they are not desirable when derived from those sources; just as wealth is desirable, but not if won by treachery, or health, but not at the
10 cost of eating anything and everything. Or (c) we may say that pleasures differ in specific quality; since (α) those derived from noble sources are not the same as those derived from base sources, and it is impossible to feel the pleasures of a just man without being just, or the pleasures of a musician without being
11 musical, and so on. And also (β) the distinction between a friend and a flatterer seems to show that pleasure is not a good, or else that pleasures are specifically different; since a friend is thought to aim at doing good to his companion, a flatterer at giving pleasure; to be a flatterer is a reproach, whereas a friend is praised because
12 in his intercourse he aims at other things. And (γ) no one would choose to retain the mind of a child throughout his life, even though he continued to enjoy the pleasures of childhood with undiminished zest; nor (δ) would anyone choose to find enjoyment in doing some extremely shameful act, although it would entail no painful consequences. Also (ε) there are many things which we should be eager to possess even if they brought us no pleasure, for instance sight, memory, knowledge, virtue. It may be the case that these things are necessarily attended by pleasure, but that makes no difference; for we should desire them even if no pleasure resulted from them.

13　It seems therefore that pleasure is not the good, and that not every pleasure is desirable, but also that there are certain pleasures, superior in respect of their specific quality or their source, that are desirable in themselves.

Let this suffice for a discussion of the current views about pleasure and pain.

iv　We may ascertain the nature and quality of pleasure more clearly if we start again from the beginning.

Now the act of sight appears to be perfect at any moment of its duration; it does not require anything to supervene later in order to perfect its specific quality. But pleasure also appears to be a thing of this nature. For it is a whole, and one cannot at any moment put one's hand on a pleasure which will only exhibit its specific quality perfectly if its duration be prolonged.

2   It follows also that pleasure is not a form of motion.[11] For every motion or process of change involves duration, and is a means to an end, for instance the process of building a house; and it is perfect when it has effected its end. Hence a motion is perfect either when viewed over the whole time of its duration, or at the moment when its end has been achieved. The several motions occupying portions of the time of the whole are imperfect, and different in kind from the whole and from each other. For instance, in building a temple the fitting together of the stones is a different process from the fluting of a column, and both are different from the construction of the temple as a whole; and whereas the building of the temple is a perfect process, for nothing more is required to achieve the end proposed, laying the foundation and constructing the triglyphs are imperfect processes, since each produces only a part of the design; they are therefore specifically different from the construction of the whole, and it is not possible to lay one's finger on a motion specifically perfect at any moment of the process of building, but only, if at all, in the whole of its duration.

3   And the same is true of walking and the other forms of locomotion. For if locomotion is motion from one point in space to another, and if this is of different kinds, flying, walking, leaping and the like, and not only so, but if there are also differences in walking itself (for the terminal points of a racecourse are not the same as those of a portion of the course, nor are those of one portion the same as those of another; nor is traversing this line the same as traversing that one,[12] for the runner does not merely travel along a certain line but travels along a line that is in a certain place, and this line is in a different place from that) – however, for a full treatment of the subject of motion I must refer to another work,[13] but it appears that a motion is not perfect at every moment, but the many move-ments which make up the whole are imperfect; and different from each other in kind, inasmuch as the terminal points of a

4   movement constitute a specific quality. The specific quality of

pleasure on the contrary is perfect at any moment. It is clear therefore that pleasure is not the same as motion, and that it is a whole and something perfect.

This may also be inferred from the fact that a movement necessarily occupies a space of time, whereas a feeling of pleasure does not, for every moment of pleasurable consciousness is a perfect whole.

These considerations also show that it is a mistake to speak of pleasure as the result of a motion or of a process of generation. For we cannot so describe everything, but only such things as are divided into parts and are not wholes. Thus an act of sight, a geometrical point, an arithmetical unit are not the result of a process of generation (nor is any of them a motion or process).[14] Pleasure therefore also is not the result of a motion or process; for pleasure is a whole.

5   Again, inasmuch as each of the senses acts in relation to its object, and acts perfectly when it is in good condition and directed to the finest of the objects that belong to it (for this seems to be the best description of perfect activity, it being assumed to make no difference whether it be the sense itself that acts or the organ in which the sense resides), it follows that the activity of any of the senses is at its best when the sense-organ being in the best condition is directed to the best of its objects; and this activity will be the most perfect and the pleasantest. For each sense has a corresponding pleasure, as also have thought and speculation, and its activity is pleasantest when it is most perfect, and most perfect when the organ is in good condition and when it is directed to the most excellent of its objects; and the pleasure

6 perfects the activity. The pleasure does not however perfect the activity in the same way as the object perceived and the sensory faculty, if good, perfect it; just as health and the physician are not in the same way the cause of being healthy.

7   (It is clear that each of the senses is accompanied by pleasure, since we apply the term pleasant to sights and sounds;[15] and it is also clear that the pleasure is greatest when the sensory faculty is both in the best condition and acting in relation to the best object; and given excellence in the perceived object and the percipient organ, there will always be pleasure when an object to cause it and a subject to feel it are both present.)

8   But the pleasure perfects the activity, not as the fixed disposition does, by being already present in the agent, but as a supervening perfection, like the bloom of health in the young and vigorous.

So long therefore as both object thought of or perceived, and subject discerning or judging, are such as they should be, there will be pleasure in the activity; since while both the passive and the active parties to a relationship remain the same in themselves and unaltered in their relation to one another, the same result is naturally produced.

9   How is it then that no one can feel pleasure continuously? Perhaps it is due to fatigue, since no human faculty is capable of uninterrupted activity, and therefore pleasure also is not continuous, because it accompanies the activity of the faculties. It is for the same reason that some things please us when new, but cease to give so much pleasure later; this is because at first the mind is stimulated, and acts vigorously in regard to the object, as in the case of sight when we look at something intently; but afterwards the activity is less vigorous and our attention relaxes, and consequently the pleasure also fades.

10   It might be held that all men seek to obtain pleasure, because all men desire life. Life is a form of activity, and each man exercises his activity upon those objects and with those faculties which he likes the most: for example, the musician exercises his sense of hearing upon musical tunes, the student his intellect upon problems of philosophy, and so on. And the pleasure of these activities perfects the activities, and therefore perfects life,
11   which all men seek. Men have good reason therefore to pursue pleasure, since it perfects for each his life, which is a desirable thing. The question whether we desire life for the sake of pleasure or pleasure for the sake of life, need not be raised for the present. In any case they appear to be inseparably united; for there is no pleasure without activity, and also no perfect activity without its pleasure.

V   This moreover is the ground for believing that pleasures vary in specific quality. For we feel that different kinds of things must have a different sort of perfection. We see this to be so with natural organisms and the productions of art, such as animals, trees, a picture, a statue, a house, a piece of furniture. Similarly we think

that that which perfects one kind of activity must differ in kind
2 from that which perfects another kind. Now the activities of the
intellect differ from those of the senses, and from[16] one another, in
kind: so also therefore do the pleasures that perfect them.

This may also be seen from the affinity which exists between
the various pleasures and the activities which they perfect. For an
activity is augmented by the pleasure that belongs to it; since
those who work with pleasure always work with more discern-
ment and with greater accuracy – for instance, students who are
fond of geometry become proficient in it, and grasp its various
problems better, and similarly lovers of music, architecture or the
other arts make progress in their favourite pursuit because they
enjoy it. An activity then is augmented by its pleasure; and that
which augments a thing must be akin to it. But things that are
akin to things of different kinds must themselves differ in kind.

3 A still clearer proof may be drawn from the hindrance that
activities receive from the pleasure derived from other activities.
For instance, persons fond of the flute cannot give their attention
to a philosophical discussion when they overhear someone
playing the flute, because they enjoy music more than the
activity in which they are engaged; therefore the pleasure
afforded by the music of the flute impairs the activity of study.
4 The same thing occurs in other cases when a man tries to do two
things at once; the pleasanter activity drives out the other, the
more so if it is much more pleasant, until the other activity ceases
altogether. Hence, when we enjoy something very much, we
can hardly do anything else; and when we find a thing only
mildly agreeable, we turn to some other occupation; for instance,
people who eat sweets at the theatre do so especially when the
5 acting is bad. And since our activities are sharpened, prolonged
and improved by their own pleasure, and impaired by the
pleasures of other activities, it is clear that pleasures differ widely
from each other. In fact alien pleasures have almost the same
effect on the activities as their own pains;[17] since, when an
activity causes pain, this pain destroys it, for instance, if a person
finds writing or doing sums unpleasant and irksome; for he stops
writing or doing sums, because the activity is painful. Activities
then are affected in opposite ways by the pleasures and the pains
that belong to them, that is to say, those that are intrinsically due

to their exercise. Alien pleasures, as has been said, have very much the same effect as pain, for they destroy an activity, only not to the same degree.

6   Again, since activities differ in moral value, and some are to be adopted, others to be avoided, and others again are neutral, the same is true also of their pleasures: for each activity has a pleasure of its own. Thus the pleasure of a good activity is morally good, that of a bad one morally bad; for even desires for noble things are praised and desires for base things blamed; but the pleasures contained in our activities are more intimately connected with them than the appetites which prompt them, for the appetite is both separate in time and distinct in its nature from the activity, whereas the pleasure is closely linked to the activity, indeed so inseparable from it as to raise a doubt whether the activity is not
7   the same thing as the pleasure. However, we must not regard pleasure as really being a thought or a sensation – indeed this is absurd, though because they are inseparable they seem to some people to be the same.

As then activities are diverse, so also are their pleasures. Sight excels touch in purity, and hearing and smell excel taste; and similarly the pleasures of the intellect excel in purity the pleasures of sensation, while the pleasures of either class differ among themselves in purity.

8   And it is thought that every animal has its own special pleasure, just as it has its own special function: namely, the pleasure of exercising that function. This will also appear if we consider the different animals one by one: the horse, the dog, man, have different pleasures – as Heraclitus says, an ass would prefer chaff to gold, since to asses food gives more pleasure than gold. Different species therefore have different kinds of pleasures. On the other hand it might be supposed that there is no variety
9   among the pleasures of the same species. But as a matter of fact in the human species at all events there is a great diversity of pleasures. The same things delight some men and annoy others, and things painful and disgusting to some are pleasant and attractive to others. This also holds good of things sweet to the taste: the same things do not taste sweet to a man in a fever as to one in good health; nor does the same temperature feel warm to an invalid and to a person of robust constitution. The same holds

good of other things as well.

10   But we hold that in all such cases the thing really is what it appears to be to the good man. And if this rule is sound, as it is generally held to be, and if the standard of everything is goodness, or the good man, *qua* good, then the things that seem to him to be pleasures are pleasures, and the things he enjoys are pleasant. Nor need it cause surprise that things disagreeable to the good man should seem pleasant to some men; for mankind is liable to many corruptions and diseases, and the things in question are not really pleasant, but only pleasant to these particular persons, who are in a condition to think them so.

11   It is therefore clear that we must pronounce the admittedly disgraceful pleasures not to be pleasures at all, except to the depraved.

But among the pleasures considered respectable, which class of pleasures or which particular pleasure is to be deemed the distinctively human pleasure? Perhaps this will be clear from a consideration of man's activities. For pleasures correspond to the activities to which they belong; it is therefore that pleasure, or those pleasures, by which the activity, or the activities, of the perfect and supremely happy man are perfected, that must be pronounced human in the fullest sense. The other pleasures are so only in a secondary or some lower degree, like the activities to which they belong.

vi   Having now discussed the various kinds of virtue, of friendship and of pleasure, it remains for us to treat in outline of happiness, inasmuch as we count this to be the end of human life. But it will shorten the discussion if we recapitulate what has been said already.

2   Now we stated[18] that happiness is not a certain disposition of character; since if it were it might be possessed by a man who passed the whole of his life asleep, living the life of a vegetable, or by one who was plunged in the deepest misfortune. If then we reject this as unsatisfactory, and feel bound to class happiness rather as some form of activity, as has been said in the earlier part of this treatise, and if activities are of two kinds, some merely necessary means and desirable only for the sake of something else, others desirable in themselves, it is clear that happiness is to be classed among activities desirable in themselves, and not among

those desirable as a means to something else; since happiness lacks nothing, and is self-sufficient.

3　　But those activities are desirable in themselves which do not aim at any result beyond the mere exercise of the activity. Now this is felt to be the nature of actions in conformity with virtue; for to do noble and virtuous deeds is a thing desirable for its own sake.

But agreeable amusements also are desirable for their own sake; we do not pursue them as a means to something else, for as a matter of fact they are more often harmful than beneficial, causing men to neglect their health and their estates. Yet persons whom the world counts happy usually have recourse to such pastimes; and this is why adepts in such pastimes stand in high favour with princes, because they make themselves agreeable in supplying what their patrons desire, and what they want is amusement. So it is supposed that amusements are a component part of happiness, because princes and potentates devote their leisure to them.

4　　But (i) perhaps princes and potentates are not good evidence. Virtue and intelligence, which are the sources of man's higher activities, do not depend on the possession of power; and if these persons, having no taste for pure and liberal pleasure, have recourse to the pleasures of the body, we must not on that account suppose that bodily pleasures are the more desirable. Children imagine that the things they themselves value are actually the best; it is not surprising therefore that, as children and grown men have different standards of value, so also should the 5 worthless and the virtuous. Therefore, as has repeatedly been said, those things are actually valuable and pleasant which appear so to the good man; but each man thinks that activity most desirable which suits his particular disposition, and therefore the 6 good man thinks virtuous activity most desirable. It follows therefore that happiness is not to be found in amusements.

(ii) Indeed it would be strange that amusement should be our end – that we should toil and moil all our life long in order that we may amuse ourselves. For virtually every object we adopt is pursued as a means to something else, excepting happiness, which is an end in itself; to make amusement the object of our serious pursuits and our work seems foolish and childish to excess: Anacharsis's motto, play in order that you may work, is felt to be the right rule. For amusement is a form of rest; but we need rest because we are not able to go on working without a break, and therefore it is not an end, since we take it as a means to further activity.

(iii) And the life that conforms with virtue is thought to be a happy life; but virtuous life involves serious purpose, and does not consist in amusement.

7   (iv) Also we pronounce serious things to be superior to things that are funny and amusing; and the nobler a faculty or a person is, the more serious, we think, are their activities; therefore, the activity of the nobler faculty or person is itself superior, and therefore more productive of happiness.

8   (v) Also anybody can enjoy the pleasures of the body, a slave no less than the noblest of mankind; but no one allows a slave any measure of happiness, any more than a life of his own.[19] Therefore happiness does not consist in pastimes and amusements but in activities in accordance with virtue, as has been said already.

vii   But if happiness consists in activity in accordance with virtue, it is reasonable that it should be activity in accordance with the highest virtue; and this will be the virtue of the best part of us. Whether then this be the intellect, or whatever else it be that is thought to rule and lead us by nature, and to have cognisance of what is noble and divine, either as being itself also actually divine, or as being relatively the divinest part of us, it is the activity of this part of us in accordance with the virtue proper to it that will constitute perfect happiness; and it has been stated already[20] that this activity is the activity of contemplation.

2   And that happiness consists in contemplation may be accepted as agreeing both with the results already reached and with the truth. For contemplation is at once the highest form of activity (since the intellect is the highest thing in us, and the objects with which the intellect deals are the highest things that can be known), and also it is the most continuous, for we can reflect
3   more continuously than we can carry on any form of action. And again we suppose that happiness must contain an element of pleasure; now activity in accordance with wisdom is admittedly the most pleasant of the activities in accordance with virtue: at all

events it is held that philosophy or the pursuit of wisdom contains pleasures of marvellous purity and permanence, and it is reasonable to suppose that the enjoyment of knowledge is a still

4 pleasanter occupation than the pursuit of it. Also the activity of contemplation will be found to possess in the highest degree the quality that is termed self-sufficiency; for while it is true that the wise man equally with the just man and the rest requires the necessaries of life, yet, these being adequately supplied, whereas the just man needs other persons towards whom or with whose aid he may act justly, and so likewise do the temperate man and the brave man and the others, the wise man on the contrary can also contemplate by himself, and the more so the wiser he is; no doubt he will study better with the aid of fellow-workers, but

5 still he is the most self-sufficient of men. Also the activity of contemplation may be held to be the only activity that is loved for its own sake: it produces no result beyond the actual act of contemplation, whereas from practical pursuits we look to secure

6 some advantage, greater or smaller, beyond the action itself. Also happiness is thought to involve leisure; for we do business in order that we may have leisure, and carry on war in order that we may have peace. Now the practical virtues are exercised in politics or in warfare; but the pursuits of politics and war seem to be unleisured – those of war indeed entirely so, for no one desires to be at war for the sake of being at war, nor deliberately takes steps to cause a war: a man would be thought an utterly bloodthirsty character if he declared war on a friendly state for the sake of causing battles and massacres. But the activity of the politician also is unleisured, and aims at securing something beyond the mere participation in politics – positions of authority and honour, or, if the happiness of the politician himself and of his fellow-citizens, this happiness conceived as something distinct from political activity (indeed we are clearly investigating it as so

7 distinct).[21] If then among practical pursuits displaying the virtues, politics and war stand out pre-eminent in nobility and grandeur, and yet they are unleisured, and directed to some further end, not chosen for their own sakes: whereas the activity of the intellect is felt to excel in serious worth,[22] consisting as it does in contemplation, and to aim at no end beyond itself, and also to contain a pleasure peculiar to itself, and therefore augmenting its

activity:[23] and if accordingly the attributes of this activity are found to be self-sufficiency, leisuredness, such freedom from fatigue as is possible for man, and all the other attributes of blessedness: it follows that it is the activity of the intellect that constitutes complete human happiness – provided it be granted a complete span of life, for nothing that belongs to happiness can be incomplete.

8   Such a life as this however will be higher than the human level:[24] not in virtue of his humanity will a man achieve it, but in virtue of something within him that is divine; and by as much as this something is superior to his composite nature, by so much is its activity superior to the exercise of the other forms of virtue. If then the intellect is something divine in comparison with man, so is the life of the intellect divine in comparison with human life. Nor ought we to obey those who enjoin that a man should have man's thoughts[25] and a mortal the thoughts of mortality,[26] but we ought so far as possible to achieve immortality, and do all that man may to live in accordance with the highest thing in him; for though this be small in bulk, in power and value it far surpasses all the rest.

9   It may even be held that this is the true self of each,[27] inasmuch as it is the dominant and better part; and therefore it would be a strange thing if a man should choose to live not his own life but the life of some other than himself.

Moreover what was said before will apply here also: that which is best and most pleasant for each creature is that which is proper to the nature of each; accordingly the life of the intellect is the best and the pleasantest life[28] for man, inasmuch as the intellect more than anything else is man; therefore this life will be the happiest.

viii   The life of moral virtue, on the other hand, is happy only in a secondary degree. For the moral activities are purely human: justice, I mean, courage and the other virtues we display in our intercourse with our fellows, when we observe what is due to each in contracts and services and in our various actions, and in our emotions also; and all of these things seem to be purely

2   human affairs. And some moral actions are thought to be the outcome of the physical constitution, and moral virtue is thought to have a close affinity in many respects with the passions.

3 Moreover, prudence is intimately connected with moral virtue, and this with prudence, inasmuch as the first principles which prudence employs are determined by the moral virtues, and the right standard for the moral virtues is determined by prudence. But these being also connected with the passions are related to our composite nature; now the virtues of our composite nature are purely human; so therefore also is the life that manifests these virtues, and the happiness that belongs to it. Whereas the happiness that belongs to the intellect is separate:[29] so much may be said about it here, for a full discussion of the matter is beyond

4 the scope of our present purpose. And such happiness would appear to need but little external equipment, or less than the happiness based on moral virtue.[30] Both, it may be granted, require the mere necessaries of life, and that in an equal degree (though the politician does as a matter of fact take more trouble about bodily requirements and so forth than the philosopher); for in this respect there may be little difference between them. But for the purpose of their special activities their requirements will differ widely. The liberal man will need wealth in order to do liberal actions, and so indeed will the just man in order to discharge his obligations (since mere intentions are invisible, and even the unjust pretend to wish to act justly); and the brave man will need strength if he is to perform any action displaying his virtue; and the temperate man opportunity for indulgence: otherwise how can he, or the possessor of any other virtue, show

5 that he is virtuous? It is disputed also whether purpose or performance is the more important factor in virtue, as it is alleged to depend on both; now the perfection of virtue will clearly consist in both; but the performance of virtuous actions requires much outward equipment, and the more so the greater and more

6 noble the actions are. But the student, so far as the pursuit of his activity is concerned, needs no external apparatus: on the contrary, worldly goods may almost be said to be a hindrance to contemplation; though it is true that, being a man and living in the society of others, he chooses to engage in virtuous action, and so will need external goods to carry on his life as a human being.

7 The following considerations also will show that perfect happiness is some form of contemplative activity. The gods, as we conceive them, enjoy supreme felicity and happiness. But

what sort of actions can we attribute to them? Just actions? but will it not seem ridiculous to think of them as making contracts, restoring deposits and the like? Then brave actions – enduring terrors and running risks for the nobility of so doing? Or liberal actions? but to whom will they give? Besides, it would be absurd to suppose that they actually have a coinage or currency of some sort! And temperate actions – what will these mean in their case? surely it would be derogatory to praise them for not having evil desires! If we go through the list we shall find that all forms of virtuous conduct seem trifling and unworthy of the gods. Yet nevertheless they have always been conceived as, at all events, living, and therefore living actively, for we cannot suppose they are always asleep like Endymion. But for a living being, if we eliminate action, and *a fortiori* creative action, what remains save contemplation? It follows that the activity of God, which is transcendent in blessedness, is the activity of contemplation; and therefore among human activities that which is most akin to the divine activity of contemplation will be the greatest source of
8 happiness.

A further confirmation is that the lower animals cannot partake of happiness, because they are completely devoid of the contemplative activity. The whole of the life of the gods is blessed, and that of man is so in so far as it contains some likeness to the divine activity; but none of the other animals possess happiness, because they are entirely incapable of contemplation. Happiness therefore is co-extensive in its range with contemplation: the more a class of beings possesses the faculty of contemplation, the more it enjoys happiness, not as an accidental concomitant of contemplation but as inherent in it, since contemplation is valuable in itself. It follows that happiness is some form of contemplation.

9 But the philosopher being a man will also need external well-being, since man's nature is not self-sufficient for the activity of contemplation, but he must also have bodily health and a supply of food and other requirements. Yet if supreme blessedness is not possible without external goods, it must not be supposed that happiness will demand many or great possessions; for self-sufficiency does not depend on excessive abundance, nor does
10 moral conduct, and it is possible to perform noble deeds even without being ruler of land and sea: one can do virtuous acts with

quite moderate resources. This may be clearly observed in experience: private citizens do not seem to be less but more given to doing virtuous actions than princes and potentates. It is sufficient then if moderate resources are forthcoming; for a life of virtuous activity will be essentially a happy life.

11   Solon also doubtless gave a good description of happiness,[31] when he said that in his opinion those men were happy who, being moderately equipped with external goods, had performed noble exploits and had lived temperately; for it is possible for a man of but moderate possessions to do what is right. Anaxagoras again does not seem to have conceived the happy man as rich or powerful, since he says that he would not be surprised if he were to appear a strange sort of person in the eyes of the many; for most men judge by externals, which are all that they can

12   perceive. So our theories seem to be in agreement with the opinions of the wise.

Such arguments then carry some degree of conviction; but it is by the practical experience of life and conduct that the truth is really tested, since it is there that the final decision lies. We must therefore examine the conclusions we have advanced by bringing them to the test of the facts of life. If they are in harmony with the facts, we may accept them; if found to disagree, we must deem them mere theories.[32]

13   And it seems likely that the man who pursues intellectual activity, and who cultivates his intellect and keeps that in the best condition, is also the man most beloved of the gods. For if, as is generally believed, the gods exercise some superintendence over human affairs, then it will be reasonable to suppose that they take pleasure in that part of man which is best and most akin to themselves, namely the intellect, and that they recompense with their favours those men who esteem and honour this most, because these care for the things dear to themselves, and act rightly and nobly. Now it is clear that all these attributes belong most of all to the wise man. He therefore is most beloved by the gods; and if so, he is naturally most happy. Here is another proof that the wise man is the happiest.

ix   If then we have suffiently discussed in their outlines the subjects of happiness and of virtue in its various forms, and also friendship and pleasure, may we assume that the investigation we proposed is now complete? Perhaps however, as we maintain, in the practical sciences the end is not to attain a theoretic knowledge of the various subjects, but rather to carry out our

2 theories in action. If so, to know what virtue is is not enough; we must endeavour to possess and to practise it, or in some other manner actually ourselves to become good.

3 Now if discourses on ethics were sufficient in themselves to make men virtuous, 'large fees and many' (as Theognis[33] says) 'would they win', quite rightly, and to provide such discourses would be all that is wanted. But as it is, we see that although theories have power to stimulate and encourage generous youths, and, given an inborn nobility of character and a genuine love of what is noble, can make them susceptible to the influence of virtue, yet they are powerless to stimulate the mass of mankind to

4 moral nobility. For it is the nature of the many to be amenable to fear but not to a sense of honour, and to abstain from evil not because of its baseness but because of the penalties it entails; since, living as they do by passion, they pursue the pleasures akin to their nature, and the things that will procure those pleasures, and avoid the opposite pains, but have not even a notion of what is

5 noble and truly pleasant, having never tasted true pleasure. What theory then can reform the natures of men like these? To dislodge by argument habits long firmly rooted in their characters is difficult if not impossible. We may doubtless think ourselves fortunate if we attain some measure of virtue when all the things believed to make men virtuous are ours.

6 Now some thinkers hold that virtue is a gift of nature; others think we become good by habit, others that we can be taught to be good. Natural endowment is obviously not under our control; it is bestowed on those who are fortunate, in the true sense, by some divine dispensation. Again, theory and teaching are not, I fear, equally efficacious in all cases: the soil must have been previously tilled if it is to foster the seed, the mind of the pupil must have been prepared by the cultivation of habits, so as

7 to like and dislike aright. For he that lives at the dictates of passion will not hear nor understand the reasoning of one who tries to dissuade him; but if so, how can you change his mind by argument?

And, speaking generally, passion seems not to be amenable to reason, but only to force.

8   We must therefore by some means secure that the character shall have at the outset a natural affinity for virtue, loving what is noble and hating what is base. And it is difficult to obtain a right education in virtue from youth up without being brought up under right laws; for to live temperately and hardily is not pleasant to most men, especially when young; hence the nurture and exercises of the young should be regulated by law, since temperance and hardiness will not be painful when they have 9 become habitual. But doubtless it is not enough for people to receive the right nurture and discipline in youth; they must also practise the lessons they have learnt, and confirm them by habit, when they are grown up. Accordingly we shall need laws to regulate the discipline of adults as well, and in fact the whole life of the people generally; for the many are more amenable to compulsion and punishment than to reason and to moral ideals.

10   Hence some persons hold,[34] that while it is proper for the lawgiver to encourage and exhort men to virtue on moral grounds, in the expectation that those who have had a virtuous moral upbringing will respond, yet he is bound to impose chastisement and penalties on the disobedient and ill-conditioned, and to banish the incorrigible out of the state altogether.[35] For (they argue) although the virtuous man, who guides his life by moral ideals, will be obedient to reason, the base, whose desires are fixed on pleasure, must be chastised by pain, like a beast of burden. This indeed is the ground for the view that the pains and penalties for transgressors should be such as are most opposed to their favourite pleasures.

11   But to resume: if, as has been said, in order to be good a man must have been properly educated and trained, and must subsequently continue to follow virtuous habits of life, and to do nothing base whether voluntarily or involuntarily, then this will be secured if men's lives are regulated by a certain intelligence, 12 and by a right system, invested with adequate sanctions. Now paternal authority has not the power to compel obedience, nor indeed, speaking generally, has the authority of any individual unless he be a king or the like; but law on the other hand is a rule, emanating from a certain wisdom and intelligence, that has compulsory force. Men are hated when they thwart people's

inclinations, even though they do so rightly, whereas law can
13 enjoin virtuous conduct without being invidious. But Sparta
appears to be the only or almost the only state in which the
lawgiver has paid attention to the nurture and exercises of the
citizens; in most states such matters have been entirely neglected,
and every man lives as he likes, in Cyclops fashion 'laying down
the law for children and for spouse'.[36]

14   The best thing is then that there should be a proper system of
public regulation; but when the matter is neglected by the
community, it would seem to be the duty of the individual to
assist his own children and friends to attain virtue, or even if not
able to do so successfully,[37] at all events to make this his aim. But
it would seem to follow from what has been said before, that he
will be more likely to be successful in this if he has acquired the
science of legislation. Public regulations in any case must clearly
be established by law, and only good laws will produce good
regulations; but it would not seem to make any difference
whether these laws are written or unwritten, or whether they are
to regulate the education of a single person or of a number of
people, any more than in the case of music or athletics or any
other form of training. Paternal exhortations and family habits
have authority in the household, just as legal enactments and
national customs have authority in the state, and the more so on
account of the ties of relationship and of benefits conferred that
unite the head of the household to its other members: he can
count on their natural affection and obedience at the outset.
15 Moreover individual treatment is better than a common system,
in education as in medicine. As a general rule rest and fasting are
good for a fever, but they may not be best for a particular case;
and presumably a professor of boxing does not impose the same
style of fighting on all his pupils. It would appear then that private
attention gives more accurate results in particular cases, for the
particular subject is more likely to get the treatment that suits
him. But a physician or trainer or any other director can best
treat a particular person if he has a general knowledge of what is
good for everybody, or for other people of the same kind: for the
16 sciences deal with what is universal, as their names[38] imply. Not
but what it is possible no doubt for a particular individual to be
successfully treated by someone who is not a scientific expert, but

has an empirical knowledge based on careful observation of the effects of various forms of treatment upon the person in question; just as some people appear to be their own best doctors, though they could not do any good to someone else. But nevertheless it would doubtless be agreed that anyone who wishes to make himself a professional and a man of science must advance to general principles, and acquaint himself with these by the proper 17 method: for science, as we said, deals with the universal. So presumably a man who wishes to make other people better (whether few or many) by discipline, must endeavour to acquire the science of legislation – assuming that it is possible to make us good by laws. For to mould aright the character of any and every person that presents himself is not a task that can be done by anybody, but only (if at all) by the man with scientific knowledge, just as is the case in medicine and the other professions involving a system of treatment and the exercise of prudence.

18   Is not then the next question to consider from whom or how the science of legislation can be learnt? Perhaps, like other subjects, from the experts, namely the politicians; for we saw[39] that legislation is a branch of political science. But possibly it may seem that political science is unlike the other sciences and faculties. In these the persons who impart a knowledge of the faculty are the same as those who practise it, for instance physicians and painters; but in politics the sophists, who profess to teach the science, never practise it. It is practised by the politicians, who would appear to rely more upon a sort of empirical skill than on the exercise of abstract intelligence; for we do not see them writing or lecturing about political principles (though this might be a more honourable employment than composing forensic and parliamentary speeches), nor yet do we notice that they have made their own sons or any 19 others of their friends into statesmen. Yet we should expect them to have done so had they been able, for they could have bequeathed no more valuable legacy to their countries, nor is there any quality they would choose for themselves, and therefore for those nearest to them, to possess, in preference to political capacity. Not that experience does not seem to contribute considerably to political success; otherwise men would never have become statesmen merely through practical association with politics; so it would appear that those who aspire to a scientific

knowledge of politics require practical experience as well as study.
20 On the other hand those sophists who profess to teach politics are found to be very far from doing so successfully. In fact they are absolutely ignorant of the very nature of the science and of the subjects with which it deals; otherwise they would not class it as identical with, or even inferior to, the art of rhetoric.[40] Nor would they imagine that it is easy to frame a constitution by making a collection of such existing laws as are reputed to be good ones, on the assumption that one can then select the best among them; as if even this selection did not call for understanding, and as if to judge correctly were not a very difficult task, just as much as it is for instance in music. It is only the experts in an art who can judge correctly the productions of that art, and who understand the means and the method by which perfection is attained, and know which elements harmonise with which; amateurs may be content if they can discern whether the general result produced is good or bad, for example in the art of painting. Laws are the product, so to speak, of the art of politics; how then can a mere collection of laws teach a man the science of legislation, or make him able to judge
21 which of them are the best? We do not see men becoming expert physicians from a study of medical handbooks. Yet medical writers attempt to describe not only general courses of treatment, but also methods of cure and modes of treatment for particular sorts of patients, classified according to their various habits of body; and their treatises appear to be of value for men who have had practical experience, though they are useless for the novice. Very possibly therefore collections of laws and constitutions may be serviceable to students capable of studying them critically, and judging what measures are valuable or the reverse, and what kind of institutions are suited to what national characteristics. But those who peruse such compilations without possessing a trained faculty cannot be capable of judging them correctly, unless they do so by instinct, though they may very likely sharpen their political intelligence.
22 As then the question of legislation has been left uninvestigated by previous thinkers, it will perhaps be well if we consider it for ourselves, together with the whole question of the constitution of the state, in order to complete as far as possible our philosophy of human affairs.

23   We will begin then[41] by attempting a review of any
pronouncements of value contributed by our predecessors in this
or that branch of the subject; and then on the basis of our
collection of constitutions[42] we will consider what institutions are
preservative and what destructive of states in general, and of the
different forms of constitution in particular, and what are the
reasons which cause some states to be well governed and others
the contrary. For after studying these questions we shall perhaps
be in a better position to discern what is the best constitution
absolutely, and what are the best regulations, laws, and customs
for any given form of constitution. Let us then begin our
discussion.

NOTES TO BOOK TEN

1 As we should say, 'gravitate towards'. Eudoxus, an unorthodox pupil of Plato, was an astronomer, and seems to have imported physical terminology into ethics.

2 *Philebus*, 60 d ff.

3 *i.e.*, incapable of being improved by the addition of something else. But the sentence looks like an interpolation.

4 These are Speusippus and the Academics of Aristotle's day; see VII, note 82 on p. 201.

5 *Philebus*, 24 e and 31 a.

6 *i.e.*, when they attribute 'indefiniteness' to pleasure, they are really thinking of the 'mixed' pleasures only; it does not apply to the 'pure' pleasures, in which there is no admixture of pain; and the distinction between these two kinds of pleasure is Plato's own.

7 *Philebus*, 53 c − 54 d.

8 This motion being uniform, it can only be spoken of as quick or slow in comparison with some other motion, not absolutely, *i.e.*, in comparison with itself at some other time.

9 *Philebus*, 31 e − 32 b and 42 c.

10 *i.e.*, we do not say a cut is a pain, but it is accompanied by pain.

11 κίνησις here has its wider sense of any process of change that actualises what is potentially; it includes generation, of which building is an instance. In its proper sense κίνησις is limited to change of quality, quantity, or place.

12 The lecturer appears to draw a line representing a racecourse, and divide it into two parts, representing two sections of the course (not two lines *across* the course). The motion of traversing one section is not the same as that of traversing the others, if only because they are in different places.

13 *Physics*, VI–VIII.

14 This parenthesis is perhaps an interpolation.

15 As well as to tastes, scents, and contacts, which are more obviously pleasant.

16 A variant reading gives 'and these [*sc.* the activities of the senses] from one another'.

17 *i.e.*, the special pain accompanying a particular activity when it functions badly or in relation to a bad object. -

18 See I, viii, 9.

19 *cf. Politics*, III, ix, 1280 a 32 'Slaves and lower animals are not members of the state, because they do not participate in happiness nor in purposeful life.'

20 This does not appear to have been stated exactly, but in Book VI (see especially v, 3 and xiii, 8) it was shown that σοφία, the virtue of the higher part of the intellect, is the highest of the virtues.

21 Probably the sentence should be curtailed to run 'or in fact the happiness of himself and his fellow–citizens; and happiness we are clearly investigating as something distinct from the art of politics [whose object it is].'

22 This should almost certainly be emended to 'excel in leisuredness'.

23 a reminder of v, 2.

24 This section and viii, 7 and 13 interpret I, ix, 3.

25 Euripides. fr. 1040.

26 Pindar, *Isthm.* 4, 16.

27 *cf.* IX, iv, 3 and 4; and viii, 6.

28 *cf.* I, viii, 14.

29 In *De anima*, III, v Aristotle distinguishes the active from the passive intellect, and pronounces the former to be 'separate or separable (from matter, or the body), unmixed and impassible.'

30 *cf.* vii, 4; viii, 9 and 10; and I, viii, 15-17.

31 Solon in his conversation with Croesus (Herodotus, i, 30-32; see I, note 62 on p. 29) says that Tellus the Athenian was the happiest man he ever knew. Tellus was well off, he lived to see his children's children, and he died gloriously in battle.

32 This section concludes the subject and prepares for the transition to politics in the next chapter; § 13 would come better after § 7: it looks back to I, ix, 1-3.

33 Theognis, 432 ff.

> εἰ δ' Ἀσκληπιάδαις τοῦτό γ' ἔδωκε θεός,
> ἰᾶσθαι κακότητα καὶ ἀτηρὰς φρένας ἀνδρῶν,
> πολλοὺς ἂν μισθοὺς καὶ μεγάλους ἔφερον.

> If to physicians God had given
> The power to cure mankind of sin,
> Large fees and many would they win.

34 Plato, *Laws*, 722 d ff.

35 Plato, *Protagoras*, 325 a.

36 Homer, *Odyssey*, ix, 114 f., quoted in *Politics*, 1252 b 22.

37 This clause, literally 'and to be able to do it', Bywater would place here; it comes in the manuscripts after 'public regulation' above.

38 *e.g.*, medicine is 'the science of healing', not 'the science of healing Brown or Jones'.

39 See VI, viii, 2.

40 Isocrates, *Antidosis* § 80.

41 This section roughly gives the contents of Aristotle's *Politics*, excepting Book I; 'a review', etc., is Book II, 'then', etc., Books III–VI, 'what is the best constitution', etc., Books VII and VIII.

42 Aristotle compiled, or caused to be compiled, descriptions of the constitutions of 158 Greek states: of these the *Constitution of Athens* alone survives.

WORDSWORTH CLASSICS
OF WORLD LITERATURE

APULEIUS
The Golden Ass

ARISTOTLE
The Nicomachean Ethics

MARCUS AURELIUS
Meditations

FRANCIS BACON
Essays

JOHN BUNYAN
The Pilgrim s Progress

KARL VON CLAUSEVITZ
On War (ABRIDGED)

CONFUCIUS
The Analects

CHARLES DARWIN
The Voyage of the Beagle

RENÉ DESCARTES
*A Discourse on Method
& other Essays*

SIGMUND FREUD
The Interpretation of Dreams

EDWARD GIBBON
*The Decline and Fall of the
Roman Empire* (ABRIDGED)

KHALIL GIBRAN
The Prophet

HERODOTUS
The Histories

HORACE
Selected Odes

LAO TSU
Tao te Ching

T. E. LAWRENCE
Seven Pillars of Wisdom

SIR THOMAS MALORY
Le Morte Darthur

JOHN STUART MILL
*On Liberty & The Subjection
of Women*

SIR THOMAS MORE
Utopia

THOMAS PAINE
Rights of Man

MARCO POLO
Travels

SAMUEL PEPYS
Selections from the Diary

PLATO
*The Symposium &
The Death of Socrates
The Republic*

LA ROCHEFOUCAULD
Maxims

JEAN-JACQUES ROUSSEAU
The Confessions

SUETONIUS
The Twelve Caesars

THUCYDIDES
*The History of the
Peloponnesian War*